WILL YOU CHOOSE THE WILDERNESS?

SAMUEL WHITEFIELD

ONE KING PUBLISHING

Will You Choose the Wilderness?
By Samuel Whitefield

Published by OneKing Publishing
PO Box 375
Grandview, MO 64030

Email: contact@oneking.online
Web: https://oneking.online

Dedicated to the many unknown saints who have chosen the wilderness. May they provoke us to follow the same path.

Table of Contents

A Life in the Wilderness 1

The Prototype

An Enigma or Something More? 11

More Than a Man—A Prototype 19

Barrenness Sets the Stage for God's Glory 29

Forged in the Wilderness...39

The Bridegroom in the Wilderness 49

Courage to Choose the Wilderness 61

Confidence in God's Leadership...73

The Messenger Is the Message..81

Suddenly the Word of the Lord Came..................................89

John Never Left the Wilderness..93

Do Hearts Move When You Quote Bible Verses?..............103

You Have the Words of the Uncreated God 113

Recovering the Prophetic 121

A Voice Crying in the Wilderness.......................................129

The Friend of the Bridegroom 137

John's Grand Finale...149

John's Greatest Achievement 161

The Path into the Wilderness

A People Who Choose the Wilderness 167

Weakness Is a Canvas for God's Glory 169

More Than a Prophet 181

The Priest Who Became a Messenger............................191

The Call to a Priestly Life...199

God Knows Your Address 209

The Path to John's Joy...219

Information without Demonstration Is Hypocrisy 227

The Fasted Lifestyle 235

John's Life Must Inform the Church's Assignment 241

The Forerunner Community 247

God's Delight in Hiddenness...253

Urgency Comes from Intimacy.......................................257

A Life in the Wilderness

Is it possible we have overlooked and neglected the biblical path to greatness? The man Jesus considered the greatest spent his life in the wilderness, but we avoid it. Are we too compelled by non-biblical definitions of success to follow the ancient paths?

Before Jesus came, God formed and fashioned a man in the wilderness for thirty years. The Spirit rested on this man as he ministered to the Lord and discipled a small group hidden away from the crowds of Jerusalem.

That man had learned a secret:

Crowds are seducing, but the wilderness is where the fire burns, the burning bush appears, and God speaks.

Jesus considered this man one of the greatest men who had ever lived because the man *chose* the wilderness. And before Jesus returns, a people will follow in this man's footsteps and discover what he found in the wilderness. Do you want to be a part of that people?

Perhaps you have avoided the wilderness because it does not seem to offer influence, popularity, comfort, or success. However, the wilderness offers something you cannot find anywhere else: the potential of undistracted communion with God. There are simply some encounters with God that are found only in the wilderness.

If you are satisfied with influence, popularity, comfort, and success, you can avoid the wilderness. If, on the other hand, you want the knowledge of God, He asks one question:

Will you choose the wilderness?

Wilderness "Seasons"

Many people use the words *wilderness season* to describe a period of time that feels difficult or unproductive. We tend to view the "wilderness" as a temporary season when our goal is to persevere through it so we can get to the season of blessing. And in the process, we overlook Jesus' definition of greatness.

Seeing the wilderness as a temporary season is not entirely wrong. There are figures in Scripture who passed through seasons of difficulty that prepared them for a unique assignment, but the Bible calls us to embrace a way of life that is compared to life in the wilderness.[1] This call to the wilderness is found throughout the Scripture, and it will grow louder and become more intense the closer we come to the return of Jesus.

The call to the wilderness is not a call to isolation. It is not a call to abandon our families or shirk our responsibilities, and for most, it is not a call to leave the place where the Lord has placed them. The call to the wilderness is an invitation to choose a life before the Lord that is not possible as long as we continue to give place and time to competing distractions.

Many people avoid the wilderness, but the Lord wants this generation to answer His question: Will you choose the wilderness?

We have a generation of Christians hoping for temporary wilderness seasons so they can enjoy great success outside the wilderness. This assumption overlooks something significant: *Jesus said no person was greater than John the Baptist, and John spent his entire life in the wilderness.* John did not go to the wilderness to prepare for a fruitful ministry and then leave. He completely fulfilled his assignment by staying in the wilderness. We think of the wilderness as negative, but John's life in the wilderness is presented in a positive light in the Gospels.[2]

It has become common to call people to endure the wilderness and look forward to a time of greater fulfillment outside the wilderness.

---

[1] We are called to be pilgrims and exiles in this age (Hebrews 11:13; 1 Peter 1:1, 17; 2:11).

[2] "Although most often associated in the Pentateuchal narratives as a place of testing in which the elements needed to sustain life are scarce (Num 14:26–35; Deut 9:7), for Luke the wilderness also has positive connotations. It is a place where prophets are called (1:80; 3:2) and a deeper relationship with God can be cultivated (1:80; 4:42; 5:16)." Clint Burnet, "Eschatological Prophet of Restoration: Luke's Theological Portrait of John the Baptist in Luke 3:1–6." *Neotestamentica* 47.1 (2–13). 9.

Today, it is time to issue a new call. *It is time to challenge a generation to embrace an entire life in the wilderness.*

Embracing the wilderness requires a profound shift in mindset, and that shift is required for the days that are now upon us. That shift does not necessarily require changing where you live or pursuing a new assignment. It means adopting a set of values that lead you to live in a very different way from the prevailing culture.

It is time to stop seeing the wilderness as something to be endured or avoided but as a process and a destination.

Maybe you have tried for years to find satisfaction in many things, even religious things, that seem to satisfy others and yet you feel a growing ache—an inability to be at rest. Perhaps you cannot simply go along with superficial answers and shallow lifestyles. The reason is simple: *You were born for the wilderness.* As long as you resist the wilderness, the ache will remain, but it is never too late to break free and discover a superior pleasure in places others fear to go.

Embracing the Path for Formation

John's life can give you critical insight into God's process of formation. If you do not know the way God forms people for His purposes, you can accidentally resist His process. You can resist God by becoming discouraged by circumstances or assuming you are stuck in a wilderness season when God may be intentionally forming you for His purposes. You can also resist His leadership by adopting unbiblical definitions of success and confusing activity with impact.

The thing you think is your greatest hindrance could in fact be God's leadership over your life and the thing forming you for His purposes.

Jesus put John in the top tier of all humans who had lived even though he:

- Only had a visible ministry for 6–18 months.
- Was in jail longer than he was a public figure.
- Was never invited to serve, travel, or minister with Jesus.
- Lived in a small, isolated place.
- Did not lead any kind of large movement.
- Did not do any miracles.
- Did not speak about visionary encounters with God.
- Did not give any new prophecies.

Jesus did this so we would carefully examine John's life to determine what greatness is and how God shapes a person for it. According to Jesus, neither Moses nor Isaiah nor Daniel nor David exceeded John, but the other "greatest" men in the Bible[3] have been studied much more than John. Jesus' evaluation of John should provoke us to value John's life as much as Jesus did.

The Lord determines the scope and expression of your assignment, but He typically uses specific patterns of preparation to shape and prepare you for your assignment. If you cooperate with God's path of preparation, you can operate in the fullness of your assignment. If you neglect certain values or the path of preparation, you will forfeit your assignment or operate in much less than God has for you.

God's Patterns of Formation

John's assignment was unique, but the patterns of formation we find in John's life need to be understood by every believer so we can recognize God's work in our lives, embrace His ways, and fully cooperate with Him. People who do not recognize God's processes of formation can easily lose heart or become discouraged.

Many people do not grasp how God works and what He wants, so they unintentionally resist Him. Others end up offended with God because of their unmet expectations or the difficulty of the process. All the while God is often orchestrating circumstances in our lives to produce what He wants.

We can be so eager to take on assignments from the Lord that we overlook the biblical process of formation. However, God has not changed. He still uses the process of formation. That process may vary from person to person, but there are profound patterns to God's work. Though we should not try to "become" John the Baptist, his life gives us a unique demonstration of the profound ways God forms a messenger for his assignment.

Regardless of your assignment from the Lord, you must see yourself as a carrier of the gospel and recognize that you play a profound role in the expansion of the church. Even if the Lord only

---

[3]The truth is we do not really know who the greatest men and women are. Our evaluation in this age is not the same as God's evaluation (1 Samuel 16:7; Matthew 8:11–12; 19:30; 20:16; Mark 10:31; Luke 13:28–30).

gives you influence with a small number of people, that influence matters to Him and can produce significant fruit. We tend to be driven by numbers, but in the parable of the talents, the Lord commended the faithful servants who had two talents and who had five with the same words.[4] Remember many that we do not think are great are great in the Lord's eyes. He simply does not evaluate the way we do.[5]

We all pass through God's process of formation, but when God gives unusual assignments, He often leads people through much longer and more involved processes. In this book, I refer to people with unusual assignments as "messengers." This is not in any way meant to diminish the role of every believer as a messenger of the gospel. It is simply a broad term to identify those given an assignment to communicate the gospel in an unusual way. Regardless of the sphere of influence or gifts, do not despise what you have been given. Every one of us is called to be fully engaged in God's mission and live according to the way of the wilderness.

A "messenger" assignment does not necessarily involve vocational ministry or even a large platform. We tend to think of messengers as preachers with large audiences, but that kind of messenger was very rare in the Bible. Biblically speaking, messengers can include those with a gift to proclaim the gospel but also can include singers, writers, and other gifts of communication. And of course, the term includes every believer making Jesus known according to the gifts and influence they are given. Most messengers will not have a big public platform. In fact, many of the best known messengers in the Bible had greater influence after they died than they had during their own lives.

Regardless of the way the Lord has gifted you, to some degree the Lord will lead you through a process of formation. If you have been given an unusual assignment, you should expect the process of formation to be more intense and typically more difficult.

Remember God does not shape people by formulas. Yet we can see patterns in His work. He guides our lives in whatever way He wants to

---

[4]Matthew 25:14–30.

[5]1 Samuel 16:7; Matthew 8:11–12; 20:16; 19:30; Mark 10:31; Luke 13:28–30.

produce what He wants. We should be aware of these patterns yet not turn them into formulas by which we order or evaluate our lives.

The Forerunner of a Generation

John lived in a focused way to prepare his people for Jesus' first coming. While John's personal assignment was unique, as we will see, his message was not fulfilled in his lifetime. John was not the end of something that was passing; he was the beginning of something new, and his life set something into motion that continues in our day. As we will see, John is a prototype of a global church that will prepare the earth for the return of Jesus by her message *and* her lifestyle.

It is time for a generation to carefully study the life of John the Baptist and be provoked to embrace the same lifestyle.

I have to warn you that the life of John the Baptist will challenge and expose you. His life will *confront*, but it does not *condemn*. His life is a gift that can liberate you from things you do not know are holding you back from wholeheartedness.

John's life will force you to look in the mirror and ask serious questions. If you follow his path, it will cost you your life. And by that, I do not necessarily mean you may face martyrdom. Following his path will go much deeper than that. It will cost you a much higher price. It will radically reorient who you are and the life you live in the day-to-day, moment-by-moment rhythm of your life. And it is not primarily an external transformation. You cannot follow John's example by taking on a set of rules or requirements. You can only follow his path by allowing your life to be consumed by God's life.

Proceed with caution, but know that a generation is coming who will embrace John's path. The question is will you be part of that people?

A mature church is coming that will embrace John's wholeheartedness. She will not be "superior" to other people. Rather, she will be very aware of her own weakness. The mature church will not be "elite." Instead, she will end up becoming a servant of all.[6] Most of those in the church will be unknown, and many will be despised. But they will be part of the Father's extravagant gift to His Son.

---

[6]Mark 9:35; 10:42–45; Luke 14:11; 18:14; John 13:12–16.

God will mature His entire church in His timing, but He is issuing an invitation *now* to embrace His process with wholeheartedness. As we will see, John's life was a preview of what is coming, and the Lord wants to release a preview again through those who hear His invitation.

Perhaps the Lord wants you to hear the invitation. And maybe He is waiting for you to respond.

Will you choose the wilderness?

If you want to understand the invitation to the wilderness, you need to understand the man Jesus considered one of the greatest.

The Prototype

An Enigma or Something More?

John the Baptist is often treated as some sort of eccentric. Most movies depict him as a strange and odd hermit who looks like he hasn't bathed in weeks but nevertheless carries a prophetic message. These portraits of John are not accurate. John was not a bizarre person. He was a man who lived a focused, intentional life shaped by his confidence in the Scriptures. John was anointed by heaven to proclaim the Scriptures with unprecedented power to prepare his people for Jesus.

Announced by Gabriel

Gabriel was sent from heaven to announce John's birth. This announcement is the first indicator of the magnitude of John's life:

> *And there appeared to him an angel of the Lord standing on the right side of the altar of incense. And Zechariah was troubled when he saw him, and fear fell upon him. But the angel said to him, "Do not be afraid, Zechariah, for your prayer has been heard, and your wife Elizabeth will bear you a son, and you shall call his name John." (Luke 1:11–13)*

Gabriel only made four recorded appearances in Scripture, two in the book of Daniel[1] and two in the New Testament. Gabriel described himself as one who "stands in the presence of God,"[2] indicating his position.

---

[1] Note Daniel 7:16 is likely a third appearance of Gabriel in Daniel. See Daniel 8:15–17; 9:21–24; Luke 1:13, 19, 26–27.

[2] Luke 1:19.

Gabriel only predicted two births in history: the births of Jesus and John. To put that in perspective, Gabriel predicted the birth of God and only one other man.

The First New Testament Messenger

New Testament preaching did not begin in the book of Acts. It began in the Gospels and specifically with the preaching of John:

> *The beginning of the gospel of Jesus Christ, the Son of God. As it is written in Isaiah the prophet, "Behold, I send my messenger before your face, who will prepare your way, the voice of one crying in the wilderness: 'Prepare the way of the Lord, make his paths straight,'" John appeared, baptizing in the wilderness and proclaiming a baptism of repentance for the forgiveness of sins. (Mark 1:1–4)*

Mark described John's preaching as the "beginning of the gospel of Jesus." Luke also described John's ministry as the gospel:

> *So with many other exhortations he preached the gospel to the people. (Luke 3:18 NASB)*

Gospel preaching obviously goes beyond John's message, but if you want to know the gospel, you need to know John's message.

Furthermore, John was the first "sent" messenger in the New Testament:

> *There was a man sent from God, whose name was John. (John 1:6)*

The word *sent* (ἀποστέλλω, *apostéllō*) is the word we derive *apostle* from. While John obviously did not play the same role the other apostles did, he is the first man *sent* in the New Testament, and the apostles who followed built on his foundation.

John was the first to make the transition to New Testament preaching:

> *For all the Prophets and the Law prophesied until John. (Matthew 11:13)*

The word *until* (ἕως) indicates John was part of a transition. This *until* does not mean John was the last of the Old Testament prophets; it indicates he was the *first* of a new kind of messenger. As a messenger, he was a prophetic hinge connected to the past but setting into motion a new phrase of proclamation, expectation, and expression. While John did not live to see the crucifixion, the resurrection, and the outpouring of the Spirit, John should not be viewed as the *end* of something. He should be seen as the *beginning* of something.[3]

John did not add to biblical prophecy; instead, he took what had already been written and began to proclaim it as descriptions of Jesus. (As the psalmist wrote, Jesus' days had been written down before He came.[4]) John boldly proclaimed Jesus was the divine Human who had come to fulfill everything the prophets had spoken.

"No Man Was Greater"

Jesus' assessment of John is the greatest indicator of John's significance. During His ministry, Jesus frequently asked His disciples *not* to tell people who He was,[5] but He submitted to John's baptism and allowed John to publicly present Him to Israel. Jesus had incredibly high esteem for a man He probably only saw once in His adult life.[6]

Jesus did not speak about anyone else the way He spoke about John:

> *What then did you go out to see? A prophet? Yes, I tell you, and more than a prophet. This is he of whom it is written, "Behold, I send my messenger before your face, who will prepare your way before you."'* (Matthew 11:10)

Jesus referred to John as "more than a prophet" and "My messenger." John was not a "privileged prophet"; he was *more* than a prophet. We will see what Jesus meant by this phrase in a later chapter, but for now,

---

[3]For example, John Holland wrote, "...the beginning point for the new situation can hardly exclude John." John Holland, *Luke 9:21–18:34*, vol. 35B, Word Biblical Commentary (Dallas: Word, Incorporated, 1993), 820.

[4]Psalm 139:16.

[5]Matthew 16:20; Mark 8:29–30.

[6]John did not know who Jesus was apart from the Spirit's witness, indicating he was not familiar with Jesus' appearance as an adult (John 1:33).

we must note the word *prophet* was incapable of fully describing who John was. But Jesus did not stop there in His evaluation of John.

Jesus is the greatest judge of character who has ever lived. No one can deceive Him. He can see directly into the soul of a man, and His judgment is completely unbiased.[7] This makes His assessment of John staggering:

> *Truly, I say to you, among those born of women there has arisen no one greater than John the Baptist. (Matthew 11:11)*

Let those words sink in: *No one is greater than John the Baptist.* The statement is shocking, and the implications are profound. Jesus looked down throughout history, and *no one had exceeded John.*[8]

This includes:

- Job, the man who endured agony and suffering but refused to curse God even when God seemed to completely forsake him.
- Enoch, the man who walked so closely with God he was taken by God before he died.
- Noah, the preacher of righteousness[9] who alone survived the flood and became a "second Adam."
- Abraham, the man God made covenant with and chose as the father of all the faithful.
- Joseph, a foreshadowing of Jesus who endured suffering, imprisonment, and betrayal yet refused to compromise or blame God.
- Moses, the meekest man in his generation who delivered a nation, led the nation to audibly make covenant with God,

---

[7]John 8:16.

[8]Many people take this to mean John is the greatest human ever born, but this is not precisely what Jesus said. Jesus said *no one greater*, meaning no one had exceeded John. It is a small difference but a significant one. For example, Craig Keener writes, "Calling John the 'greatest' was a typically Jewish form of praise, which could be applied to more than one person at a time; rabbis, for instance, could in the same breath speak of both Joseph and Moses as the greatest figures of Israel's history." Craig S. Keener, *The IVP Bible Background Commentary: New Testament* (Downers Grove, IL: InterVarsity Press, 1993), Mt 11:11.

[9]2 Peter 2:5.

experienced the manifest glory of God for over forty years, spoke to God face to face, and was the human instrument of the most powerful signs and wonders in history. No other generation since has seen anything like the exodus, but Moses did not exceed John.

- Ruth, the woman who left her land, forsook her family, and rejected her gods to follow the God of Israel and join herself to His people.
- David, the man "after God's own heart" who was promised a son who would rule forever.
- Elijah, the man who stood before God, called fire down from heaven, controlled the rain with his words, and was carried into the heavens in a chariot of fire.
- Daniel, the man who was faithful and without compromise as a slave under three different pagan rulers, numbered among the greatest intercessors in history, and the wisest man in his generation.
- Esther, the woman who endured suffering and life in the palace of a pagan king to risk everything to save her people.
- Isaiah, the man who was given profound and stunning visions of Jesus and His coming reign.
- Jeremiah, the man who was God's mouthpiece to Judah, confronted false prophets, endured the siege of Jerusalem, endured suffering, and wept God's tears over the fall of Jerusalem.

Each of these seem far more impressive than John:

- *John did not have a long ministry*—His public ministry only lasted six to eighteen months.
- *He did not do any miracles*—His public ministry did not include signs or miracles like Moses' or Elijah's ministry.
- *He did not lead a nation like David*—He never left the wilderness and was not a "leader." Only a few disciples followed him.
- *He was not given prophetic insights and visions like Isaiah or Ezekiel*—He did not make new predictions or add to biblical prophecy. He has no recorded encounters. He simply proclaimed Bible verses recorded by other messengers.

- *He was not in a great city*—He lived in a small place.
- *He did not live a long life of faithfulness like Daniel*—He died in a filthy prison as a young man when a party went wrong.
- *He was not a part of Jesus' life or ministry*—Jesus did not invite John to be part of His ministry. Instead, Jesus chose others to be His disciples. When Jesus began to minister, John went to jail and was overshadowed by Jesus while he was still alive.

At first glance, there is nothing in John's life that merits Jesus' evaluation. *We would not write a story like John's and then say "no man was greater."* After all, John's ministry was brief. He did not add to Scripture. His death seemed like a tragic waste. He was not invited to be a part of Jesus' ministry. He did not live to see the things he proclaimed. Only a remnant responded to John's message. Considering the prophetic revelation given to men like Isaiah and unparalleled ministry of signs and wonders that men like Moses and Elijah had over decades, Jesus' assessment of John's ministry is shocking.

Jesus' assessment of John demonstrates God does not define greatness the way we do. His assessment of John and His relationship to John confront us. They require us to examine John's life carefully to discover what Jesus considers to be great.

If you do not discover why Jesus considered John to be great, you may in fact be living your life according to the wrong definitions of "greatness."

Before we move on, we have to briefly consider the second half of Matthew 11:11, where Jesus said:

> *Truly, I say to you, among those born of women there has arisen no one greater than John the Baptist. Yet the one who is least in the kingdom of heaven is greater than he.*

Many people quickly read the second half of Matthew 11:11 and assume it means everyone who comes after John is automatically greater than him. But we must read the phrase "least in the kingdom" in its full context. There is a very real privilege to living after Jesus' suffering, death, and resurrection, but Jesus' comment about this privilege was a *christological* statement—an assertion of Jesus' worth—not a reduction of John's.[10]

The message is that anyone who experiences Jesus' ministry, even the "least," has an incredible advantage because access to Jesus and life in the Spirit is a superior privilege to what John had access to. The statement reveals the *privilege* of access to Jesus, and it does not diminish the magnitude of who John was.[11]

This raises a profound question: *Why did Jesus need to assert the superiority of His ministry over John's?*

Jesus was not insecure and did not engage in self-promotion,[12] so His statement reflects the incredible esteem the people had for John. For example, Josephus wrote that Herod:

> *feared that the great influence John had over the masses . . . for they seemed ready to do anything he should advise. . . .[13]*

John had clearly been great, and his words were accompanied by immense power, but Jesus had to set His ministry apart from John's so there would be no confusion: John had been great, but *Someone far greater* had now arrived. *Something greater* than John had arrived: enjoying *access to Jesus.*

---

[10]Donald A. Hagner, *Matthew 1–13*, vol. 33A, Word Biblical Commentary (Dallas: Word, Incorporated, 1993), 306.

[11]New Testament scholar Craig Keener explains it this way, "This comparison elevates Jesus' disciples rather than demeans John. One may compare the early rabbinic saying that Johanan ben Zakkai, one of the most respected scholars of the first century, was the 'least' of Hillel's eighty disciples; this saying was not meant to diminish Johanan's status but to increase that of his contemporaries and thus that of his teacher." Craig S. Keener, *The IVP Bible Background Commentary: New Testament* (Downers Grove, IL: InterVarsity Press, 1993), Lk 7:28.

[12]John 5:31; 8:54; Hebrews 5:5–9.

[13]Josephus, *A.J.* 18.118.

More Than a Man—A Prototype

If we see John as a strange individual who briefly emerged to announce Jesus' ministry and then quickly faded into history, we will overlook the full message of his life. When Jesus said John was "more than a man," He was referring to the role John would play as a prototype.

John was a forerunner of the task given to the church: to proclaim the prophetic Scriptures as a witness of Jesus.[1]

If John troubles you or confronts you, do not superficially resolve or dismiss the discomfort of the confrontation. Do not dismiss John as "unusual" or "unbalanced." Instead, pursue the revelation of God that John had. He received that revelation by the indwelling Spirit, the Word of God, and his life in community—and *so can you*. You need to look at his message and life for your example.

It's time for a generation to embrace the values that governed John's life to prepare the church and provoke the nations before the great and terrible Day of the Lord.

John Boldly Proclaimed Things That Still Have Not Happened

John proclaimed Jesus as the "Lamb of God"[2] *and* as the One who would:

> *baptize you with the Holy Spirit and fire. His winnowing fork is in his hand, and he will clear his threshing floor and gather his wheat into the barn, but the chaff he will burn with unquenchable fire. (Matthew 3:11–12)*

---

[1]John 5:39.

[2]John 1:29, 36.

The majority of John's message in Matthew 3:11–12 refers to Jesus' second coming and not the first. John's message was not fulfilled in Jesus' first coming. In fact, John preached Jesus' second coming as the primary motivation to prepare for Jesus' first coming:[3]

> *Bear fruit in keeping with repentance. . . . Every tree therefore that does not bear good fruit is cut down and thrown into the fire. I baptize you with water for repentance, but he who is coming after me is mightier than I, whose sandals I am not worthy to carry. He will baptize you with the Holy Spirit and fire. His winnowing fork is in his hand, and he will clear his threshing floor and gather his wheat into the barn, but the chaff he will burn with unquenchable fire." (Matthew 3:8, 10–12)*

John proclaimed Jesus' second coming to the generation who only experienced Jesus' first coming, and John's preaching reminds us the gospel is the good news of Jesus' first *and* His second comings. Regardless of whether people live to see the return of Jesus, this is the gospel. John preached this way, the apostles preached this way,[4] and we should preach this way.

If the message of Jesus' second coming was critical to prepare Israel to receive redemption in His first coming, how much more is that message needed to prepare Israel and the nations for the second coming?

Any gospel that does not include the second coming of Jesus is an incomplete gospel[5] because the first coming of Jesus did not *fulfill* all the promises of God; it *secured* them.[6] We have only received a

---

[3]See also Luke 3:7–17.

[4]For example, see Acts 10:42; 17:30–31.

[5]This does not mean every time we share the gospel we must speak of the first and second comings. It simply means the gospel includes both. Any part of the gospel message carries great power for salvation.

[6]For more on this, see the book *It Must Be Finished*.

downpayment of what God has promised, and our gospel is ultimately ?
meaningless without Jesus' return.[7]

The Apostles Expounded on John's Message

John's message can be summarized as follows:

- Jesus is the One predicted by the prophets.[8]
- Jesus will execute God's judgment.[9]
- Jesus is the Bridegroom coming for a people who are the Bride.[10]
- Jesus is the Lamb of God who secures atonement.[11]
- Because Jesus is coming to bring salvation and release judgment, we should respond by repenting of our sins and being baptized.[12]
- Jesus will baptize a repentant people in the Holy Spirit.[13]
- History and heredity are not sufficient to ensure participation in Jesus' kingdom. Repentance is required, and it involves something more than temple sacrifices. We must change our lifestyle and turn from sin. [14]

It is easy to see John's message was a summary of the gospel carried by the apostles. The New Testament apostles took this basic message,

---

[7]Acts 1:11; 28:20; Romans 8:18–25; 1 Corinthians 15:19; Galatians 5:5; 1 Thessalonians 2:19; 3:13; 1 Timothy 6:14–16; 2 Timothy 1:12; Titus 2:13; Hebrews 10:37; 1 Peter 1:13; 2 Peter 3:4–14; 1 John 3:2–3.

[8]Matthew 3:3; Mark 1:3, 7; Luke 3:16; John 1:23, 26–27, 30, 34; 3:31.

[9]Matthew 3:12; Luke 3:17.

[10]John 3:29.

[11]John 1:29, 36.

[12]Matthew 3:2, 11; Luke 3:3; John 1:31.

[13]Matthew 3:11; Mark 1:8; Luke 3:16; John 1:33.

[14]Matthew 3:8–10; Mark 1:4–5; Luke 3:3, 8–9.

expounded on it, and carried it everywhere, demonstrating John's ministry was a prototype for what would come.

John boldly proclaimed the day of Jesus' judgment and called people to repentance in light of the coming judgment. When that judgment did not come in the first century, the apostles understood a "delay" of judgment had been given to allow additional time for repentance:

> *The Lord is not slow to fulfill his promise as some count slowness, but is patient toward you, not wishing that any should perish, but that all should reach repentance. (2 Peter 3:9)*

The apostles understood John began a ministry of preparation that must continue until the day of judgment comes. John was sent as the first messenger who prepared the way of the Lord, and the church has been given an assignment to continue to prepare the way before the Lord.

If God extravagantly raised up a man to prepare Israel, how much more will He prepare the church at the end of the age to prepare the nations for the arrival of His Son?

John's personal assignment was unique, but his message was not new. He continued the prophets' message of repentance, salvation, and judgment. Yet John's ministry carried an elevated intensity because Jesus' appearing was imminent. While we cannot (and should not) predict the day of Jesus' return, we should expect an increase in the intensity of the church's witness about Jesus as the day of His return comes closer.

Some believers are wary of the idea of preparing the earth for the return of Jesus because a handful of people have tried to "prepare" for Jesus' return in unbiblical ways.[15] The issue, though, is not whether or not we prepare—Jesus commanded us to prepare.[16] The issue is *how* we prepare.

---

[15]This includes trying to guess the timing of Jesus' return or becoming more preoccupied with prophetic theories than building the church.

[16]Matthew 24:42–44; 25:1–13.

The church's mission in this age is to obey Scripture and cooperate with God to prepare the earth for the return of His Son.

Jesus summarized this task in Matthew 24:

And this gospel of the kingdom will be proclaimed throughout the whole world as a testimony to all nations, and then the end will come. (v. 14)

Jesus predicted the gospel must be given as a *witness* to all nations before the end. Jesus is so kind He will not fulfill end-time events until the entire earth is given a witness through the church. That witness will prepare the earth for the events that will accompany Jesus' return.

God did not release the flood until Noah prophesied for some time.[17] God did not release His plagues on Egypt until He first sent Moses as a messenger to warn Pharaoh. God also sent numerous prophets to Israel before the Assyrian invasion and before the Babylonian siege on Jerusalem. Jesus did not come until John warned the people to prepare for His arrival.

God has always prepared His people. If the end of the age produces the greatest calamity and deliverance in history, it means it must be accompanied by the greatest prophetic witness in history. If we perceive the church's responsibility to prepare the nations for the coming Day of the Lord, it requires us to consider John's ministry more carefully.

Before Jesus returns, God is going to release a witness through the church to the "whole world" and "all nations," indicating the end-time witness of the church will be much larger than John's ministry. Some assume no witness is necessary because we have the witness of Scripture. Yet previous generations had the witness of Scripture as well.

When we carefully consider everything the Bible says about the first and second comings, it raises a critical question:

If John's life of devotion and bold message were necessary to prepare Israel to receive mercy, how much more will something similar be required to prepare the nations to receive Jesus' mercy and His judgments?

---

[17]It is traditionally assumed the ark may have taken around a century to build though the Scripture does not explicitly give the time frame (2 Peter 2:5).

John Is the Only Human Filled with the Spirit in His Mother's Womb

John was a dedicated and focused man, but his dedication is not what made him unique. There were many other dedicated communities in the wilderness. John was unique because he was given a gift no other messenger was given; he was filled with the Spirit in his mother's womb:

"He will be filled with the Holy Spirit, even from his mother's womb." (Luke 1:15)

This gift put John in a unique light: John died before Pentecost, but he enjoyed a measure of the gift that came on Pentecost. The Holy Spirit in John is what made John who he was. If we view John as a superior human, we miss the point. John had to respond to the Lord and live intentionally, but the Spirit in John is what made John who he was.

This point is emphasized by the lack of miracles in John's ministry and no mention of any unusual spiritual encounters. The background of John's ministry can be summarized by three verses:

"He will be filled with the Holy Spirit, even from his mother's womb." (Luke 1:15)

And the child grew and became strong in spirit, and he was in the wilderness until the day of his public appearance to Israel. (Luke 1:80)

During the high priesthood of Annas and Caiaphas, the word of God came to John the son of Zechariah in the wilderness. (Luke 3:2)

John was defined by three things:

1. He was filled with the Holy Spirit and submitted to the Spirit. His public ministry was the result of God coming to him and speaking through him in God's timing and at God's initiation rather than through human strategy.
2. He lived an intentional life in a small place over a long period of time.
3. He treasured the Word of God, meditated on it deeply, and allowed it to shape His life.

These three simple factors produced John's revelation of God, his insight into the Scripture, and the power of his ministry. John did not shake a nation because he was impressive, but because of his life in the Spirit. In fact, as we will see, his life was likely marked by weakness.

As far as we know, John did not experience the presence of God the way Moses did. We have no record of John's experiencing the kind of encounters Ezekiel and Daniel had. Gabriel came to John's father to predict his birth, but we have no record that an angel ever appeared to John. John received revelation and was transformed as he encountered God by the Spirit and through the Word and lived an intentional lifestyle in a small place.

John's life is a description of New Testament life in the Spirit, which means John is an incredible preview of the prophetic church.

John's life was a foreshadowing of Paul's descriptions of life in the Spirit:[18]

> *For those who live according to the flesh set their minds on the things of the flesh, but those who live according to the Spirit set their minds on the things of the Spirit. (Romans 8:5)*

> *I have been crucified with Christ. It is no longer I who live, but Christ who lives in me. And the life I now live in the flesh I live by faith in the Son of God, who loved me and gave himself for me. (Galatians 2:20)*

As we will see, incredible power flowed through John, but that power did not come from dramatic miracles, new revelations, or unusual encounters. John accessed the power of God by walking the same path we are called to walk. In 2 Corinthians, Paul reminded the Corinthians that they had access to a greater glory than Moses experienced because they had the gift of the Spirit. John was a living example of the glory available through the gift of the Spirit.

---

[18]Romans 6:3–14; 8:3–10; 2 Corinthians 4:7–12; Galatians 2:19–21; 5:16, 24–26; Ephesians 2:4–6; Colossians 1:26–29; 2:11–14; 3:1–4; Philippians 3:7–11; 2 Timothy 2:7–12.

John's life models the way we are to live, the way we become a witness of Jesus, and the way we prepare a people for His coming. Do you have confidence that the gift of the Spirit can produce in you what it produced in John?[19]

A Spirit-Filled Preview

John emerged just before Jesus began preaching, and his life was a foreshadowing of what was coming.

One of the most unusual aspects of John's life was being filled with the Spirit while he was still in his mother's womb. This infilling was a unique gift and a powerful preview of what was coming. John did not have the fullness of what was coming on the day of Pentecost, but he had a substantial, demonstrable deposit of what was coming before it came. John did not only carry a message, he *was* a message.

John prepared the way for Jesus by demonstrating in part something that would come in fullness when Jesus appeared. John resembled Jesus so much he was asked if he was the Messiah.[20] This is a preview of the end-time church that will resemble Jesus far more than we currently anticipate.

John emerged suddenly just before Jesus' ministry as one of the greatest men of all history, and the mature end-time church also will seem to emerge suddenly just before Jesus returns. And the church will emerge as a mature, corporate people. Many people are discouraged by the compromise they perceive in the church, but we must form our opinions about God's people from Bible verses.[21] God is going to shock and amaze the world and the powers by bringing His people to maturity before Jesus returns. God is going to form a beautiful, mature people who resemble His Son and become the glorious answer to His Son's prayer in John 17.[22]

---

[19]This does not mean the Spirit will give you the kind of ministry John had. But He wants to give us the burning heart John had.

[20]John 1:19–20; 3:28.

[21]For example, see Romans 6:5; 8:17–29; Philippians 3:20–21; 2 Thessalonians 2:14; 1 John 3:2.

[22]For more on this, see *What Does God Want?*.

Just as John demonstrated a measure of the power of what was coming, so also the end-time church will be a demonstration of what is coming. We will not have the fullness of what will come after Jesus returns, but the end-time church will be an undeniable and visible foreshadowing of the glory that will come after Jesus appears again. John provided a picture of the future of the church. For nearly two thousand years, the church has been a people who point to the age to come and the return of the King. As the King and the next age come closer, this assignment will intensify dramatically.

A Life and a Prediction

Throughout the Bible, there are people whose lives are a prophecy, picture, and prototype of something that is coming. When we read their stories, we are reading real, historical events, but we are also reading prophecies of something that must come.

For example, the story of Jacob's transformation into Israel is a prophetic picture of Israel's history. The life of Joseph is an incredibly detailed foreshadowing of Jesus' life. Daniel was another example. He lived through the reign of Nebuchadnezzar who was an antichrist prototype that destroyed Jerusalem, enslaved God's people, and commanded people to worship an image. Throughout the story, Daniel was completely faithful to God and without any flaws. He was a prototype of the mature, end-time church that is faithful and loyal to Jesus even during the rule of the antichrist.

Prototypes are common in the Bible, and when we carefully examine John's life, message, and ministry, we discover he is also one of these prototypes.

John the Baptist was not strange or bizarre as many people have thought. John was not an impossible ideal; he was a weak man like us who demonstrated what is possible in the grace of God. While John's assignment was certainly unique, the Bible presents John as a person to *emulate*, not just a person to *esteem*. We should not try to mimic John's individual assignment, but we must learn greatness from him.

John was not extreme—His way of life was a reasonable response to His knowledge of God.

People who are wholehearted only seem extreme to us if we lack the revelation they have. World-class musicians do not consider their practice regimen extreme because they have a revelation of what is possible when they play their instrument. Olympic athletes do not think it is strange to carefully order every moment of their lives and deny themselves because they have been captivated by the possibilities of competition. When people *love* something, they consider what others find extreme the only reasonable response.

If you find John's life extreme, it is only because you do not yet have the revelation of God he had.

John's life does not primarily expose our lack of discipline; it confronts our lack of *revelation* and our lack of *desire*. The revelation of anything desirable—whether it is exceptional musical skill, an Olympic medal, or the possibilities of a romantic relationship—has incredible power. When our deepest desires are stirred and love is kindled, we eagerly reorder our lives and do what others consider extreme in response to those desires.

If you see God as John did, you can live the way John lived. This is the desperate need of our time. God is looking for people whose lives will be defined by their pursuit of that revelation.[23]

The last time God was about to come to the earth, He filled a man with the Sprit, put him in the wilderness for decades, gave him profound revelation from the Word, and then anointed him with unusual power to proclaim the Word.

God is preparing to come again, and every time He comes, it increases in intensity. The last time God used John to prepare a small people group (Israel) for His arrival. This time, He wants to use a corporate witness to prepare every people group for His arrival.[24] But first He is looking for a remnant who will study His ways and become part of His process to prepare His people for His coming.

---

[23] 1 Corinthians 2:2; Philippians 3:8, 10.

[24] Matthew 24:14.

Barrenness Sets the Stage for God's Glory

Many avoid the wilderness because it appears "barren." Most people do everything they can to avoid their own barrenness, but we must face our own barrenness. The wilderness removes everything superficial and confronts us with who we really are and what we can produce in our own strength. When we come to the end of our own strength, our barrenness sets the stage for God's glory.

John became the most powerful preacher in the nation, but his story began with barrenness:

> *In the days of Herod, king of Judea, there was a priest named Zechariah, of the division of Abijah. And he had a wife from the daughters of Aaron, and her name was Elizabeth. And they were both righteous before God, walking blamelessly in all the commandments and statutes of the Lord. But they had no child, because Elizabeth was barren, and both were advanced in years. (Luke 1:5–7)*

Barrenness is incredibly painful, and it can easily lead to despair. However, if we bear the pain of barrenness, it can produce things that do not come any other way.[1] Does your life feel "barren"? Do you think the church is barren?

God does not always answer the pain of barrenness the same way, but the anguish of barrenness is an invitation into the knowledge of God and a taste of the pain God has felt waiting for the maturity of His people.

God's glory is most brilliant when human strength fails, and He often uses barrenness to set the stage for His glory.

---

[1]God does not always respond to barrenness in the same way, but the anguish of barrenness is an invitation into the knowledge of God.

John's parents lived under a cloud of shame. In a culture that intensely valued children and the family line, Elizabeth could not conceive. For decades, they wept and prayed. Discouragement turned to despair and finally a long-term sadness. They never imagined Elizabeth's barren womb would produce one of the greatest messengers in history.

There are times God lets routine things break down to demonstrate man cannot do anything to bring about the promises of God. And there are key moments—often when God wants a deliverer—when He sets barrenness into motion.[2] For example, the entire promise of salvation depended on Abraham having a son, but for decades, Sarah's womb was shut.

Hannah is another example. Her barrenness caused her to cry out for a son, but we are told the Lord had shut Hannah's womb.[3] Why did He shut it? Because the priesthood was corrupt, and He wanted a messenger who would be the product of intercession. Hannah's intercession produced that messenger, Samuel, and he confronted a corrupt priesthood. Being the wife of a priest,[4] Elizabeth probably read Hannah's story repeatedly and shed tears hoping she also would be the mother of a priest who would confront the corruption in the priesthood.

Our confidence in our own ability is an expression of pride, and it limits our ability to experience the power of God. As a result, there are times God makes a promise that may seem barren for a time. There are some things so precious to Him that He will not bring them to pass

---

[2] Barrenness is an incredibly painful condition, and not every story of barrenness ends the same way. The truth is we do not always fully grasp God's design and purpose in our own pain. Barrenness drives us to intercession and ultimately leaves the result in God's hands. The answer is not always a child, but these stories also indicate barrenness should not automatically be interpreted as a judgment or statement of God's displeasure. God does not always resolve barrenness the same way, but if we turn to Him in our barrenness, He will do surprising things in the midst through an agonizing dilemma.

[3] 1 Samuel 1:6.

[4] Hannah's husband, Elkanah, may have been a Levite.

until we have been emptied of our confidence in human strength and have nothing left but intercession.

Reproduction is a normal, natural human process. The vast majority of humans reproduce. Babies are conceived, carried, and born every day. Because reproduction feels so natural, we assume we can accomplish our destiny in our ability. God gave man an assignment to multiply, fill the earth, and take dominion,[5] but barrenness is a painful demonstration that we cannot accomplish any assignment God has given us in our own strength.

Barrenness is an extreme demonstration of our true condition.

Without God, we cannot do the basic things we have been commanded to do, whether that is multiplying physically or demonstrating the glory of God. The truth is we cannot even breathe without Him,[6] and John knew everything he was came from God's decision to put life in a dead womb. He understood his story began at the end of human strength.

No matter how gifted you are, you must become disillusioned with what you can produce and get a vision for what God alone can produce.

Until this happens, you are not safe to carry the glory of God because the power of God requires weakness. His glory will not fully rest on the confident, the proud, and the strong because God resists the proud.[7] As a result, those who are aware of their human weakness can steward the power of God in a way others cannot. God is not looking for "better" humans, nor is He impressed with you.

God may ask you to fulfill your assignment by walking a path that does not make sense by human definition. As we will see, God chose John the Baptist to prepare a nation, but John lived in a small place, disconnected from national leaders, and only publicly ministered for a few months. Most of John's life appeared "barren" in light of his assignment, but John's "barren" life was one of the most fruitful lives in all history.

---

[5]Genesis 1:28; Psalm 115:16.

[6]Job 33:4; Acts 17:28.

[7]Isaiah 2:11–12, 17; 57:15; Proverbs 3:34; Matthew 23:12; Luke 14:11; 1 Peter 5:5–6; James 4:6.

God loves to demonstrate His glory when people no longer have confidence in their own strength.

A Barren Couple and a Barren Nation
Zechariah and Elizabeth's condition was a reflection of their nation.

Israel had just emerged from a brief period of political independence under the Hasmonean dynasty. The dynasty had begun with the fierce zeal of the Maccabees who refused to submit to forced Greek religion or tolerate religious compromise among their people. Tragically, the dynasty quickly succumbed to political strife and serious corruption. This strife set the stage for Herod, an Edomite, to become the ruler of Israel. The Hasmonean dynasty had been Israel's greatest hope since the Babylonian invasion five hundred years earlier, but it failed to restore Israel's glory and instead delivered the nation into the hands of another foreign occupier.

Israel's government was demonstrably barren—unable to produce the promises of God. More importantly, Israel's priesthood had failed. Under the Hasmonean dynasty, the religious leadership of Israel had become a political game, and the high priest had become a political prize. This priesthood had been corrupted.

Herod had heavily invested in the temple and turned it into a structure more visibly impressive than the temple Solomon had built. The temple was the crown of Jerusalem and filled with activity, but the fire that fell on Solomon's temple never fell on Herod's temple. To emphasize the point, the holy of holies, where God's presence dwelled above the ark, was empty because the ark of the covenant had been lost.

The priesthood had political influence but, like the temple, was barren.

Once in a Lifetime
Over decades, Zechariah and Elizabeth were forced to accept her barrenness, and then one day, Zechariah was invited to offer incense in the temple. It was a special privilege because Zechariah probably only offered incense in the temple once in his life. As a priest, this was a moment he lived his entire life for. Zechariah was probably nervous, but he was completely unprepared for what was coming.

As he stood before the altar offering incense, Gabriel suddenly appeared:

> *Now while he was serving as priest before God when his division was on duty, according to the custom of the priesthood, he was chosen by lot to enter the temple of the Lord and burn incense. . . . And there appeared to him an angel of the Lord standing on the right side of the altar of incense. And Zechariah was troubled when he saw him, and fear fell upon him. But the angel said to him, "Do not be afraid, Zechariah, for your prayer has been heard, and your wife Elizabeth will bear you a son, and you shall call his name John. And you will have joy and gladness, and many will rejoice at his birth." (Luke 1:8–9, 11–14)*

This was an incomparable event because Gabriel had only appeared one other time in Israel's history in the book of Daniel. Gabriel's message contained an even greater shock, *"your wife Elizabeth will bear you a son."* Gabriel included a staggering four-fold summary of this son's assignment:

> *For he will be great before the Lord. And he must not drink wine or strong drink, and he will be filled with the Holy Spirit, even from his mother's womb. And he will turn many of the children of Israel to the Lord their God, and he will go before him in the spirit and power of Elijah, to turn the hearts of the fathers to the children, and the disobedient to the wisdom of the just, to make ready for the Lord a people prepared. (Luke 1:15–17)*

In short, John:

- would be great before the Lord.
- would be filled with the Holy Spirit before birth.
- would turn many in Israel to the Lord.
- would go before God in the spirit and power of Elijah to prepare a people.

Elizabeth's barrenness had been her shame, but like Sarah, Rachel, Hannah, and others, it would become her glory.[8]

---

[8]Genesis 11:30; 25:21; 29:31; Judges 13:2; 1 Samuel 1:1–5; Isaiah 54:1.

John's life was an answer to Zechariah and Elizabeth's intercession.[9] Like Hannah, they had groaned for a priestly son, and their intercession had combined with God's desire for a messenger.

What prayers are you praying that may in fact be God's desire?

Gabriel's announcement was a shock. Elizabeth's pregnancy was so miraculous and surprising that Gabriel referred to it as "impossible" and used it to encourage Mary who would also conceive a son outside natural processes.[10] Zechariah found the prophecy impossible to believe. Because of his doubt, Zechariah was struck mute until John's birth.

After Elizabeth conceived, she went into seclusion. Her heart was filled with all kinds of emotion as she suddenly found herself carrying a child long after she had given up all hope of giving birth. She likely wrestled with fears of miscarriage, but her mute husband was a living testimony that this was a miraculous pregnancy and the child she carried was not a product of her own strength.

Understanding Times and Seasons

After predicting John's birth, Gabriel visited Mary to predict her pregnancy. In short time, both Elizabeth and Mary gave birth. Two visits from Gabriel, two miraculous births, and two dramatic prophecies shattered four hundred years of prophetic silence. Within only a few months, things seemed to fall silent again for nearly thirty years.

The people who experienced two astonishing births had to wait nearly thirty years to see the full manifestation of what God had done. Twenty- and thirty-year-olds who watched these events with intensive speculation would be in their fifties and sixties before they saw the fruit of what God had set into motion. Zechariah and Elizabeth would not even be alive when John's voice shattered the darkness and Jesus took the stage.

Luke referenced the story of Samuel to describe the next three decades of John's life:

---

[9]Luke 1:13.

[10]Luke 1:36–37.

Now the boy Samuel continued to grow both in stature and in favor with the LORD and also with man. (1 Samuel 2:26)

And Samuel grew, and the LORD was with him and let none of his words fall to the ground. (1 Samuel 3:19)

And the child grew and became strong in spirit, and he was in the wilderness until the day of his public appearance to Israel. (Luke 1:80)

John's life was very similar to Samuel's:

- John was born to a woman who had been barren.
- His life was the product of intercession.
- He was born at a time when the priesthood was corrupt and had failed.
- He would live as a priest.
- He was a prophetic voice to the priesthood.
- He would grow in the Lord over time.
- He would know the Lord's voice.

For the next three decades, John and Jesus followed a very similar path in obscurity in small places:

And the child [Jesus] grew and became strong, filled with wisdom. And the favor of God was upon him. . . . And Jesus increased in wisdom and in stature and in favor with God and man. (Luke 2:40, 52)

The lack of information in the Gospels on the next thirty years reveals just how quiet and ordinary these years were. (In fact, 90 percent of Jesus' life was apparently too ordinary and mundane to write down in the Gospels.) These seemingly quiet years illustrate a profound principle: God accomplishes His purposes through a combination of His sudden, direct activity and a slow and steady process of growth that feels ordinary and mundane. God is both patient and urgent all at the same time.

Most people do not embrace both aspects of God's work. They either neglect the need for God's miraculous activity *or* the need for faithfulness and growth over long periods of time. Yet both are necessary, and God *enjoys* both the moments of sudden transition and the mundane days of steady growth.

John and Jesus were both born in miraculous circumstances, and then God used thirty years of normal human life and process to mature both of them.

God enjoys this process so much He chose it. When God became a man, He could have come any way He wanted. He simply could have descended from heaven as some sort of superhero and delivered His people. Instead, He *chose* to be born. He *chose* to learn language. He *chose* to live a mundane, ordinary human life in ancient Israel. He *chose* to get up each day, go to work, share meals, and repeat it again. He *chose* to grow in wisdom and stature.[11] Furthermore, God *enjoyed* it.

This is the way of God, and if you do not understand it, you can become offended, discouraged, or disillusioned.

A Priest Who Became a Prophet

God intentionally answered Zechariah's cry for a son in the one moment in his life that Zechariah stood in the holy place. Gabriel's appearance in that moment communicated a message: God was going to give Zechariah a priestly son.

Zechariah's encounter was a summary of John's life. Zechariah stood in the holy place to offer incense once in his life, but John would spend a lifetime offering another kind of incense as he ministered to God day after day in the wilderness. Many other priests would be caught up in politics and other distractions, but John was born to minister to God.

We tend to think of John mainly as a messenger, but this does not describe John accurately. John was primarily a priest who became a public messenger for a very short period of time—likely only 6–18 months.

John's life and everything that accompanied it were all about the priesthood. If we miss this, we will miss the full message of John's life. John was more than a prophet announcing Jesus' arrival. He was a priest whose life was a rebuke to a corrupt, political priesthood.

---

[11]Luke 2:40, 52.

God chose a priestly man to prepare the way for Him, and He still looks for priestly ones to prepare the way for Him.[12]

The family line was very important in Israel, and everyone assumed John was a gift from God to continue Zechariah's family line. The community expected him to be given a family name, but the child would not be named after Zechariah. When John was born, Zechariah confidently wrote, "His name is John," and then prophesied the unique future of the child.

This break with custom was incredibly significant. This miraculous child had not been given to continue Zechariah's priestly line. He would be a priest, but a priest of a different kind. He did not belong to Zechariah; he belonged to God. He was Zechariah's son, but he was not going to continue Zechariah's ministry. God had something different in mind.

John is typically referred to as a messenger, a prophet, or the "forerunner." All those things are true, but they describe what John *did*. They do not capture the essence of who John *was*.

Above everything else, John was a priest, but a priest of a different kind. Instead of standing in the temple to burn incense, he stood in the wilderness and ministered to God as a different kind of priest and a prototype of a new priesthood.

When Jesus spoke about John, He asked a series of penetrating questions:

What did you go out into the wilderness to see? A reed shaken by the wind? What then did you go out to see? A man dressed in soft clothing? Behold, those who wear soft clothing are in kings' houses. What then did you go out to see? (Matthew 11:7–9)

In this section, Jesus asked the same question three times: *What did you go out to see?* No doubt, every time He asked this question, people in the crowd responded, "A prophet," but Jesus continued to press the question. Any time Jesus asks the same question three times in a row it

---

[12]For example, the apostle Paul was launched out of Antioch when he and the other leaders were "ministering" to the Lord (Acts 13:2), which was language typically applied to the priestly ministry. The early church understood churches were temples and believers were priests.

means the assumed answer is not correct. Jesus' question carried a simple message: The crowds had not fully understood what they had seen and heard.

This forces us to ask a serious question: *If the crowds who saw and heard John did not grasp who he truly was, have we truly grasped who he was?*

Like the crowds, we know information about John but have not grasped who John truly was.

Forged in the Wilderness

Many people want to be a "voice," but they cannot become a voice automatically.[1] If you want to be a voice, you must take on God's yoke and embrace the path of formation. He prepares His vessels for years —usually for decades. He has methods of preparation, but He does not have formulas.

Out of the sight of everyone in Jerusalem, God formed and fashioned John in the wilderness for a long thirty years. The spirit of Elijah rested on John as he stood before the Lord and ministered to Him hidden away from the crowds:

> *And the child grew and became strong in spirit, and he was in the wilderness until the day of his public appearance to Israel. (Luke 1:80)*

Crowds are seducing, but the wilderness is where the fire burns, the burning bush appears, and God speaks.

In the wilderness, John lived in communion with God, and a fire burned stronger and stronger in his inner man. John was fully alive as he stood before God and ministered to Him as a priest.

John was called to "go before the face of God,"[2] so he had to live before the face of God.

John had to live before the Lord for thirty years before he was ready to confront the corruption in the priesthood. Many people are eager to "correct" and "confront," but having right information—even if it's biblical—is not enough to give a messenger the right to publicly

---

[1]We must also remember that God defines a "voice" differently than we do. Most of the greatest messengers in the Bible were not preachers and did not work in full-time ministry.

[2]Luke 1:76.

confront God's people. You have to live before the face of God. And let Him transform you.

More Than One Wilderness

There is more than one kind of wilderness, and it is critical to understand the difference. There is the wilderness of testing and the wilderness of communion.

The wilderness of testing is a place of battle, and it is temporary. Faith is tested and refined in this wilderness. The goal is to pass the test and to emerge with power. For example, after Jesus was baptized, He went into the wilderness to be tested for forty days, but He did not stay there. After the test, He left the wilderness with power:

> *And Jesus, full of the Holy Spirit, returned from the Jordan and was led by the Spirit in the wilderness for forty days, being tempted by the devil. . . . And Jesus returned in the power of the Spirit to Galilee, and a report about him went out through all the surrounding country. (Luke 4:1–2, 14)*

However, there is an entirely different kind of wilderness—the wilderness of communion. John is not the only one who lived here. Jesus also retreated to the wilderness as often as He could. Jesus exited the wilderness of testing, but His soul yearned for communion with His Father in the wilderness. Jesus' life in the wilderness was vital to His life and His ministry, so He frequently withdrew to the wilderness:[3]

> *And rising very early in the morning, while it was still dark, he departed and went out to a desolate place, and there he prayed. (Mark 1:35)*

> *But he would withdraw to desolate places and pray. (Luke 5:16)*

Most people focus on leaving the wilderness, but the wilderness must be understood and embraced according to its purpose.

The Crucible of the Wilderness

The wilderness is a crucible that tests the issue of unmet expectations. The wilderness closes in on us and asks a penetrating question: *Is God enough?* When we are asked this question, we all think, *Yes, of course God*

---

[3]See also Matthew 14:23; Mark 6:46; Luke 6:12; John 6:15.

is enough, but the wilderness forces us to face our real answer. The wilderness exposes the deepest desires of our hearts because it seemingly offers only one thing: *the possibility of deep communion with the uncreated God.*

John was probably a gifted man. He was born into a priestly family, which meant he could have ministered in a temple that was more magnificent than the one Solomon built. However, John abandoned the hope of service in the temple and the sense of importance life in Jerusalem carried for the sake of a life in a small, isolated place.

The wilderness not only exposes our deepest desires, but it can also shape our deepest desires. Day in and day out, the wilderness closed in on John and challenged his decisions. Yet John remained in the wilderness devouring the Word of God, establishing a life of prayer, and discipling a small group. He let the crucible of the wilderness mold him into the most powerful messenger in his generation.

Most believers recognize that Jesus' victory over temptation in the wilderness was symbolic. Israel had failed in the wilderness, but Jesus, as the ultimate Israelite, overcame in the wilderness. John's life in the wilderness was symbolic as well. Like Jesus, John lived Israel's wilderness story the way it was meant to be lived. His life was a picture of God's original desire for Israel to be an obedient people who enjoyed communion with God in the wilderness *more* than their inheritance in the land.

John did not take his place at the temple in Jerusalem because he would not prioritize his inheritance over intimacy. He risked everything in the wilderness and abandoned the mirage of "success" in this age. Instead, he pursued the knowledge of God. He stood in the wilderness and pursued intimacy with God before he sought a public assignment. John understood this was what God had intended for Israel after the exodus, and he seized the opportunity to pursue the knowledge of God in a small place.

As we will see, John did all this for one reason: *Jesus' inheritance was more precious to John than his own.*[4]

---

[4]John 3:29–30.

The Test of Unmet Expectations

The story of Israel in the wilderness reveals how much is at stake in the wilderness. When God brought Israel out of Egypt, He did not lead her directly into the Promised Land even though it was a short journey. He led her on a longer journey into the wilderness and gathered her around Mount Sinai. Around that mountain, God revealed Himself to Israel in an unprecedented event that has never been repeated.

God came down on the mountain in smoke and fire. He spoke audibly. The earth shook at His presence. His desire was clear. He had come down to reveal Himself to His people and forge a deep covenant relationship with them. Because God came down *as God*, the people were so terrified they could not endure His presence.

Moses' description of the scene is stunning:

Now Mount Sinai was wrapped in smoke because the LORD had descended on it in fire. The smoke of it went up like the smoke of a kiln, and the whole mountain trembled greatly. (Exodus 19:18)

Now when all the people saw the thunder and the flashes of lightning and the sound of the trumpet and the mountain smoking, the people were afraid and trembled, and they stood far off and said to Moses, "You speak to us, and we will listen; but do not let God speak to us, lest we die." (20:18–19)

The Israelites were terrified by God's presence, but within a short period of time they had made a golden calf, called it YHWH, and worshipped it with pagan practices.[5] How did Israel so quickly transition from the terror of God's presence to bold idolatry at the foot of the mountain?

The answer is simple: *unmet expectations.*

God led Israel into the wilderness to reveal Himself and form covenant with the nation before He brought her into the land. Though Israel wanted the Promised Land, she wanted her "destiny" *and* her "inheritance." The irony of the situation is God had already promised Israel a profound inheritance and vividly demonstrated His ability to fulfill His promises.

---

[5]Exodus 32:1–7.

This wilderness is the place where God lovingly calls us to come away and allow Him to shape new dreams and new desires. God gathered Israel in the wilderness to enter into covenant and ask Israel a deep question: *Am I enough for you?*

God did not bring Israel into the wilderness for punishment. God designed the wilderness to be a place of tender encounter where Israel entered into deep covenant with Him. In a sense, it was a "honeymoon" before He brought Israel into the land and gave her an inheritance. God wanted a kind of communion with Israel that would not be possible once her people spread out and began enjoying their inheritance in the land. The wilderness only became a place of hardship and judgment because of Israel's disobedience.

Even though Israel failed in the wilderness, God's deep desire for His people caused Him to view Israel's time in the wilderness with deep affection centuries after the exodus:[6]

Go and proclaim in the hearing of Jerusalem, Thus says the LORD, *"I remember the devotion of your youth, your love as a bride, how you followed me in the wilderness, in a land not sown." (Jeremiah 2:2)*

The exodus demonstrates a profound pattern: God seeks intimacy and covenant with us in the wilderness before He seeks "ministry" or "impact."

You can see God's desire in His first statement to Pharaoh:

Afterward Moses and Aaron went and said to Pharaoh, "Thus says the LORD, *the God of Israel, 'Let my people go, that they may hold a feast to me in the wilderness.'" (Exodus 5:1)*

God obviously planned to give Israel her inheritance in the land, but He commanded Pharaoh to let Israel go so she could worship, feast, and enjoy God's presence. Communion was first, then inheritance. Relationship was on God's mind before assignment.

Ancient people associated the greatness of a nation with the power of its gods. When Israel saw YHWH demonstrate His superiority over

---

[6]See also Ezekiel 20:35–36. When Israel sinned, Moses would go outside the camp away from the people to commune with YHWH (Exodus 33:7).

the gods of Egypt,[7] the Israelites reasonably assumed YHWH would quickly form her into a nation much greater than Egypt had ever been. In a sense, Israel expected to become "Egypt 2.0." The Israelites assumed their newly liberated nation would glorify YHWH with its prosperity, might, and grandeur. They wanted an inheritance among the nations, not a camping trip in the wilderness.

Israel valued the hope of a nation more than the divine presence among the barrenness of the wilderness. Because YHWH did not do what Israel expected when Israel expected it, Israel took things into her own hands. Israel made a God in her own image and called it YHWH. The Israelites did not abandon YHWH; they just redefined Him according to their own desires. Israel's idolatry illustrates that what we think is for "God's glory" can be more directly connected to our own hopes, dreams, and expectations.

Unmet expectations fueled Israel's idolatry. They ended up worshipping a calf because they did not have a vision for communion with God in the wilderness.

Israel assumed God wanted a glorious nation, which was true. However, God wanted something else first—*priests:*

"And you shall be to me a kingdom of priests and a holy nation.' These are the words that you shall speak to the people of Israel." (Exodus 19:6)

God always intended to take Israel into the land, but Israel had to be established as a priestly people *before* a king could be given or the land could be taken. When God organized Israel in the wilderness, He placed the tribes of Israel around the tabernacle as a visual statement that the nation was a priestly people gathered around God's dwelling place.

God wanted a people who stood before Him before they took their place among the nations. Tragically, Israel rejected the intimacy God offered her in the wilderness because she was more interested in an immediate inheritance in the land than the inheritance of God in her midst. Ironically, Israel's fixation on her inheritance ended up delaying her entry into the Promised Land.

Unmet expectations are one of your biggest enemies in this age.

---

[7]Exodus 12:12.

A Wilderness People

If we only see the wilderness as a place to "pay the price" to obtain our inheritance, we will suffer tremendous loss—a loss of *the knowledge of God.* Have we heeded the warning of Israel's story? Or do we still avoid the wilderness more eager for impact than intimacy? Israel's failure in the wilderness set up the tragedy that unfolded when she entered the land. Do you realize there will be future consequences for not embracing the purpose of the wilderness of this age?

Our life in this age is an encounter in the wilderness. It is a unique opportunity that will never come again to forge relationship with God.

The Bible presents our walk with God in this age as a "pilgrimage" where we are "strangers" waiting for a future inheritance,[8] yet Christian conferences, books, and ministries incessantly call us to pursue our inheritance, our destiny, and find fulfillment in this age. The concept of our "destiny" is so strong that the task of missions is being affected by the pursuit of destiny. It is now common to hear people speak more about their "calling to missions" than their burden to empty out their lives on behalf of another people.[9]

Many members of the body of Christ are currently paralyzed by a relentless pursuit of fulfillment in their assignment.

We need to carefully examine our expectations, our motivations, and even our gospel. Like Israel, we long to escape any wilderness in this age. Like Israel, we have great expectations of success, fulfillment, and inheritance. Like Israel, we are slowly making God into our image and using Him to pursue our inheritance instead of bearing the tensions of living in the wilderness of this age.

The church is a wilderness people, and we must be reoriented to a wilderness mindset before the return of Jesus.

---

[8]Matthew 6:19–20; Romans 8:23; 1 Corinthians 9:25; 2 Corinthians 1:22; 5:5; Ephesians 1:14; 4:30; Colossians 1:5; 1 Timothy 6:18–19; 2 Timothy 4:8; Hebrews 11:9–10, 13–16; 25–26; James 1:12; 1 Peter 5:4.

[9]Of course, it is not wrong to feel a compelling burden for a missionary assignment, but that call is about emptying your life for another people, not finding your identity in the assignment.

Jesus is not returning for a church satisfied with her success in this age. He is returning for a church dissatisfied with His absence, a church filled with longing for Jesus to receive the final reward of His suffering.

The Father loves His Son far too much to send Him to a people who are satisfied with His absence.

God raised up John and placed Him outside the land to confront Israel with the reality of her condition and call her to prepare for the arrival of God. In the same way, God is going to raise up messengers again to call His people back to the wilderness. Most of them will be unknown. Like John, they will be great, but by a definition of greatness that is foreign to most people.

Messengers may challenge people with their words, but God typically makes His biggest statement through their lifestyles. For example, John never left the wilderness. His entire life was a profound statement calling people to reorient their lives to the message he proclaimed. Like John, we are called to be a people who live our lives differently. Our lifestyle should provoke people to re-evaluate their own lives.

A wilderness lifestyle seems radical to many, but it is not radical at all. It is a reasonable response to the Word of God and the possibilities of communion in the wilderness.

Far too often we dismiss people who take the Bible seriously as extreme, but God raised up an extreme man to prepare the way for His Son's first coming, and we should expect something similar to prepare the way for His Son's second coming. God will raise up messengers, but more than that, He is going to form His church into a corporate messenger. A people who have more pain over His absence than delight in their success will prepare the way for Jesus.

It's time for a generation to emerge that will not claim its inheritance until Jesus receives His.

Jesus is fully God, and this means He was the One who stood on Mount Sinai,[10] clothed with fire and surrounded by earthquakes and thunder. Can you imagine Jesus gazing at Israel with great desire, longing for her affections and watching as Israel turned aside to worship a golden calf?

---

[10]Exodus 19:18–20.

Jesus now looks from heaven upon His people who live in the wilderness of this age. His eyes are filled with the same desire. What does He see? Does He see a people gazing back at Him? Or does He see a people distracted with the gods of this age, using His name but seeking pleasure in their own idols?

Israel experienced fire on a mountain, and we have been given something greater: a fire within through the Spirit. Will we go the way of Israel or the way of John?

Regardless of what Jesus sees now, we know what He is going to see before this is over. He is going to see a people filled with longing, a people who desire Him with a desire that corresponds to His own desire. Jesus' return is referred to as a wedding celebration.[11] No one wants to delay the day of their wedding, and yet many of Jesus' people are not thinking about the day of their wedding. *It will not end this way, however.* God is going to get a people who are more captivated by Him than the things of this age.

Far too many in the church are unknowingly living according to an unbiblical paradigm of seeking their inheritance in this age when the biblical framework is to live for Jesus' inheritance in this age.

Captivated before the Crisis

Crises enable us to quickly focus our attention on the things that are most valuable and ignore the things that are superficial. The trouble that will come at the end of the age will serve a similar purpose. It will disrupt our comfort and cause us to turn our affections to Jesus and set our hope on His return. In short, it will align our agenda with God's.

In the future, when we lose the comforts we currently enjoy and the diversions that presently take our time, it will give us a chance to focus our gaze on Jesus.

Trouble will come, but we do not know when that disruption will come, and we do not have to wait for it. We have an invitation *right now* to turn aside, take the Word of God seriously, and ask the Holy Spirit to align our affections with His. If we respond, we can begin to live wholeheartedly as a wilderness people even if we live in a comfortable, prosperous, and distracting place.

---

[11]Matthew 22:2; 2 Corinthians 11:2; Ephesians 5:32; Revelation 19:7.

Many believers assume crisis will be required to bring the church to maturity. While the Lord can (and does) use crisis, it is not required. The early church took root in prosperous regional cities, because there is a divine person who is more captivating than pleasure, comfort, and success. Many people assume the gospel is most powerful among the poor and in the midst of calamity, but that is the opposite of Paul's church planting strategy.

The first apostles planted churches in powerful, affluent cities, demonstrating the gospel is stronger than affluence. Jesus can be loved wholeheartedly *before* the end-time crisis.

God is raising up people and churches that will begin to embrace the way of the wilderness in the midst of prosperity, peace, trouble, and disruption. The invitation is being given now. You do not have to wait for end-time events to unfold.

Can you hear the invitation?

The Bridegroom in the Wilderness

Regardless of where you live, you are called to a wilderness lifestyle so God becomes your inheritance and a relationship is forged in intimacy. You will always get off track if you set your hope on fulfillment in this age. Consequently, the New Testament describes us as "sojourners" and "exiles" in this age:[1]

> *Beloved, I urge you as sojourners and exiles to abstain from the passions of the flesh. (1 Peter 2:11)*

Far too many people think their "assignment"[2] in this age is their inheritance. Our assignments are not our inheritance because God did not create us merely for work. He made us for relationship, and if you make your "work" (or ministry) your reward, it reduces your value to a function.

The true value of our assignment is not what we accomplish, the accolades we earn, or the sense of satisfaction they may bring. The true value of our assignment is that we get to labor with God, discover who He is in the labor, and spend our strength to give Him His inheritance.

God Himself is our inheritance, not our assignment. Therefore, the wilderness is not a delay; it is the place where we begin to encounter our true reward and enjoy our true inheritance.

---

[1] See also Hebrews 11:13; 1 Peter 1:1, 17.

[2] People often use the word *calling* when they mean their assignment in this age. The New Testament almost always uses the word *calling* to describe our lives before God, not our vocation (Romans 1:1, 6–7; 8:28, 30; 9:26; 11:29; 1 Corinthians 1:1–2, 9, 24, 26; 7:18, 20–22, 24; 15:9; Galatians 1:6, 15; Ephesians 1:18; 4:1, 4; Philippians 3:14; Colossians 3:15; 1 Thessalonians 2:12; 4:7; 5:24; 2 Thessalonians 1:11; 2:14; 1 Timothy 6:12; 2 Timothy 1:9; Hebrews 3:1; James 2:7; 1 Peter 1:15; 2:9, 21; 2 Peter 1:10; Jude 1).

John referred to himself as the "friend of the bridegroom"[3] because He had a revelation of God as a divine bridegroom. When John spoke about God as a bridegroom, his audience immediately understood it was a reference to God's revelation of Himself as the divine Bridegroom in the wilderness of Sinai. God's encounter with Israel at Mount Sinai was modeled after a wedding ceremony because Israel was brought into the wilderness to become God's covenant companion. Centuries after the exodus, God continued to use passionate language to speak about Israel's time in the wilderness.[4]

God came to Israel in the wilderness as a bridegroom because the wilderness is about covenant, communion, and intimacy with God.

The wilderness is the place God forges a relationship with His people that is not possible in the midst of other distractions. In the wilderness, God offers us the most expensive gift He can give: *Himself.*

A People Shaped by the Wilderness

We are far too eager to receive certain "blessings," and as a result, we are missing a profound opportunity to forge covenant with God in the wilderness of this age.

This age only has two primary purposes:[5]

- It is a stage for God to reveal Himself in a way He was not previously known.
- It is a context designed by God to forge a companion for His Son.

This age is God's immersive classroom[6] where He reveals Himself to us and then conforms us to His image. This age is not the place for our ultimate purpose; it is the place of our preparation. To use an analogy, this entire age is a preschool. A student should be diligent in preschool, but preschool is not the student's ultimate purpose. Your true purpose

---

[3]John 3:29.

[4]Ezekiel 16:8; Jeremiah 2:2; Hosea 2:15.

[5]For more on this see the book *What Does God Want? Aligning Your Life with God's Desire.*

[6]A phrase developed by Stuart Greaves in numerous teachings.

and identity will not be revealed in this age,[7] and if you do not recognize this, you can waste your life on the wrong pursuits.

There will be incredible weeping and wailing at the Lord's return when millions suddenly realize they missed the entire purpose of this age.

Millions of saints will sob uncontrollably when the façade of this age is finally broken.[8] They will be saved by God's mercy, but when they stand before Him, He will be a distant Savior and not a familiar friend. As one preacher used to say, "The opportunity of a lifetime must be seized during the lifetime of the opportunity."[9] This age is a unique opportunity to forge relationship with God and learn His ways —an opportunity that will never come again in this way.

God's plan in this age will produce a people who are brilliant and stunning—prepared to be His eternal companion.

This age has been designed by God to shape us so we become *like* Him and can be *joined to* Him in deep intimacy.[10] Once the Bride (church) is mature, this age will be over:

> *After this I heard what seemed to be the loud voice of a great multitude in heaven, crying out, "Hallelujah! Salvation and glory and power belong to our God. . . ." Then I heard what seemed to be the voice of a great multitude, like the roar of many waters and like the sound of mighty peals of thunder, crying out, "Hallelujah! For the Lord our God the Almighty reigns. Let us rejoice and exult and give him the glory, for the marriage of the Lamb has come, and his Bride has made herself ready; it was granted her to clothe herself with fine linen, bright and pure"—for the fine linen is the righteous deeds of the saints. (Revelation 19:6–8)*

The implications of this song are stunning—a day is going to come when the church comes to maturity and becomes so much like Jesus that heaven will declare the church to be a fitting companion for God. Think about what this communicates: Married spouses are not

---

[7] 1 John 3:2.

[8] 1 Corinthians 3:10–15.

[9] A phrase often repeated by Leonard Ravenhill.

[10] See the book *What Does God Want? Aligning Your Life with God's Desire.*

identical, but they must be compatible. We will not be made divine, but we are going to be made compatible to God—so much like Him that marriage is the closest analogy for how we will relate to Him.

Notice also the angels do not cry out, "This is unjust!" when the church is joined to Jesus. They do not question whether the church is an appropriate companion for Jesus; instead, they look on in awe and amazement, wondering how God used this age to make a fallen people compatible to Himself.

This is our future, and we are prepared for it by treating this age like a wilderness.

As long as this age fascinates us, it obscures our glorious future, so we need a wilderness mentality that scoffs at the things that capture men's affections in this age. If we cannot see this age clearly, we will not live in it correctly nor utilize this time properly. Tragically, most people do not have any substantial vision for their lives beyond this age even though the New Testament repeatedly sets our focus on our eternal calling as God's companion.[11]

God is not committed to your "success" (by human definition) in this age, but He is committed to making you like Himself.

A Call to the Wilderness

When we seek fulfillment and inheritance in this age, we demonstrate a profound ignorance of God's eternal plan.

Billions of people live fascinated with this age because they either do not grasp what God wants, or they have no desire to embrace a wilderness approach to this age for the sake of intimacy with God. But it will not end this way.

God is going to confront our apathy toward Him with a people who are no longer enamored with this age. This people will live in small places or big places, but they will treat this age like a wilderness and live careful lives pursuing an intimacy with God that was not possible when their hearts were still gripped by competing affections.

This people will pursue God with a fierce tenacity that will surprise many and even shock others.

---

[11]Romans 8:29; 1 Corinthians 15:49; 2 Corinthians 3:18; 4:10–11; Ephesians 5:31–32; 1 John 3:2; Revelation 19:7.

They will abandon comforts, success, and human praise in this age, considering the prize of intimacy with God more precious than anything they may forfeit. They will eagerly pursue changes in their lifestyle that others would never consider. To the world, this people will appear as bizarre as John did in his generation. To heaven, they will appear rational and reasonable.

Many will consider them to be too extreme, but they will dramatically advance the cause of world evangelism in two ways. First, they will jolt the church out of her fascination with this age and point her to her glorious inheritance in God. This will set the church free from many of the chains that currently hold the church back, and it will play a profound part in mobilizing the global church for end-time missions. Second, the world will see a people whose lifestyle corresponds to their message. This combination of the message and demonstration of the gospel will produce a great witness of the gospel.

The world is not provoked by the gospel when they see Christians captured by the same dreams that capture everyone else.

When Christianity becomes a more "religious" option to achieving success and Jesus is presented as a way to achieve our human goals and obtain eternal bliss, it does not provoke the world. The world sees through our charade when we adopt certain practices or moral codes but remain captivated by the same things that motivate everyone else. However, the world is confronted any time a people willingly and joyfully dismiss any inheritance in this age.

It is time for the church to become a people who embrace the wilderness.

God is looking for a people, not isolated individuals, who will hear this call. The call to the wilderness is a call to a corporate way of life—not an insular one.

The God of the Wilderness

The wilderness is more than a test to pass or a temporary season. It is a place where our thinking and our affections are transformed. Before this age is over, there will be a people who not only embrace the lifestyle of the wilderness—they will seek it out.

When individuals are addicted to drugs, they must go through a painful detox to become free. When they begin detox, they may feel like they are going to die, but as they persist, they begin to regain freedom from their life of addiction. Through this painful process, they rediscover true life.

We do not realize the spirit of the age is like an addictive drug that offers destructive pleasures and distorts our thinking.

When we are under the influence of the spirit of the age, we cannot grasp the pleasures of spiritual sobriety that are found in the wilderness. So many are genuinely saved and intensely loved by God, but they are still under the grip of an addiction to the narcotic of this age.

The wilderness is the place where we are weaned off our addiction to this age. This detox only feels like a punishment when other desires are greater than the desire for communion. Detox can feel excruciating in the beginning, but then it produces life and freedom.

Many taste the wilderness when they intentionally engage in spiritual disciplines or embrace a time of fasting. Tragically, many experience momentary spiritual growth through intentionality, but they may prematurely abandon the wilderness and revert back to their previous lifestyle. As a result, the spiritual vibrancy they have tasted soon fades back to spiritual dullness.

I want to give you courage. Once you have tasted the pleasures of the wilderness, *you do not have to go back* to old ways of living. Life in this age tries to make incredible demands on our time. It requires we fill our time with various activities, stay current with the sway of the culture, and keep up with popular entertainments. *You do not have to yield to these demands.* You can continue to forge a new path—and continue to pursue wholeheartedness. If you do, you will find a new dimension of life. You will discover spiritual sobriety. And when you do, you will see the fog of this age clearly. You may find a new life by making certain disciplines lifelong practices.

Once you taste the power of the wilderness, you do not have to leave the wilderness.

The wilderness was the place Israel heard God's audible voice, saw Him in smoke and fire on the mountain, and experienced earthquakes that accompanied His presence. When they entered the land, His presence was hidden in the holy of holies.

There are some revelations of God you only encounter in the wilderness.

It is possible to obtain an inheritance in the land but lose the manifestation of His presence. Israel's love for Egypt's glory and her desire for the land clouded her vision because she valued her inheritance more than the manifest presence of God. In the same way, fascination with this age obscures the glories of deep communion with God through the indwelling Holy Spirit.

We tend to avoid the wilderness so we can chase impact which typically means popularity and success in this age. We usually say (and perhaps sincerely feel) we want to make an impact for God, but many times our pursuit of impact is more connected to our own glory than God's. We want to be known and celebrated in a way that does not seem possible in the wilderness.

Like Israel, we can pursue the promises of God in an idolatrous way when we neglect the wilderness of communion.

It should alarm us that preaching in the affluent world often centers on God's benefits in this age. God often graciously saves people despite this message, but it is a distorted message that sets people up for idolatry. God loves to bless His people, but He will not be reduced to the means of our blessing, nor is He forming us for success in this age. In fact, He warns of the opposite.[12] If God is your *true* dream, He will graciously give you many things. But He will not be reduced to a means to a desired end.

God loves to bless us, but He does not exist for us. We exist for Him. Far too often, we are honoring a Jesus we have shaped according to our own image and desires rather than Jesus as He has chosen to reveal Himself. This utilitarian way of relating to God is very close to idolatry, and it often leads there.

Utilitarian relationships with God are as dangerous as utilitarian marriages because, if something "better" comes along, your loyalties will shift.

You must ask soberly—what is the *true* dream of your heart?

- Is it God?
- Or your calling?
- Or your "destiny"?
- Or something else?

---

[12]John 16:33.

Because he was born in the priestly line, John could have had an inheritance in Jerusalem in the temple. Instead, he pursued a different inheritance in the wilderness and became a priest of a different kind. If you understand you will be a priest *forever*, you will reshape your priorities in this age in light of your eternal future. *If you do not realize the priesthood is your only permanent vocation, you will overemphasize your assignments in this age.*

You do not need to pursue "weird" ways of living for the sake of being different, nor should you seek to stand out, but as long as you are enamored with the culture, you cannot be a messenger to it. Many people are trying to become "successful" to "bring the kingdom" to society, but the job of the church is to demonstrate another definition of success and, in the process, expose the falsehoods of this age. This age promises much, but in reality the emperor of this age has no clothes. It is all a mirage that has no substance though it makes incredible demands of us.

The spirit of this age is so pervasive and has so much momentum few are willing to question or confront the illusion—even in the church. However, the church is called to confront and expose this illusion in the way we live.

John's message of repentance was shocking because John first called *Israel* to repent. Israel expected God to deliver her from gentile oppressors like Rome, but gentile oppressors were not the real problem. John addressed the much bigger problem: Israel was not compatible with God. God could end the rule of Rome in a moment, but Israel was not ready for His rule.

Do we truly want God, or do we simply want God to change our situation?

When God delivered Israel from Egypt, the exodus quickly deteriorated into idol worship and divine judgment because the people did not truly want God. *So what do you want?*

Perhaps you are beginning to feel conviction because of your own fascination with this age. This conviction is *good*, and it is not *condemnation*. Remember God revealed Himself to Israel in the wilderness when Israel was in compromise, and He will do the same for you. The call to the wilderness is an *invitation*, not an *evaluation*. He is not looking for those who have obtained perfection. He is looking for those who will embrace the process.

If you embrace the process, He will bring the transformation. If you will follow Him into the wilderness, He will take care of the rest.

Leaving Lesser Lights

For thousands of years, skies across the earth were dark at night, but due to electricity, modern cities are no longer dark. Instead, they seem to glow because of artificial light. Modern lighting enables a "night life" in cities, but it has another consequence: It is no longer possible to see the brilliance of the stars in the sky. Our electric lights cannot remotely compare with the brilliance of a single star (our sun is only a medium-sized star[13]), but artificial lights can obscure the brilliance of thousands of stars. This phenomena is known as "light pollution."

Living in this age is like living in a modern city at night. It is a mix of darkness and artificial lights. There is an illusion of light, but it obscures your vision of "heavenly" light. If you live in a modern city, the only way to see the brilliance of the stars is to get outside the city and head to the wilderness. Accordingly, the only way to get a vision of "heavenly" light is to get into the wilderness.

Just as the stars in the sky are more visible and more brilliant when you are away from the lights of the city, so too the Person of God burns most vividly in the wilderness.

Divine Jealousy

The wilderness is a place where God removes distractions and eliminates other options. There are times God restricts and reduces us to mature us. He will even prevent your temporary success because He is more zealous for who you become than what you accomplish. When God restricts and reduces you, it is not rejection—it is a demonstration of His jealousy for you. But if your assignment is your highest joy, it will feel like a punishment. You may even mistake it for spiritual "warfare."

In the wilderness, John submitted to God's jealousy over his life, and if you follow the same path, you you will discover the burning emotions of a God who is jealous for a relationship not possible in the middle of distractions and competing affections.

---

[13]Tim Sharp, "How Big is the Sun?" Space.com, October 31, 2017, https://www.space.com/17001-how-big-is-the-sun-size-of-the-sun.html/.

God's activity cannot be understood apart from His jealousy. It is one of the most overlooked parts of His character, but it is so central He *named* Himself "Jealous":

> For the LORD, *whose name is Jealous.* . . . *(Exodus 34:14)*
>
> For the LORD *your God in your midst is a jealous God.* . . . *(Deuteronomy 6:15)*

We usually consider jealousy a negative emotion because we often confuse jealousy and envy. *Jealousy* is intense desire for something that belongs to you and is being threatened by someone else. *Envy* is intense desire for something that belongs to someone else. Jealousy is right, and envy is wrong. For example, a man should be jealous if someone tries to seduce his wife because he is in covenant with her. In fact, if a husband lets another man seduce his wife with no emotion and no response, something is intrinsically wrong. We instinctively know he should be jealous. On the other hand, if a man has desire for another man's wife, that is envy, and it is obviously wrong.

Any time a covenantal relationship is threatened, jealousy is the normal and expected response.

Jealous husbands are not careful, and they are not concerned about collateral damage. They are only concerned with the object of their affection. Jealousy is not rational or reasonable because it flows from intense desire. We understand this in human relationships, but we tend to overlook it in God's relationship with us because we forget He is a real person. God's jealousy is a beautiful expression of the intensity of His commitment to His people. His jealousy undergirds the most intense biblical descriptions of His salvation and His judgments. God's jealousy is a biblical description of His love. And divine jealousy is much, much more intense than human jealousy.

God's name is Jealous, and He relates to His people as a jealous husband. Until you know God as the jealous God, you do not truly know Him.

If you are in Jesus, you are in a covenantal relationship with God, and God relates to you as a jealous bridegroom. This is beautiful, but it can be terrifying. For example, if believers wholeheartedly pursue sin after coming into covenant with Jesus, they will quickly discover the jealousy of God. They will find sin that used to be enjoyable is no longer satisfying. It may even lead to depression and misery because they cannot find any relief in their compromise. God will surround a compromised believer "with thorns,"[14] meaning He will use difficulty to provoke them to return to Him. The reason for this is simple: *Once you belong to God, He will not share you.*

The Lord will cut you off from *anything* that competes with Him. He will not be one affection among competing affections—even "Christian" ones. He wants to be your supreme love who determines every other aspect of your life. He wants you to love Him as wholeheartedly as He loves you. He is not hoping His people will love Him. He has predicted His people *will* love Him, and He is able to fulfill His promise.[15]

In His jealousy, God did not hesitate to shatter Israel's idols—even when they were promised blessings—and He will not hesitate to remove anything that competes with Him, even a "successful" business or ministry.

God's jealousy is central to His character. It is a demonstration of the strength of His love. If we are uncomfortable with His jealousy, we are uncomfortable with His love.

---

[14]Hosea 2:6.

[15]Genesis 17:8; Exodus 6:7; 19:5; Leviticus 26:11–12; Ruth 1:16; Song of Songs 2:16; 6:3; Jeremiah 7:23; 11:4; 30:22; 31:33; Ezekiel 36:28; 37:26–28; Zechariah 2:11; 8:8; Revelation 21:3.

Courage to Choose the Wilderness

Do you have the courage to *choose* the wilderness? *This way of living comes at a high cost because communion with God requires you to cut other things off.*

We live in a time of unprecedented leisure time[1] with seemingly unlimited options to fill that time. Furthermore, social and visual media have created a deep and profound fear casually referred to as FOMO: the Fear Of Missing Out. Even though our lives are jammed with activity, we continually fear we will "miss something" because we are constantly bombarded with images and advertisements of everything else we could be doing. Social media adds to the pressure by giving us a constant glimpse of everyone else's carefully curated lives.

Millions live FOMO-driven lives, constantly checking their social media in case they might be missing out on something. Are you one of them?

God is not something you add to your life for a little more excitement, a sense of meaning, or an emotional boost. He is not something meant to fill in the "empty" space in our lives. People often speak about God as if He exists for us, but in reality, we exist for Him.

Our God is a consuming fire,[2] *and if you open yourself to Him, He will consume your life.*

Jesus terrified the Israelites when He consumed the top of Mount Sinai in fire,[3] and His suffering did not diminish His majesty. It *increased* it. His sacrifice did not make Him less of a consuming fire; it enabled

---

[1]Brian Harris, "Sorry, I've no time. Really?" June 20, 2019, https://brianharrisauthor.com/sorry-ive-no-time-really/.

[2]Hebrews 12:29.

[3]Exodus 19:16–20; 20:18–21.

us to approach the consuming fire and survive. He is both fear and pleasure, terror and majesty. His presence is accompanied by earthquakes, thunder, lightning, hurricanes, and wind storms,[4] all things we cannot control that can also terrify us. God made all these things, and they are all *less* terrifying than His glory.

Jesus is not content to be an accessory to your life. His love consumed Him to the point of self-sacrifice, and He is going to form a people similarly consumed by their love for Him. The fact He tolerates so much of our deep self-centeredness is a profound demonstration of His humility, kindness, patience, love, and long-suffering.

A New Kind of FOMO

It is time to call a generation to a new kind of FOMO.

The idea of FOMO is right; we should fear "missing out." The problem is we fear missing out on the wrong things. As a result, we try to add God as an accessory onto lives, yet we are still largely consumed with the same things that drive the prevailing culture.

You have been trained by media and peer pressure to fear missing out on amusements, but you need a God-given fear—a terror really—that your lifestyle is causing you to miss out on the knowledge of God.

When you breathe your final breath, you will not be concerned about the trivial things that pervade social media and so easily dominate your life. You cannot remember what grabbed your attention on Instagram a year ago, and I guarantee you will not be able to recall it on your deathbed either.

As you breathe your final breath with the ocean of eternity in front of you, will you be crushed by the weight of thousands of hours of time that could be have been spent pursuing the knowledge of God but were instead given to things so trivial you will not even be able to recall them?

You need a God-saturated FOMO—a terror that you can live eighty years coasting through this age like it is an amusement park. For humans, this age only has two real purposes—one is to reveal God to

---

[4]Exodus 19:16–20; 20:18–21; Isaiah 6:1–4; Ezekiel 1; Revelation 4.

us, and the second is that we would become like God.⁵ However, how can you become like a person you do not even know?

We have reduced becoming like Jesus to learning His moral code, so we think, if we can resist stealing and pornography, we have become like Jesus. There are many different methods people can use to change their behavior, though. God is after much more than modified behavior; He wants people who are *like* Him. When you assume the knowledge of God is found in adopting behaviors rather than becoming like a person, you become a hypocrite trying to shape your external life to demonstrate an internal reality you do not have.

To be transformed, you must behold the glory of God:⁶

And we all, with unveiled face, beholding the glory of the Lord, are being transformed into the same image from one degree of glory to another. For this comes from the Lord who is the Spirit. (2 Corinthians 3:18)

You behold this glory through the work of the Holy Spirit in your inner man.⁷ Through His work, what is recorded in Scripture becomes alive in your inner man. It takes time to behold this glory. It does not always feel exciting in the moment, but it produces something tremendous over time. You also behold this glory *together* with others. It is not an isolated pursuit. Holy conversations and true fellowship in the church fuel your desire for God and are part of the path to maturity.⁸

Our lifestyles often allow room for some Christian information and biblical insights, but by and large we are not beholding the glory of the Lord together in our FOMO-driven lives. Too often we are simply trying to fit God in the gaps with a little meditation, occasional Bible reading, a prayer offered, and a few Sunday services. We even treat conversations with Him far more casually than we would a conversation with any other person. If this is your present condition,

---

⁵See the book *What Does God Want? Aligning Your Life with God's Desire.*

⁶For more on the centrality of beholding, see *Discipleship Begins with Beholding.*

⁷John 16:12–15.

⁸Proverbs 18:21; Malachi 3:16; Ephesians 4:1–16; Hebrews 10:24–25.

God may have genuinely saved you, but you are missing out on the knowledge of God.

It's time for eternity-driven FOMO.

John had to make choices. If he had stayed in Jerusalem, he could have been a part of the temple system and a faithful priest. Perhaps he would have become an influential rabbi. He could have pursued activity and influence, but he had a fear of missing out, so he lived in the wilderness where he became the priest he was born to be and the messenger God wanted him to be.

Will you choose the way of the wilderness?

You may not need to leave where you live, but we all need a radical reorientation toward the life of the wilderness. Everyone wants to be a "voice" that speaks truth, but very few are willing to live a lifestyle against the grain of the culture. You cannot confront our generation if your life is consumed by the same passions, hopes, dreams, and fears as everyone else in our generation.

Going "against the tide" does not primarily mean criticizing what is wrong in the culture. You should not expect the culture of this age to follow God's ways.[9] It does not mean being strange for the sake of being strange or being overly critical. It means you begin to live with different dreams, hopes, joys, and fears. In short, it means you begin to order your life as though the Bible is true.

The Joy of Missing Out

There is a realm of pleasure only found when you make a decisive move to cut distractions and needless activity for a greater purpose. Compromise can never produce it. Endless activity, hobbies, and variety cannot produce it. Entertainment cannot produce it. Human affirmation and accolades cannot produce it.

It's time to exchange our FOMO for *JOMO:* the Joy of Missing Out.

If a young man wants to experience the full pleasure of taking a wife, he has to cut some things off. Previous pastimes must be abandoned. Old friendships change dramatically, and some must be cut off. His entire lifestyle must change. He must lose "his freedom," and

---

[9] 2 Corinthians 4:4.

yet he does it willingly. *Why?* Because he discovered a superior pleasure in the demands of a relationship that is not possible as long as he maintains his freedom, independence, options, and amusements.

We love our freedom and our options so much it has cost us the pleasure of knowing God.

God is a *person*. Intimate relationship with Him will cost us our freedom, and it will cost us many of our amusements. Relationship with a divine person demands real time and real attention. Single men know what it is like to "lose" a friend to a marriage. However, young men gladly "lose" certain things to gain intimacy with a desirable companion. You must learn the lesson of a man in love: As long as you keep certain options open, you can never obtain what your heart craves. Many people have genuine desire for the knowledge of God, but they are kept from the thing they seek by keeping other options open.

Perhaps we have gone as far as we can go in God without cutting off some of our "options."

Why do men enter into marriage, cut off options, abandon freedom, and risk long-time friendships? *Love.* This forces a question: *Are you willing to "lose" areas of your life in order to gain God?* If not, why not? If we are willing, then why does it seem so rare to see people "losing" things in order to gain God?

The answer is the same as it is for marriage: *love.* If you are captured by love, then losing something to obtain greater intimacy with the object of your affection is worth it. The cost may feel great, but love values the pleasure of intimacy with a treasured person more than the cost of that intimacy. However, if you are not captured by love, the cost required for relationship with another person seems too high. Accordingly, the cost of the knowledge of God can seem "too high" if you do not have a revelation of His beauty.

The value of something—or Someone—is expressed by what you are willing to give up to obtain it.

When you are reluctant to lose something else in order to obtain the knowledge of God, you demonstrate your perception of the value of the knowledge of God. We are quick to receive the "free gift" of salvation yet seem reluctant to pay much in return. This may indicate we do not value our salvation as much as we think we do.

Imagine if a young man told a potential spouse, "I love you the most, but I would like to spend some time each week enjoying and getting to know other women. I just need some downtime and would enjoy some recreation with them, but I won't sleep with them. I only want ultimate intimacy with you." What woman would accept such a proposal?

No woman would be delighted with her husband's intimacy with a myriad of other women as long as he committed to avoid additional sexual partners. However, this is essentially how we treat God. We reserve our deepest commitment for Him yet continue to seek pleasure, rest, and recreation in competing affections. We think if we do not cross certain lines it is okay, but in reality it is like offering a spouse an exclusive sexual relationship while enjoying every other kind of intimacy with many others.

A young man in love often takes time to carefully consider certain "costs" of obtaining his wife, and you may experience a difficult struggle as you carefully consider what adjustments are necessary to obtain the knowledge of God. God has incredible patience as you seek the wisdom of Scripture and struggle with the cost of the knowledge of God. Our problem is not that God is unreasonable or impatient, but that this kind of struggle hardly exists. We seem to be more driven by what we will lose than what we will gain if we pursue God with all our strength. As a result, the idea of living a life out of step with the culture is quickly dismissed. At times, we even use Scripture out of context to explain away the need to pursue God wholeheartedly.

We desperately need messengers who are so captivated by the beauty of Jesus they proclaim the reward of the knowledge of God with such conviction that the reward of God far outshines the costs to obtain that reward.

Will you become one of those messengers? God will determine the scope and expression of your ministry, but He is looking for those who will rearrange their lives to become fascinated by divine beauty. And He especially looks for the church to become a corporate messenger. *And she will.*

God's instructions can be reduced to two commandments, and the first is:[10]

You shall love the Lord your God with all your heart and with all your soul and with all your mind. (Matthew 22:37)

Loving God with all your heart will mean conversations will change, entertainment will shift, priorities will be altered, relationships will be affected, and your lifestyle will be transformed over time. It does *not* mean abandoning your family or trying to avoid work and other biblical responsibilities. John discipled a group of young men, and you should also serve others and invest in your family. The question is are you leading your family and others into the light of the knowledge of God? Does your lifestyle teach others to trade lesser pursuits for a greater pleasure, or are you leading others to tolerate cultural compromise?

John's life is an invitation to live by the same values that shaped his life and to obtain a similar accolade from Jesus.

Trading Compromise for Wholehearted Living

Embracing the wilderness means cutting off certain freedoms and abandoning endless possibilities. It means you seriously engage the God who is a consuming fire, fully expecting He will come to you as He is and fully consume you.

Moderation can be a value in some things, but at times a full commitment is necessary to obtain what we truly desire. Trying to remain "balanced" and being fearful of being "extreme" can keep you from what you truly want. What is holding you back from wholeheartedness? What decisions do you need need to make either for a season or for a lifetime?

A young man truly in love is not "balanced," and he cannot secure the wholehearted love of a wife if he wants to avoid the "extreme" commitment of marriage and keep his options open. If he seeks balance among different loves, it will prevent a deeper experience of intimacy.

Why is there so much demand for balance in our love of God?

---

[10]Matthew 22:37–40.

While we need wisdom,[11] the idea of balance in our relationship with God would be foreign to the apostle Paul. You cannot have a balanced relationship with a divine person named "Jealous"[12] who is a consuming fire.[13]

An Olympic athlete cannot live a balanced life. There are things he cannot eat. There are things he cannot do. There are things in his schedule that are non-negotiable. If he tried to "balance" every area of life, he would be unable to do what is required to perform at an Olympic level. A "balanced" life would leave an Olympic athlete constantly filled with angst, knowing he was capable of setting world records but could not because he was not taking the steps necessary to perform at that level. So he would arrange his life around a single pursuit.

Do you prioritize the knowledge of God with the same intensity an athlete prioritizes athletic competition?[14]

People who make a profound difference do not live balanced lives. They make calculated decisions and deliberate sacrifices to pursue an objective wholeheartedly. In the same way, we need to make calculated decisions to trade some things in order to obtain something else. You cannot have everything. You cannot do everything. You cannot keep up to date with all the latest movies and have a spirit of revelation.

Once an Olympic athlete decides to pursue his goal, he makes the necessary sacrifices because his goal is set. He has weighed the cost and the reward. There is no more compromise. He will never wonder if he could have set a world record. He will focus his life toward his objective and discover how far he can go. Once calculated decisions are made, you will find a peace that was not possible when you were trying

---

[11]Pastoral wisdom is necessary when people are prone to truly unhealthy mental or physical extremes.

[12]Exodus 34:14.

[13]Hebrews 12:29.

[14]1 Corinthians 9:24–27; Galatians 2:2; 5:7; Philippians 2:16; 2 Timothy 4:7; Hebrews 12:1.

to keep up with everyone else. Like an athlete, you discover the joy of missing out on many other things to pursue your deepest desire.

This is what the wilderness is about—cutting off competing affections and setting your primary focus in a specific direction.

Many people feel an inner turmoil because they *know* what is true but are not *living* in light of what they know. Whenever you do not live in agreement with what you know, it creates inner conflict. You can try to ignore that conflict, but it will not go away. The reason is simple:

> *"No one can serve two masters, for either he will hate the one and love the* *other, or he will be devoted to the one and despise the other. You cannot serve God and money." (Matthew 6:24)*

Many Christians are frustrated because they are still trying to live with multiple goals or, more precisely, multiple masters. They have not decided to abandon the demands of the culture and go wholeheartedly in one direction. This conflict will only be resolved when we decide to live in agreement with what the gospel says is true. This is a process, it is difficult, and your response will not always be perfect, but the Holy Spirit will help you.

When you decide to live with a narrow focus—like an Olympic athlete—you will find a profound peace that cannot be found as long as you try to stay in the place of compromise and "moderation."

God wants His gospel not only proclaimed, but demonstrated in the flesh and blood of the proclaimer. That demonstration will be imperfect because of the limitations of our human frame, but it must be genuine. The power of the gospel is not primarily in the logic of the words, but in the transformation it produces in the life of the one who proclaims it and the one who hears it.

When we reduce the gospel to information to be considered, we lose sight of the scope of the gospel. And if we reduce the gospel to information, we will not experience the full power of the good news.

When you reject the demands of popular culture and decide to live in agreement with the gospel, you discover the "Joy of Missing Out." And you find an ocean of pleasure that the powers of this age do not want you to discover. Your life and schedules slowly find a rhythm. Your thoughts and emotions become settled. You are freed from the weariness and tensions that come from compromise. You are liberated from the frantic demands of FOMO style living.

The call to the wilderness is a call to JOMO. It is an invitation to choose a way of life designed to produce a life of communion with God—a life that produces a joy simply not possible any other way.

Psychologists tell us the human mind is not designed for multitasking and does its best work when it focuses wholeheartedly in one direction at a time. You are not designed to multitask. You can have multiple areas of responsibly (family, church, work, etc.), but you cannot live in multiple directions.

We endlessly crave "more" in order to fill in the ache in our souls. However, your ache will only be satisfied when you embrace the "less" of the wilderness. You need to be faithful to what the Lord asks you, but you should be more carefully considering what you should say *no* to and what you say *yes* to. When you embrace the wilderness, you say *no* to some opportunities to protect your pursuit of the knowledge of God. Just as a young man says *no* to other women to enjoy the one woman who is the object of his affection.

Exit the System

As long as you allow the pressures of the culture to define the way you live, you cannot expect to enjoy all the pleasures of intimacy with God, nor can you become a voice. You have the ability, though, to exit the system. No one is making you stay. Exiting the system simply means you are no longer dominated by the demands of the popular culture. There are a few things exiting the system does *not* mean:

- It does not mean living aloof with a spirt of elitism.
- It does not mean abandoning your families to live like a hermit.
- It does not necessarily mean you need to change jobs or locations.
- It does not mean you dishonor governmental leaders and those God has put in authority.[15]
- It does not mean you become excessively critical toward unbelievers.

---

[15]Romans 13:1–7; 1 Peter 2:17.

- It does not mean you have a critical spirit toward the church. The church is imperfect, but it is Jesus' body. True devotion to Jesus will lead to deeper love for His people.

The culture cannot demand your affections—it can only solicit them. The pressure is real, but you have an option. The question is *will you do this?* It means others may find you odd, but the Bible calls you to live in this age as a stranger and pilgrim.[16] It may mean you "miss out" on many of the amusements people consider essential, but if your life makes sense to the world, something is wrong.

How do you know if the culture dominates you? You honestly examine your joys, fears, emotions, hopes, dreams, entertainments, and perhaps, most of all, your schedule. The extent these things resemble the mass culture indicates the extent to which you remain captured by the culture.

Are you ready to pursue JOMO in the wilderness? Or are lesser pleasures satisfying?

---

[16]Hebrews 11:13; 1 Peter 1:1, 17; 2:11.

Confidence in God's Leadership

The way John walked out his assignment demonstrated immense confidence in God's leadership.

No doubt Zechariah told John the story of his birth over and over, so John knew the significance of his life and message. Given his assignment to turn a nation and his priestly lineage, it would have been natural for John to place himself in Jerusalem so he could engage the theologians of Israel, be among the priests, reach the greatest number of people, and fulfill his assignment.

This makes John's decision to stay in the wilderness even more significant.

John had been commissioned from heaven to impact the entire nation, and yet he stayed in a small place that was difficult to access. According to human wisdom, embracing a life of communion in a small place would *prevent* John from fulfilling his assignment. In the wisdom of God, it did the opposite—it *prepared* him for it.

John lived under the weight of urgency his entire life. No doubt the passing of time weighed down on him as he wondered, *Is now the time?* John knew he was too weak to accomplish the assignment that had been given to him, so instead of seeking influence, he followed the Lord's leadership into a small place. He did not form a plan or try to become a national figure, he waited for the Word of the Lord to come to him. He submitted his urgency and his assignment to God's leadership.

We tend to celebrate—even idolize—the strength of youth, but there is another strength we know little about: the strength of God that comes on vessels prepared in weakness over decades.

Many receive an assignment from the Lord and immediately run to do it in their own strength, but John stewarded the assignment of God by living before the face of God. John did not set his public ministry into motion on the basis of his calling; he stewarded his calling for decades by living intentionally in a small place.

Abraham had to wait for a miracle son. Joseph had to wait for God to call him out of prison. Moses waited until the burning bush appeared. Elijah appeared suddenly. Many overlook the fact that Paul was commissioned directly by Jesus but was not sent to the Gentiles by the Holy Spirit for fifteen years. John and Paul had direct commissions from heaven, but both let God initiate their public ministry, and neither were considered disobedient for waiting for the Spirit's leadership.

John and Paul both knew their assignments had been given by God and could only be accomplished in God. They were not passive—they faithfully labored where they were and allowed God to do what only He could do. As a result, both their lives produced something only God could produce. Sadly, a lot of what is done today does not require God. It can be produced by human talent and effort.

When you stand at the judgment seat, the Lord is not going to say "Wow! Your marketing was impressive," and Gabriel is not following your social media. There is a desperate need for something only God can produce, but when you decide that you want something no man can produce, it will force you to submit to the sovereignty of God.

If you surrender control of your assignment and allow God to do what He wants with you, it may end up smaller or bigger than you expected. What flows from the life of God may or may not result in public accolades, but it will produce life, and it will bear fruit. What flows from human strength—no matter how impressive—will never produce the life of God.

If It Is a Divine Assignment, You Cannot Fulfill It

John followed a biblical pattern that is nearly entirely lost in our time. We prematurely launch people into their assignments, which often harms those the Lord has called and reduces the impact of their ministry. We are not called to be passive or fatalistic, but there is a waiting on the Lord that gives the Holy Spirit the right to determine our times and seasons. Until we recover this, we will not see messengers like John or Paul.

We tend to seek formulas and immediate results. People want to do a few years of Bible school and then lead for decades, but God is not like that. He often chooses to form and shape a person over a long period of time. Biblically, people typically do not enter their strength until somewhere between thirty-five and fifty-five years of age. Moses was not effective until he was eighty. Paul did not leave Antioch and enter apostolic ministry until he was around forty-five years old. Jesus spent thirty years in obscurity and only ministered publicly for about three years.

The concept of formation and waiting is almost unknown in our generation, but it is foundational, and it *must* be recovered. If it took God decades to prepare laborers in the past, what will it take Him to prepare laborers for the end-time harvest and a time unlike any other time?

Biblical "waiting" does not mean passivity. Waiting means allowing God to unfold the fullness of your assignment in His power on His timetable. Waiting should be *active*, which means we engage in the work of ministry wherever God has placed us and regardless of what our vocation is. Many people neglect actively waiting and, instead, passively wait for the "big thing." But even Jesus gave most of His strength to "small" things. He lived most of His life in a small place, focused most of His energy on twelve men, and invested uniquely in just three young men.

Sadly, many refuse to embrace in the seemingly small and weak things that God has ordained for their maturity. As a result, they do not engage with the process of transformation necessary to carry the power of God.

What you consider a delay may be a profound part of God's leadership of your life. A delay tests the human temptation to exalt ourselves and seize our inheritance. God's delays are an expression of His kindness, and if you cooperate with Him, He will prepare and transform you through consistent faithfulness in the delay.

You may ask, "But what if it never happens?" Well, if God is not going to do it, do you really want to manufacture it? Why not live like Abraham who died without his promise, looking forward to an inheritance only God could give?[1]

---

[1] Hebrews 11:8–10.

John answered, "A person cannot receive even one thing unless it is given him from heaven." (John 3:27)

The church suffers when gifted people produce things that appear spiritual but were not given from heaven. Human activity may come from a desire to fulfill an assignment, create "impact," or feel successful, but the flesh cannot produce life.[2] The only thing that brings transformation is the life of God flowing through a human vessel. If God has not given you something, you must not manufacture a substitute.

Sin is not always the greatest hindrance to the work of God. Treating the result of human effort as if it were the work of God can cause a much greater hindrance to God's purposes. We should be very alarmed that many assume they are being helpful to God when in fact they have confused human ability with divine activity.

If you want the real thing, you cannot do God's part. You must do your part, which is faithful obedience, and He must do His part, which is to bring to pass what He speaks. If you attempt to do His part, you will jeopardize your ability to experience all that God has for you.

Small Decisions Yield Big Results

When God needs a messenger or a deliverer, such a one nearly always stays hidden for decades and then suddenly emerges in power.

John did not shatter the prophetic silence by trying to be a voice. John shattered the silence by positioning himself before the Lord through a number of seemingly small decisions over years that enabled him to hear God's voice when it came to him.

We have many people who can echo spiritual truth, but we desperately need *voices* in our generation. God alone can choose and anoint a voice, but your part is to live a life that positions you to hear the Word of God when it comes. Far too many are short-circuiting their ability to be a voice by seeking activity and influence when they should be living before the Lord in their local church family.

There are some things you simply cannot get "on the go." The bigger the assignment, the more a person needs to pull away from

---

[2]John 3:6; Romans 7:5, 18; 8:8; Galatians 5:16–17.

opportunities that may seem exciting but are not truly impactful in order to live before the Lord. The failure to do this is a major hindrance to prophetic voices like John's emerging in our generation.

John had to be prepared to carry the kind of power he carried because, when God gives a man that kind of power, it can easily destroy him. History is filled with examples of people who were unusually anointed and did not end well. Perhaps God is withholding power from us in kindness because He knows what it does to unprepared vessels, and maybe we lack prophetic weight on our words because we have not embraced John's path.

Perhaps God's kindness and concern for His people keeps Him from answering some of our prayers for power and anointing.

When we cry out for the power of God, we often do not consider the risks that divine power carries. Humans were not made to be worshipped, and when God releases His power through a person, it inevitably creates incredible challenges. If you study revival history, you find the sad reality that a person can operate in divine power and also be destroyed by what that power produces.

When God gives someone a substantial assignment, He typically spends much longer on preparation than we expect. Furthermore, the fulfillment of the assignment can happen suddenly in much less time than we would have imagined. Our modern approach of educating a student for four to seven years so they can minister for forty years is not the way God typically prepares people for a weighty assignment.

God will often spend decades maturing a person before releasing the full measure of power He has for them. When God does not immediately answer the cry for power, He is not necessarily saying *no*. God is calling us to continue in a patient pursuit of Himself. He is looking for us to allow Him to transform us so we can handle His power working through us. Just as you would not give an exotic sports car to a ten-year-old, God often withholds dimensions of His power. We tend to be more concerned with getting things done, but God is more concerned with the person.

God often does not tell us when He will answer the cry for power because many of us would become discouraged and give up. Furthermore, God may answer the prayer for power by releasing unusual power on another vessel. If we are truly jealous for *His* glory, then we will not mind this. We will celebrate the release of God's power for the sake of His glory.

It is not unusual for God to spend much longer preparing a person for an assignment than it takes for the person actually to perform that assignment.

It is easy for us to become discouraged because God does not work on our timelines or frequently does His work in unexpected ways. We tend to focus on our *assignments*, but God is focused on us as His *people*. As a result, God *enjoys* our formation, but we often *despise* it. You may have an assignment from the Lord you are anxious to get to, but remember God does not *need* you to fulfill your assignment. Your assignment is simply a context for Him to enjoy working with you. It is important, but it should not become a greater reward than God Himself.

You were not made for your assignment. You were made for God. You belong to Him, and He gets to bring your assignment to pass however He wants.

When an anointed messenger emerges suddenly, their ministry seems spectacular, so we assume their preparation must have been spectacular, but this is not true. Messengers often emerge from small places. Preparation primarily takes place in the ordinary and mundane, the small and the familiar. Small, daily obedience over time is what shapes a messenger. The truth is most of life is small and mundane. Our endless search for excitement is not biblical. It is an indicator of our own unsettledness, and it resists some of God's methods of formation and maturity. Tragically, many messengers come short in their assignment because they lacked vision for faithfulness in the small and seemingly ordinary things of life over decades.

Divine Power Is Attracted to Weakness

The wilderness forces you to face your weakness and embrace it.

Many people mistakenly believe John was an incredibly strong man. They assume the strength of his message and the impact of his life flowed from his extreme dedication and internal strength. However, John was in the spirit of Elijah who was a man "with a nature like ours,"[3] a nature marked by human weakness.

---

[3]James 5:17.

John's life was very intentional, but it was not strong. John was known for his manner of life,[4] and the manner of life he chose produces weakness, not strength. John's main message was Isaiah 40, which ends with a message about weakness:

> *The grass withers, the flower fades when the breath of the* LORD *blows on it; surely the people are grass. . . . All the nations are as nothing before him, they are accounted by him as less than nothing and emptiness. . . . It is he who sits above the circle of the earth, and its inhabitants are like grasshoppers. . . . Have you not known? Have you not heard? The* LORD *is the everlasting God, the Creator of the ends of the earth. He does not faint or grow weary; his understanding is unsearchable. He gives power to the faint, and to him who has no might he increases strength. Even youths shall faint and be weary, and young men shall fall exhausted; but they who wait for the* LORD *shall renew their strength; they shall mount up with wings like eagles; they shall run and not be weary; they shall walk and not faint. (Isaiah 40:7, 17, 22, 28–31)*

John proclaimed God's grandeur and man's frailty. Furthermore, John *was* the message, which indicates he grew "faint" and was carried along by God's strength. He had to wait on the Lord to renew his strength. His was sustained by divine might, not human fortitude. If John had been an exceptionally "strong" human, he would have been out of sync with the message of Isaiah 40. Verse 29 indicates that John's weakness created a canvas for God's glory.

Our humanism leads us to assume "superior" humans are used by God in profound ways, but John did not accomplish his assignment in his own strength. John's life points in a different direction. His *weakness* became a conduit for God's glory. That weakness was not compromise, it was the result of choosing a life in the wilderness that stripped him of his human strength.

Do you want to be "strong"? Or are you willing to be reduced so you become a conduit for divine glory?

---

[4]Matthew 3:4; 9:14; 11:8, 18; Mark 1:6; 2:18; Luke 1:15; 5:33; 7:33.

The Messenger Is the Message

The messenger is the message: Who you are is more powerful than what you know. Many people want to carry a message with eloquent or powerful words, but who will allow God to shape them so *they* become the message?

Acquiring and communicating information only requires some discipline and time. Becoming the message will cost you your life.

Moses was the meekest man alive,[1] but he went through profound humiliation and breaking to get to that point. Hosea lived through a gut-wrenching marriage to produce his message on the mercy and faithfulness of God. Jeremiah endured immense suffering and wept agonizing tears to communicate God's pathos over Israel. Daniel was forced to endure a life of loss, pain, pressure, and disappointment to produce his message of unwavering confidence in the Word of God when it seems God has failed.

We tend to focus in on the information in the prophets' books but overlook the fact that these messages cost men their lives. God led them to become demonstrations of what they spoke.

You should not try to order your own circumstances to become a message. For example, you should not seek to duplicate Hosea's tragic marriage. But if you want to be a message, God will orchestrate circumstances in your life and take you where you would not go to make you into a message. In fact, things you may think are hindrances to your assignment could in fact be tools of God to shape you into something He wants.

Martyrdom is a costly sacrifice, but there is something that can be more costly: living your life week after week in obedience to God on

---

[1]Numbers 12:3.

whatever path He lays out for you. One of the reasons the biblical prophets had such power on their words is because their words were shaped and backed by their lives. If you want a similar power on your words, you must follow a similar path.

In the wilderness, John devoured the prophetic scriptures as the Spirit shaped John into the image of the words he treasured. John gained a God-centered perspective and began to look at the world through a God-saturated lens.[2] His profound grasp of God altered the way He lived.

John did not just learn information; he become a demonstration.

God wanted Israel to see a man with clarity and understanding—a man who had made profound lifestyle decisions out of desire and anticipation for the coming of the Lord. As he followed God's leadership, John became that man, and Israel was not only provoked by John's words; they were provoked by who John had become.

John was not unique because he carried a new message; he was unique because he became the message.

John's messages came from passages his audience was familiar with, yet he provoked a powerful response.[3] This illustrates a profound reality: Two different people can say the same thing with radically different effects. If you are not a demonstration of the words you speak, your words will not carry the kind of power John's words carried. God is not looking for you to discover a "new" message. He is inviting you to become the message He has already given.

Information or Transformation?

John did not bring a new message or declare things people had never heard. The fragments we have of his sermons demonstrate he preached from the Old Testament prophets, particularly Isaiah and Malachi. He shook a nation by speaking Bible verses everyone was familiar with, demonstrating the preparation of a messenger is far more important than the preparation of a message. If you focus more on the preparation of your messages than on your life before God, you

---

[2] His use of Isaiah 40 demonstrates this.

[3] Luke 3:10–14.

will be an echo and not a voice. An echo sounds like the real thing, but it is an inferior copy of the original that produces a diminished effect. *If you want to burn, you have to purchase your own oil.*

The Word of God is not something to be entertained, considered, enjoyed, and then forgotten an hour after Sunday dinner. The Word of God is not primarily *interesting*; it is primarily *transformational.* It is active. It demands a response and produces an effect. When it is spoken with power, the Word of God does not make *suggestions*; it creates a confrontation. It provokes the question, *"What do we do?"*

Too many messages produce little more than a moment of mental curiosity because the messengers have not been transformed by the message—they are not a living demonstration of the words coming out of their mouths. And if the word has not transformed the messenger, why should it transform the audience?

The heavenly seraphim are described as "burning ones." They are on fire, and their words have power because of *who* they know and how close they are to Him, not because of *what* they know. All they have to do is cry, "Holy, holy, holy is the LORD of hosts; the whole earth is full of his glory!" and the foundations of the temple shake,[4] demonstrating that simple words have tremendous power when those words have transformed the speaker.

If you have a gift of teaching, one of the greatest challenges you face is talking about Jesus more than you talk to Him.

If you speak the words of the prophets backed up with the lifestyle of the prophets, it produces a response, and that's precisely what John did. John's audience had heard the prophets read year after year, but when John spoke the words they all knew, people cried out, *"What do we do?"*[5] John's life may have seemed extreme, but the entire nation was called to live according to the same fire that burned in John's heart and drove him into the wilderness. *And so are you.*

God gives different individuals different spheres of influence and authority, so not everyone will have a ministry like John's. However, in many cases, we operate beneath the level of authority that is available

---

[4] Isaiah 6:3.

[5] Luke 3:10–14.

for us because we allow the Word of God to shape our *thinking* yet do not allow it to fully shape our *lifestyle*.

We live in what is termed "the Information Age" and Western culture in particular tends to prize information over transformation. Sadly, this thinking has crept into the church to the point that discipleship is frequently reduced to learning new information. This is not surprising because people enjoy the mental pleasure of considering new ideas and absorbing new information. The activity of learning is especially enjoyable when new information makes few requirements on the way we live.

We easily honor and esteem those who know much but are often extremely uncomfortable around people who live out Scripture in an uncompromising way. We love to remember those who lived wholeheartedly in the past, but those who attempt the same in the present deeply disturb us because zeal confronts our passivity.

To comfort ourselves, we often repeat the platitude that we should be balanced in our application of Scripture as if it were a command of Jesus. In reality, what we frequently call "balance" is often an accommodation to our culture, our comfort, and our selfish pursuits that blunts the Bible's clear call to intentional living. The Bible is practical and filled with wisdom, but it never instructs us to be balanced. If anything, it calls us to a lifestyle that is the opposite of what a modern, secularized culture would consider balanced.

We know more about the Bible than any generation in history, which means it is possible we live a smaller percentage of what we know than nearly any previous generation. There is one way forward: We need a new generation of messengers in the church who *are* the message, messengers who confront us with their lives and not just their words, and messengers who value *expression* over *information*.

As Leonard Ravenhill used to say:

> *The world does not need a new definition of Christianity; it needs a new demonstration of it.*[6]

---

[6]A phrase often repeated by Leonard Ravenhill.

You can acquire information in a moment, but it can take decades for you to be formed into a demonstration of that information.

Authority

Not only did John's audience cry out, *"What do we do?"* they came to him to be baptized with water as part of their repentance. This act was incredibly significant because in John's time the act of baptism was one of the final steps a gentile convert would make to join the Jewish people. In essence, John called Israel to be "re-converted" to their own spiritual heritage.

We also live in a time when many Christians need to be converted into biblical Christianity.

John spoke Bible verses with so much power that people sought repentance in his ministry rather than the temple.[7] It is hard to fathom how radical this was for a Jewish audience, and it provoked religious leaders to go out and confront John.[8] All of this emphasizes how much authority was resting on a man who did not do any miraculous signs.[9]

John's words were so powerful King Herod feared John:

> *When others too joined the crowds about him, because they were aroused to the highest degree by his sermons, Herod became alarmed. Eloquence that had so great an effect . . . it looked as if they would be guided by John in everything that they did.*[10]

The sermons that terrified King Herod were predominantly Bible verses spoken by a man who had been transformed into a living example of those verses.

John had something people wanted—something more than what was available at the temple.

---

[7]Matthew 3:6, 11; Mark 1:4; Luke 3:3; John 3:23.

[8]Matthew 3:7; John 1:19.

[9]John 10:41.

[10]Paul W. Hollenbach, "John the Baptist," ed. David Noel Freedman, *The Anchor Yale Bible Dictionary* (New York: Doubleday, 1992), 887.

Where did this wilderness prophet get the right to offer forgiveness for sins through repentance in the wilderness rather than through the temple service in Jerusalem? *He had authority from heaven.* The people were use to control, power, and influence but shocked at the measure of divine authority resting on John. John was a preview of what was coming, because Jesus' authority is what set Him apart from every other teacher, even more than His message.[11]

You can create a measure of influence, but you cannot manufacture authority. And when you have authority, everyone knows it.

There was a profound difference in the influence other priests had gained by political maneuvering and the authority John had from heaven. To this day, many continue to seek influence, power, and control through political and humanistic means, but authority from heaven is a completely different thing. Do you want influence, notoriety, or authority? Many people aspire to be an "influencer" in our time, but "influencers" do not have authority, do not make impact, and are unknown in heaven.

John's authority was so tangible people questioned whether he was the Messiah even though he did not do any miracles. Yet John knew his own weakness. He refused to entertain any speculation that he might be the Messiah and instead joyfully pointed to Jesus. [12]

As the people were in expectation, and all were questioning in their hearts concerning John, whether he might be the Christ, John answered them all, saying, "I baptize you with water, but he who is mightier than I is coming, the strap of whose sandals I am not worthy to untie. He will baptize you with the Holy Spirit and fire." (Luke 3:15–16)

The Word Must Become Flesh

God's plan for your life is simple:

And the Word became flesh and dwelt among us, and we have seen his glory. (John 1:14)

---

[11]Matthew 7:28–29.

[12]See also John 1:19–23; 3:28.

This verse obviously spoke about Jesus, but He is the firstborn among many brethren,[13] and His people are meant to follow this pattern. The Gospel of John introduces John the Baptist a few verses before it describes Jesus as the "Word made flesh" to make a point: John was an example of God's Word expressing itself in a man (though obviously not the unique, divine incarnation of the Word.)

God does not evaluate people by how well they speak. His evaluation is simple: *Will you let the Word become flesh in you?*

John's life was not just a demonstration of a man consumed with God. His life was a demonstration of God Himself. For example, John did not have a wife because God does not yet have His eternal companion, and John lived in the wilderness because God does not yet have His dwelling place on the earth.[14] When people heard John, they did not just hear a message from God; they experienced *God* as the Spirit that filled John spoke through him.

When people encounter us, they should *hear* about God, and they should also *encounter* God in some measure. If God is in pain, we should be in pain. If God is joyful, we should be joyful. If God is burdened, we should be burdened. We are to become manifestations of God in human flesh just as Jesus was because we are made in the image of God. Obviously, we do not become God in any way, nor are we complete manifestations of God. Jesus alone is God and is the complete revelation of who He is in flesh. Jesus is the firstborn among many who become demonstrations of who God is by the work of the indwelling Spirit.

What do you want? Many people want to amaze audiences with information. Others hope to be "prophetic" by revealing unknown things. But God is after something different. *He wants to transform people into the message, and He is going to do it.*

Will you let Him make you a message? Be forewarned it will cost you your life. If you want to become a message, God will orchestrate circumstances you would not choose and lead you where you would

---

[13]Romans 8:29.

[14]God's presence pervades the earth, but Jesus is absent, and God is not dwelling on the earth the way He will in the future (Isaiah 11:9; Habakkuk 2:14; Zechariah 14:8–9; 1 Corinthians 15:24; Revelation 21–22).

not go to produce something you cannot accomplish in your wisdom and best intentions.

John did not preach new information, and we do not need any more new information. What we desperately need is to become a people who have been transformed by the message we have already been given and have become "living messages."

Suddenly the Word of the Lord Came

John was not passive or anxious. He waited until the Word of the Lord came to him, and then thirty years of communion erupted into a few months of proclamation. For years, John submitted his assignment to God's leadership. God, and not his assignment, became his supreme delight, yet he knew one day the task Gabriel predicted would come.

Decades of faithfulness prepared John for a moment that came suddenly. The Word of God came to John in the wilderness:

> *during the high priesthood of Annas and Caiaphas, the word of God came to John the son of Zechariah in the wilderness. (Luke 3:2)*

After generations without a prophetic voice, John suddenly *shattered* the silence as his light burned brightly in the wilderness. In fact, the word *shattered* is not strong enough. A few months and a handful of sermons would create far more impact than many others who had much longer "ministries" and spent far more time publicly speaking.

Luke named the high priests to make a comparison. The high priest in Jerusalem should have had the Word of the Lord,[1] but instead it came to another priest: John the son of Zechariah. God bypassed a corrupt priesthood and found His priest in the wilderness. To further emphasize the point, the Word of the Lord came to John when he was approximately thirty years old. Under the law, priests could not publicly minister to the people until they were thirty years old. Like all priests, John had prepared for three decades. Unlike a typical priest, John's service would not last twenty years.

---

[1]Malachi 2:7.

John's decision to embrace the wilderness looked like a mistake from a human perspective, but it illustrated Ravenhill's well-known phrase:

You never have to advertise a fire.[2]

Many expend incredible amounts of energy trying to get someone to pay attention to them. In most cases, people are simply wasting their time because a well-known ministry has not been appointed for them. Moreover, being well-known is not an indicator of God's favor. The truth is God simply gives some people a more visible assignment than others.

If you have been given a unique assignment, instead of trying to draw a crowd, you should live a life that attracts the fire of God and then wait for His fire to come.

The people, hungry for a word from God, came out to hear the preacher in the wilderness:

Then Jerusalem and all Judea and all the region about the Jordan were going out to him. (Matthew 3:5)

When the Word of the Lord came to John, he did the most surprising thing possible: *John stayed in the wilderness* and traveled in a small area around the Jordan.[3] John had a national message, but he did not go to Jerusalem. In the desert, John became a *demonstration* of his message and not just a *communicator* of it.

John had divine authority to proclaim his message and a national stage, but he stewarded his assignment by living within the constraints the Lord had placed on him. He would not abandon the pleasure he had discovered in the wilderness—a pleasure that could not be replaced by the crowds in Jerusalem. In a time when travel was difficult —long before automobiles, planes, and air conditioning—the nation would have to travel into the hot wilderness if they wanted to hear John.

---

[2] A phrase often repeated by Leonard Ravenhill.

[3] Luke 3:3.

To everyone's shock, John had prepared for thirty years, but he would fulfill his immense assignment in a few short months.

John Cried Out

John did not simply speak; he *cried out*:

John bore witness about him, and cried out, "This was he of whom I said, 'He who comes after me ranks before me, because he was before me.'" *(John 1:15)*

John had pursued the knowledge of God for decades, and there was a fire in his soul that had been waiting to be released. When the time came, John could not talk about Jesus the way men talk about ordinary, mundane things. His soul erupted, and he cried out because the revelation of Jesus produces that kind of response:[4]

And one called to another and said: "Holy, holy, holy is the LORD of hosts; the whole earth is full of his glory!" And the foundations of the thresholds shook at the voice of him who called. (Isaiah 6:3–4)

The majestic and terrifying seraphim *cry out* when they behold Jesus, and when people encounter something majestic or terrifying, they do not speak quietly; they cry out. Crying out is not a premeditated style; it is an unpolished, nearly involuntary reaction to majesty. Crying out is not a communication style. John did not merely raise his voice and adopt a certain religious style of preaching. Shouting preachers do not produce the kind of response John produced.

John *cried out* because his inner man was on fire and he could not restrain his desire. Some may consider John's passionate message "radical," yet they eagerly cry out at sports events, indicating athletic competition stirs their souls more deeply than divine beauty. Somehow, we have full control of our affections when we speak of Jesus yet show raw emotion when an athlete unexpectedly scores. *Do you think this is normal?*

---

[4]This vision Isaiah saw was not simply a vision of God; it was a vision of Jesus (John 12:41).

Isaiah predicted a day is coming when the church will "lift their voices" (cry out) from the very ends of the earth because of the majesty of Jesus:[5]

> *They lift up their voices, they sing for joy; over the majesty of the* LORD *they shout from the west. Therefore in the east give glory to the* LORD; *in the coastlands of the sea, give glory to the name of the* LORD, *the God of Israel. (Isaiah 24:14–15)*

The fact we can speak about Jesus as calmly and collectedly as we do indicates we have little revelation of His glory. But it will not end this way. A day is coming when the church will be filled with the revelation of the beauty of Jesus. His majesty will produce a raw, passionate, and unmeditated response, and a people will cry out from the very ends of the earth.

John shows us we can access the majesty of God through the Spirit, the Word, and an intentional lifestyle. You do not have to have a dramatic encounter. It is possible to live fascinated in this age, and a people will emerge before the age is over who are more fascinated by Jesus than any other thing. They will long for the revelation of Jesus more than success, more than ministry, more than notoriety, more than sex, more than entertainment.

The Holy Spirit is ready to produce this cry in you if you want it. Ask Him.

---

[5]See also Psalm 96; 98; Isaiah 42:10–12.

John Never Left the Wilderness

We tend to assume we go to the wilderness to pay a price for an anointing, but as we've seen, this thinking misses the message of John's life and the point of the wilderness.

The wilderness is not a place to "earn" some kind of public ministry; it is a place to embrace a life before God until He—not crowds—becomes your reward. John did not go to the wilderness for thirty years so that he could preach for a few months. Nor did "real life" begin when his ministry became public. John was *more* than a prophet[1] because his brief prophetic ministry did not define his life.

John was fully alive as he lived in obscurity in the wilderness filled with the Holy Spirit, meditating on the Word of God, living as a priest, living in a small place, and discipling a small group. As a result, when John became a national figure, he did not leave the wilderness. Even when John went to jail, he was held in a jail in the wilderness not far from where he had ministered.[2] John's brief public ministry was a vivid demonstration of a man who had become the message and fulfilled his ministry by *not* leaving the wilderness. Though he knew he had a significant assignment, he did not seek publicity or notoriety. He only began publicly speaking when the Word of the Lord came to him.[3]

---

[1]Matthew 11:9.

[2]According to Josephus, John the Baptist was imprisoned in in the Machaerus fortress just east of the Dead Sea in the wilderness. F. F. Bruce, "Machaerus," ed. D. R. W. Wood et al., *New Bible Dictionary* (Leicester, England; Downers Grove, IL: InterVarsity Press, 1996), 712.

[3]Luke 3:2–3.

John's public ministry was the result of God's sovereign leadership of John's life, not John's ministry ambition.

John could have filled the stadiums of Israel, but he had found something in the wilderness he was not willing to surrender. Travel is not always wrong, but if you are living for public ministry and crowds, the wilderness has not done its work. John could have drawn massive crowds in the cities of Israel, but it was not the prize John was living for.

God gave John a message for the nation, but if you wanted to hear John, you had to spend significant time to travel out into the wilderness.

This was part of God's purpose because, as we saw in Matthew 11, John's life in the wilderness was part of his message. God wanted people to go and *see* John and not just *hear* him. John had discovered the revelation of God as a bridegroom and learned to minister to God. John's lifestyle was the basis of his ministry, and it was so precious to John that he refused to give it up.

It's time to stop looking for hidden wilderness seasons that prepare us for seasons of blessing. It is time for an entire generation to embrace a life in the wilderness for the sake of Jesus' joy.

God Is Not Efficient

The wilderness confronts our sense of "efficiency," but we cannot understand God's ways unless we realize He is not efficient by human standards.

God invested thirty years in John, but John only ministered publicly for a few months. God did not consider that kind of investment to be extravagant because He did not form John for a few months of ministry—He formed John to be His companion for the rest of eternity. John's notoriety in this age was a very small expression of his assignment.

The life of Moses demonstrates this perhaps more than any other messenger in the Bible. Moses was about forty years old when he killed a man and ran away from Egypt in disgrace. He had forfeited the prestige he had in Egypt and was disqualified for the redemptive assignment he had been given. Because Moses was a failure at forty, any reasonable person would have chosen someone else to fulfill Moses' assignment, but at this point, God did something truly shocking.

Instead of replacing Moses, God chose to wait *forty more* years on Moses.

The story of Moses does not make human sense. Jewish slaves continued to cry out night and day for deliverance, but God refused to choose another deliverer. Instead of replacing Moses, God patiently formed and shaped him through his menial life in the wilderness with a gentile priest.[4] And this was forty years *after* Moses had failed. In total, it took Moses eighty years before he was ready for the assignment God had given him. God's way with Moses was not unusual. It has been this way since the beginning.

God's promise to Abraham took decades to unfold. After the promise was given, Abraham and Sarah spent years trying to conceive a son. Then one day God miraculously touched Sarah's "dead" body. Once Isaac was conceived, Sarah had to carry him and give birth. It then took decades to raise the promised son. The promise was fulfilled by a combination of God's activity in a moment *and* God's activity through the mundane tasks and normal processes of daily life because this is God's way.

God accomplishes His work through the combination of human processes and sudden divine activity. We tend either to neglect the need for His activity or despise the process. God is both urgent and patient all at the same time. And He is much more committed to processes over time than we imagine. Many are rushing to get to their "promise," but God is not utilitarian. If He gives you an assignment, He also enjoys the process that will prepare you for the assignment, He enjoys the assignment, and He enjoys you after the assignment is complete.

We seek efficiency because we find identity in our assignments and our "output." God is not efficient because He seeks relationship. He is not looking for better managers for His kingdom. He is forming an eternal companion.

Divine Patterns but No Formulas
God was not efficient with any well-known man or woman in the Bible.

They endured significant delays, suffered from their failures, experienced rejection, struggled with disappointment, and many spent time in prison. We must learn God's ways, but He has no formulas. He

---

[4]Exodus 18:1.

forms people the way He wants. No one can give you "four steps to becoming anointed," nor can anyone lay hands on you and suddenly make you a "messenger" or a "prophet."

You have to be willing to walk the path He puts in front of you, and He rarely tells you precisely where that path will lead. He often gives a sense of where it will lead, but it may take surprising turns to get to the destination. Life in this age is not a straightforward roadmap; it is God's immersive classroom, designed to form people into His image, not merely accomplish a task.

God does some things suddenly, but more often than not, He shapes people over time in the ordinary and mundane. Perseverance is more important than you think.

Your wilderness expression may be very different from someone else's. And when God gives someone an unusual assignment, His process of preparation typically takes longer than we would expect. In some cases, a person's life will not make sense until the very end. It took John thirty years to prepare for an assignment that was finished within months, demonstrating that many times a person's season of fruitful public ministry may be smaller than we would expect. For example, public ministry was only 30 percent of Moses' life, 10 percent of Jesus' life, and less than 5 percent of John's life. Daniel, the prophet referenced by Jesus more than any other[5] and called *greatly beloved* multiple times,[6] probably did not have a public ministry. His "ministry" was not before men, but it challenged the spiritual powers.[7]

Decades of preparation may be necessary so that God can accomplish something through a person suddenly.

Many people think formation happens in dramatic moments, but the primary battles in life are not fought in periodic, dramatic moments. The primary battlefield is the small decisions and actions made every day. Every time you say *no* to certain things and *yes* to other things you move forward. People who are in poor physical condition cannot suddenly shift their condition. They have to embrace a daily

---

[5]See *Son of Man: The Gospel of Daniel 7.*

[6]Daniel 9:23; 10:11, 18.

[7]Daniel 10:11–12.

rhythm of small, consistent choices if they want transformation and the same is true for spiritual maturity.

Your spirituality is primarily won or lost on the battlefield of seemingly small choices made every day.

Most people begin their journey with God out of desire for some kind of success or ministry assignment. If God told most people how long it would take them to fulfill their assignment they would quit, so instead He gives them a clear direction and steady encouragement to keep going. In the process of waiting, God reshapes your values until He becomes your reward rather than your assignment. Once this happens, you can find pleasure in hiddenness and preparation because God, and not your assignment, becomes your delight.

God primarily forms His people through consistent faithfulness over time as you make small, daily decisions in the right direction. There is far more at stake in the small things than you realize.

Grand Expectations

Not only is God inefficient, He does not operate according to our expectations. When God gives a person an assignment, they make a number of assumptions about the assignment which nearly always includes expectations of success, notoriety, praise, power, and personal fulfillment, even though the Bible promises the opposite.[8]

We often add things to our assignment that the Lord never promised us, and our imagination creates profound expectations about how our assignments will unfold.

For example, many people love to receive the prediction they will stand before kings and important figures, but Jesus warned the disciples they would witness to kings as prisoners.[9] This was not unusual because many biblical figures who stood before kings did so as prisoners or slaves.

---

[8]Matthew 10:16–25; Mark 13:9–13; John 16:2, 33; Acts 3:18; 5:40–41; 9:16; 14:22; Romans 5:3–5; 8:17–18; 2 Corinthians 4:17–18; 11:23; Philippians 1:29; 3:10–11; 2 Timothy 2:10–12; Hebrews 2:10; 5:8; 10:32–37; 1 Peter 1:11; 2:19–21; 4:13–14, 19; 5:9–10; Revelation 2:10.

[9]Matthew 10:18–20.

Our expectations rarely consider the call to take up our cross, but the Lord calls us to embrace the cross over our own hopes for personal glory:

If anyone would come after me, let him deny himself and take up his cross and follow me. (Matthew 16:24)

We should walk in active obedience, but it can be very dangerous to try to force an assignment to come to pass because God's plans rarely unfold according to our expectations.

The Reward of Wilderness Communion
John shook an entire nation, and he never entered a large city.

God chose to put John and his message on public display for a few months, but when John became the most anointed man in the nation, he did not go on tour. He stayed in the wilderness and continued to cultivate the same life he had lived for decades. John never left the wilderness because he had no desire to leave. He grew in the wilderness. He discipled in the wilderness.[10] He prayed from the wilderness. He proclaimed from the wilderness. He was even imprisoned in the wilderness. John's life does not mean all of us must stay in one place our entire lives, but it should provoke us.

God is not looking for a people who will embrace the wilderness so they can leave it with more power. He is looking for a people who will embrace a wilderness lifestyle for the prize of a communion not possible any other way. When we seek the wilderness just to secure an outcome, it is a utilitarian approach to God, indicating we are more focused on the outcome than the Person we can encounter in the wilderness.

The primary reward of the wilderness is found in a life of communion with God, not in the visible ministry that may result from such a life. Faithfulness in our assignments is important, but it is not our *reward.* Many other individuals in biblical history had much more

---

[10]"Now Jesus was praying in a certain place, and when he finished, one of his disciples said to him, 'Lord, teach us to pray, as John taught his disciples'" (Luke 11:1). An ancient rabbi shared his entire way of life with his disciples, so John taught his disciples his entire lifestyle. However, it is notable prayer is the only thing that the Gospels specifically mention John teaching his disciples (Luke 11:1). This is a profound statement—communion was the defining aspect of John's life and the chief thing John passed on to his disciples.

visible ministry activity than John, yet according to Jesus, none of those figures exceeded John.

Defining Impact Correctly

To pursue a life of communion, you must define impact correctly. Every human wants their life to matter and have an impact, but most people do not define impact correctly. If you define impact correctly, you can focus your life, but if you do not, you can unknowingly waste your life.

For example, the life of Daniel had profound impact. God told Ezekiel that Daniel was one of only a handful of men whose prayers could have saved Jerusalem.[11] God implied he was the wisest human in his generation.[12] Daniel's intercession challenged the powers.[13] Furthermore, Daniel was given perhaps the most unique insights into the end times and wrote the book Jesus referenced more than any other book.[14] But Daniel never preached publicly, he worked for a pagan king who conquered his nation, and he lived his life as a slave separated from his people.

From a human perspective, Daniel's life had little impact, but from heaven's perspective, it was significant because Daniel lived a life that impacted the heavens. A life that impacts the heavens will also impact the earth, but far too many are living a life that prioritizes human impact and has little or no impact in the heavens.

Are you willing to live a life that prioritizes impact in the heavens?

Daniel challenged the powers with his life.[15] Do you? If you pursue this kind of life, people will likely find your priorities odd. You may experience loneliness and seasons with few friends. Your greatest

---

[11]Ezekiel 14:14, 20.

[12]Ezekiel 28:3.

[13]Daniel 10:12–13.

[14]For more on this see the book *Son of Man: The Gospel of Daniel 7.*

[15]Daniel 10:12–13.

impact may become visible after you die. However, heaven will call you *greatly beloved*,[16] and the spiritual powers will be challenged.

Many people try to have impact by doing "big" things. Yet the secret to impact is not mostly about doing big things. It is about the small things that you do every day. If you look at John's brief public ministry, he looks like a failure. John spent more time in jail than he did preaching. Only a remnant responded to his message, and national leaders rejected him. Yet Jesus counted him among the greatest of all human beings. Paul exhausted himself working in a small region, planting house churches, and writing letters to encourage struggling churches. His impact probably seemed small for much of his life, but two thousand years later, very few humans have had as much impact as Paul had.

Confusing Activity and Impact

We dramatically overestimate the impact of travel and events. It is ironic we live in a time when a person can have greater impact from a single place than ever in history due to technology, yet we are probably more enamored with travel and activity than any other generation. There are legitimate assignments from the Lord that involve travel and public ministry, but most prominent figures in the Bible lived their lives in a much smaller place than we imagine.

When travel or ministry activity becomes a way to escape the wilderness, it does not produce substantial impact; it serves as an escape from the place God has designed for our communion, formation, and ministry.

The Christian world is "busier" than any time in history, but this does not automatically mean we are having more impact than any other generation. In some cases, travel is used to escape boredom, but this goes unnoticed because we've confused activity and impact. Events and gatherings can be life-changing, but most are not. Events are only life-changing if there is a transformation that persists long after the event has ended, not by the enthusiasm of the moment.

Sadly, it is possible for speakers and attendees to go from conference to conference, learning information and enjoying events,

---

[16]Daniel 9:23; 10:11, 19.

but not becoming a demonstration of the Word they speak and hear. This should terrify us because this is fertile ground for hypocrisy.

Hypocrisy exists any time you are not allowing the Lord to shape your life so that it corresponds to what you know.[17]

When you try to escape boredom through diversions—whether it is social media on your phone or Christian conferences—you are simply avoiding your own barrenness by confusing activity with impact and information with transformation. That avoidance robs God of the opportunity to work something in you through your barrenness.

The enemy is not nearly as threatened by religious activity as we imagine. He does not mind if you engage in activity and even acquire information as long as you do not become a living demonstration of the Word of God.

We should weep because the truth is there is a lot of religious activity that is nothing more than activity.

Activity does not produce true impact simply because it earns accolades, gives you a sense of purpose, and convinces you that you are something you are not. However, this delusion can continue as long as you are not brave enough to shut down your busyness, stare in the mirror, examine the condition of your own soul, and confront who you really are. God can work with those who face their lack and barrenness. He cannot do a deep work in you, though, as long as you cling to the façade of strength and popularity. Who knows how many have short-circuited their assignment by excessively traveling and creating activity rather than standing before the Lord?

Travel and activity feel successful when they are accompanied by accolades, but accolades are deceptive when they are more enticing than the possibilities of a life before God in the wilderness.

Are we be brave enough to honestly examine our "Christian" activities and prayerfully evaluate how much is God and how much is human craving for activity to fill the void of our own barrenness and boredom due to the lack of an internal reality with God?

---

[17]In the process of growing in maturity, our lives do not always fully reflect what has been revealed to us, but we should be in process with the Lord to allow our lives to conform to the Word we have received. In a sense, we all live with some hypocrisy. The question is how are we responding to it?

The wilderness forged John. There were no crowds to seduce him. He was cut off from the noise and activity of the temple, so he had to face his own barrenness until God produced something in him. Any authority he gained would have to come from God.

Do Hearts Move When You Quote Bible Verses?

John did not shatter the prophetic silence with a new message. He shattered the silence by speaking the same Bible verses that were quoted year after year throughout the synagogues of Israel to produce a distant hope that one day God would come again to deliver his people. When John spoke these verses, however, the response was completely different. John did not simply read Isaiah; he spoke Isaiah under an unction from the same Spirit who gave those words to Isaiah. In John's mouth, Isaiah's predictions came like a sledgehammer and carried a weighty sense of immediacy. Distant predictions suddenly became overwhelmingly real, and Bible verses produced an immediate, raw response. People cried out, *"What do we do?"*[1]

The Word of God has explosive power because it contains the words of the uncreated, transcendent, sovereign Ruler of the cosmos. However, God does not automatically let people wield the full power of His words.

Many people are frustrated because their words lack power, so they pursue new ways to excite audiences the way an amusement park introduces new rides to keep people coming. Day after day, all sorts of new "insights" fill our websites and Christian bookstores. Like the philosophers in Athens,[2] we seem to be constantly looking for a new revelation, a previously hidden insight, a mystical experience, or some undiscovered information that will finally make our Christianity work. Most Christians do not realize this is a modern expression of

---

[1]Luke 3:10–14.

[2]Acts 17:21.

Gnosticism—an ancient heresy that sought spiritual progress through hidden insights.

The relentless search for novelty in Christian messages is often an attempt to cover up the lack of anointing.

Novelty stirs mental curiosity (and sells books), but it does not produce transformation. Christian fads are popular because information can be conveyed without sacrifice. It only requires a small amount of time and a stage presence. There is a big difference between information, charisma, and the anointing, however, and everyone knows it. If sermons and messages give people something to think about but never provoke the question, *"What must we do?"* then something is missing.

Roman soldiers followed a pantheon of gods. They had military might and thought Jewish monotheism and worship were strange, so there was little reason for a Roman soldier to do anything about John except ensure he was not stirring up political trouble. John was just another passionate Jew with a bizarre message. However, when hardened, pagan Roman soldiers heard this wilderness preacher, they cried out, *"What do I do?"*[3] That response reveals quite a bit about the power resting on John.

When John spoke Bible verses, they pierced pagan hearts.

It is easy to read the Bible in a detached way and assume John's environment was much simpler than ours, but John's world was incredibly complex. John faced a corrupt, religious priesthood who saw themselves as the true interpreters of the Scriptures. He also lived under the political and military might of Rome. Furthermore, the sensuality, humanism, and paganism of Greece were widespread. John preached in a context filled with religion, dead spirituality, military might, sensuality, and humanism.

John faced the same threats we continue to face, and he confronted them with the power of the Scripture.

People did not ask John, "What shall we *believe?*" The message John delivered demanded a response, not just intellectual agreement. John did more than address his audience's thinking—he addressed their

---

[3]Luke 3:14.

actions.[4] We tend to call people to *believe* the gospel (which is biblical), but our words should also provoke people to *obey* the gospel. You should think clearly about the gospel, but you must not substitute knowledge of the gospel for the transformational impact of the gospel. People *heard* something from John, but they also *saw* something in John.

John had lived before the face of God, so his words carried the weight of God.

Because the Word of God is living and active,[5] it can only be communicated properly when the messenger is willing to let that message transform them. The message we carry is so valuable it cannot be communicated in words alone. It must be *demonstrated* in us, the messengers. God does not require full maturity before He gives the anointing, and He is incredibly patient, but if you do not allow Him to conform you to His Word, you cannot expect the anointing to come when you speak that Word.

The Word is so valuable it makes the ultimate requirement of us—if we want to communicate it properly, it will require our lives.

We need a renewed value for the Word of God, and we need to allow that Word to transform us as we behold the beauty of Jesus in the book written about Him.[6] We don't need a "new message"; we need messengers who cause hearts to burn when they speak what God has already said, but you cannot become an expression of a message you do not know.

Do you want to be a messenger? Do you want to know if you are "anointed"? You need to ask yourself one simple question: *Do hearts move when I quote Bible verses?*

I Found Your Words, and I Ate Them

We should not expect God to speak new things to us if we do not value what He has already spoken.

When we prioritize new mystical experiences over the Word of God in the desire to be "prophetic," we miss a powerful fact: *The chariot*

---

[4]Luke 3:10–14.

[5]Hebrews 4:12.

[6]John 5:39.

the Holy Spirit rides best on the Word of God.[7] We need a fresh appreciation and value for the Word of God, and we must shatter the misconception that the activity of the Holy Spirit and the Word of God are in some sort of tension. The Holy Spirit inspired the Word, He loves the Word, and if we truly love the Word, it will cause us to treasure the Holy Spirit and yield to Him in a deeper way.

Moses commanded Israel to love the Lord with all her heart, soul, and might, and the first expression of that love was a deep value for the Word:

> *You shall love the LORD your God with all your heart and with all your soul and with all your might. And these words that I command you today shall be on your heart. You shall teach them diligently to your children, and shall talk of them when you sit in your house, and when you walk by the way, and when you lie down, and when you rise. You shall bind them as a sign on your hand, and they shall be as frontlets between your eyes. You shall write them on the doorposts of your house and on your gates. (Deuteronomy 6:5–9)*

Loving the Lord with all our soul and might begins by treasuring and valuing His Word. It means:

- We carry the Word in our hearts, which is the deepest place of our beings.
- We meditate on the Word and allow it to fill our imaginations.
- The Word stirs our emotions and guides our affections.
- We study the Word rigorously.
- We give time to the Word.
- We teach the Word diligently.
- We treasure the Word so much it becomes a subject of our daily conversation.
- God's Word begins to reshape and transform us into the image of the One who spoke these words.

If we want to be prophetic, we must treasure God's Word like Jeremiah did:

---

[7] Unknown author, site:https://ihopkcorg-a.akamaihd.net/platform/IHOP/925/583/20141114*The*Value*of*Using*Biblical*PrayersGIP08study*notes.pdf*

Your words were found, and I ate them, and your words became to me a joy and the delight of my heart, for I am called by your name, O LORD God of hosts. (Jeremiah 15:16)

When we respond to the Lord this way, the Lord will respond to us the way He did to Jeremiah:

Therefore thus says the LORD: "If you return, I will restore you, and you shall stand before me. If you utter what is precious, and not what is worthless, you shall be as my mouth." (Jeremiah 15:19)

We need to come to a place where God's words are our highest pleasure. We need to sit before the Lord, taking delight and pleasure in His words.

If you have a Bible, you hold in your hands a written record of words spoken by an uncreated God. You cannot be prophetic if you do not treasure these words.

We have reduced the prophetic gift to unusual predictions, but there is much more available to us if we will treasure the words God has already spoken to us. The prophetic gift is not in conflict with the Word of God. In fact, three of the men in Scripture who had the most unusual prophetic revelations (Ezekiel, Jeremiah, and John) were told to eat a scroll, an act which represented deep meditation on the Word of God.[8]

Make time to sit in a posture of prayer with the Bible and allow God to speak to you through His Word. His words are tender and terrifying. Tremble at them and then take delight in them. Meditate on the Word to hear His voice. It takes time, but when you hear His voice, it is worth it. If you want to be prophetic, combine the Word with a life of prayer and seasons of fasting:

You can do the prophetic without prayer and fasting, but you'll never be the prophetic in the way that God intended without embracing the grace of prayer and fasting.[9]

---

[8]Jeremiah 15:16; Ezekiel 3:1–3; Revelation 10:9–11.

[9]Mike Bickle, *Forerunners and the Spirit of Elijah*, 2002, http://www.mikebickle.org.edgesuite.net/MikeBickleVOD/2002/20020227-T-Forerunners_and_the_Spirit_of_Elijah_S&W.pdf (accessed February 7, 2013), 13.

The deepest way we can express our love for the Word is to allow the Holy Spirit to bring us into full agreement with the Word and to produce a manifestation of that Word in us—this is what John did.

John meditated on the oracles of Isaiah until they began to take deep root in his soul. He contemplated Malachi's words until they became his own words. Over decades, John lived according to the mantra, *"You are what you eat,"* and as he meditated on the Word of God, the Spirit used the Word to shape and mold John until he shared the prophets' burden and carried their passion.

It is easy to know what a person consumes. All you have to do is listen to them:[10]

> *"For out of the abundance of the heart the mouth speaks." (Matthew 12:34)*

What are you eating?

The God of Genesis 1

When God decided to form the cosmos out of nothing, He did not form a construction company. *He spoke:*

> *In the beginning, God created the heavens and the earth. The earth was without form and void, and darkness was over the face of the deep. . . . And God said. . . . (Genesis 1:1–3)*

If you read Genesis 1 as only an explanation of how the world began, you can miss the point. In this chapter, God spoke ten times, and every time He spoke, the results were explosive. Things without form suddenly took on very specific and purposeful form. Things that did not exist suddenly came into being.

The primary theme of Genesis 1 is the explosive power of God's words, and we are expected to read the entire Bible in light of Genesis 1.

Genesis 1 establishes the explosive power of God's words, and the unparalleled power of His voice is demonstrated repeatedly throughout the Bible. His voice creates, destroys, inspires awe, and produces

---

[10]See also Proverbs 4:23; Luke 6:45.

terror.[11] The great miracle of the exodus is that a people *heard* the voice of the living God and lived.[12] The prophets were undone when they recorded "thus saith the Lord." God's words are so powerful and so central to who He is that, when God became a man, He presented Himself as the "Word of God."[13]

Because you are made in God's image, the centrality of the Word is reflected in you as well. Your words are the most difficult thing to control and yet have the most destructive power.[14] Your words indicate who you really are.[15] You will be judged based on your words.[16] Even the words of a stranger have unbelievable power. Cruel words can hurt more than a physical injury, and an encouraging word from a stranger can completely shift our demeanor.

The cosmos we inhabit exists because God spoke. The Bible contains the words of the same Person, and they carry the same power.

The words God spoke after Genesis 1 are not less powerful than His first recorded words. In fact, the words of Genesis 1 are not nearly as dramatic and passionate as many of God's other words. All of God's words must be read with Genesis 1 in mind because they contain the same explosive, creative power demonstrated in creation. *And many of God's most powerful words have yet to be fulfilled.*

The effect God's voice had on the cosmos is a picture of the power God's words have in us. If you will give yourself to His words, those words will shape and form your inner man just like they shaped the cosmos. They will recreate you just as they created beauty from a dark and unshaped earth.[17]

---

[11]Genesis 1; Exodus 20:18–19; Psalm 29:3–9; Isaiah 42:13.

[12]Exodus 19:7–9, 16–18; 20:19; Deuteronomy 4:9–13, 32–36, 5:1–4, 20–23.

[13]John 1:1–13.

[14]James 3:1–12.

[15]Matthew 15:11, 18.

[16]Matthew 12:36.

[17]Genesis 1:1–2.

God is the God who speaks.

The Weight of our Words

Many people lack weight on their words because they do not know when to be silent.

If you want real power on your words, you must learn when to speak and when to be silent. The prophets not only spoke for God, they understood the need to bear the tension of His silence and not give their own "prophetic opinions" as His Word. Like the ancient prophets, John did not cry out until the Word of the Lord came to him.[18]

There are times the Lord is speaking through someone else, and we need to sit and receive what the Lord is saying instead of speaking our own opinions. When the Lord has not stirred something, it is better to wait in silence than speak prematurely in God's name. But holding the tongue is one of the most difficult and powerful things a human can do.[19] When we speak because we crave attention and have an overinflated view of our own wisdom, we limit our ability to prophesy.

Furthermore, we have more outlets to speak than any other generation. Our words are many, but they are not significant. The vast majority of our conversation is meaningless and trivial. It has no weight and produces no effect. The Lord records the conversations of the righteous,[20] which reveals just how serious our conversations are. What are the angels writing down when you speak?

We endlessly render judgment, give opinions, and speak light, frivolous words. We do not hesitate to quickly offer strong opinions on things we barely know anything about. Then we use our words to attack our church family, friends, and even those in authority. Even Michael did not rebuke Satan directly,[21] yet we feel very free with our opinions and rebukes.

---

[18]Luke 3:2–3.

[19]James 3:7–8.

[20]Malachi 3:16.

[21]Jude 9.

When our mouths are filled with cheap words, we should not expect to speak on God's behalf or have weight on our words.

You Have the Words of the Uncreated God

Do you truly believe your Bible contains the words of the living, uncreated God? Do you treasure your Bible accordingly?

Many people *study* the Word of God, but do you *meditate* with affection and longing? Do you read the Word of God over and over, carefully savoring each phrase? Do you take in every syllable of every word like a refreshing drink? Do you speak God's words back to Him because your heart has been captured and your affections stirred? Does the Word provoke songs of love? Do you read the Bible with *desire?*

A man or woman in love treasures every phrase in a letter written by a lover. They read it repeatedly, and they meditate on the words and phrases because it was written by the one they love. And they respond to their lover with similar words. If the Bible contains the words of a divine person who loves more deeply than any human can, His words should stir deeper affections than any human love letter.

How is it that so many are more moved by the words of an emotional human than the words of the uncreated God who is filled with desire?

Preachers may be well-intentioned, but many spend more time consulting secondary resources, looking for creative graphics, and searching for funny stories than they do savoring the Bible itself. Sermon aids can be helpful tools when they *support* the proclamation of the Word of God, but not when they *replace* it. Have you considered we are going to stand at the judgment seat and all the saints of history will be in utter shock at how much access we had to the Word of God?

God is going to raise up a people who treasure His Word more than they treasure their own words.

Apathy Is Apparent

A captivated messenger is like a man in love.

When he speaks, he is not just communicating facts, but he is pleading with his hearers to behold the majestic, divine Person he has discovered in the pages of Scripture. His words have a radically different effect because he speaks out of his affections.

Most people want power on their words, but words carry unusual weight when we speak about what we love and desire.

Passion is obvious, and deep desire cannot be hidden. Informed preachers can produce mental agreement, but captivated messengers penetrate the heart and confront ambivalence toward God and His Son. The gospel is the most valuable message in the world, but if God has not captivated a messenger, why should their words about God captivate an audience? Desire is obvious—and so is apathy.

A man or woman deeply in love finds words inadequate, and a man or woman who has encountered true majesty struggles to describe what they have seen and felt. Human language is incapable of fully representing things that are transcendent, which illustrates something surprising: *Many of the most powerful messengers use weak words and lack natural eloquence.*

When you read the biblical prophets, it is obvious they saw and heard things they were unable to fully convey in human language. They used the strongest words they could find, but their visions of God exceeded their human capacity. Paul also saw things he felt were not even lawful to speak in human words.[1]

When is the last time you saw a preacher at a loss for words and unable to fully describe what he had seen in the Scripture?

Eloquent words are beautiful, but we need more messengers who cannot find language to convey what they have seen and heard. We need more speakers grasping for words, obviously incapable of describing the majesty and splendor of the uncreated Person.

Words have incredible power, but sometimes a lack of words carries more power.

God is the uncreated Person who governs all of creation, and if we never run out of words to describe God, it should trouble us. Perhaps we have precise words and polished messages because our revelation of God is so small we can fully comprehend what we know of Him in

---

[1] 2 Corinthians 12:2–4.

our limited minds. If you can fully describe what you know of God, you have very little revelation of His majesty.

When people speak about a God they do not know, their lack of affection is apparent, and their words lack impact.

God's Son is the most precious and beautiful Person in the world. If a messenger values other things over Jesus—even a "ministry"—his life does not demonstrate Jesus' worth so his words cannot convey that worth. God is not going to put weight on the words of men who do not desire His Son—it's an insult to His Son.

God is desperately looking for messengers who value His Son the way He does. He is eager to anoint their words with incredible power.

Far too many sermons are not *from* the Bible; they are messages *about* the Bible. These messages may contain true and factual information, but they are sterile because the speakers were not captivated by their study of the text; they were merely informed by it.

We must not confuse the modified behavior that information and new habits can produce with the true transformation the Word of God brings. When the Word becomes flesh, it revolutionizes the inner person. It does not simply produce more "moral" behavior. There are millions of people who have modified their lives in response to "helpful" sermons but have not heard the Word of God proclaimed with power.

It will not end this way. The Word will be proclaimed in power by messengers who chose the wilderness because their affections were captured by the Man who is coming.

Will We Be Ashamed of Our Words?

When you begin to treat the Word of God as a message from the heart of the uncreated, living Person who desires intimate communion—the One whose majesty can terrify us—you will discover new authority on your words.

Have you really considered that we will stand before the judgment seat and answer for our messages?

Do you really want to stand before the uncreated God and explain why you put more confidence in stylish graphics, funny illustrations, and "thoughtful" quotes from unbelievers than you did in the words of the uncreated God? Have we forgotten the extraordinary nature of our call? We are finite, created beings who live in time and yet have been commissioned as the primary messengers of the infinite, uncreated God who rules eternity, but we cannot accurately describe someone we do not know.

When you stand before the terrifying, uncreated Lord of glory, will your sermons, songs, or words be an accurate portrayal of His beauty and His nature? Every sermon, Bible lesson, and song in this age is utterly incapable of fully expressing His majesty, but are any even accurate? Do you lead people into the knowledge of God or give them some self-help combined with a promise to escape hell?

Furthermore, when all our teaching (including singing, which is perhaps the most effective form of teaching) is collected, what will the main message be? Will the words we have spoken throughout our lives primarily reveal the knowledge of God or something else?

If you are a teacher, when you stand before God, He will not compliment you on the way you quoted the *New York Times* in your sermon. His fiery eyes will instantly center on what you communicated about His Son because this is the task you have been given.[2] You are His image. You represent *Him*. You must commit not to stand before the throne with little more than years of proclaiming pithy quotes, singing self-centered ballads, and teaching human maxims for a prosperous life in the name of God.

This entire fallen age came about because the first humans put more confidence in their perception than in what God had said. Is it possible that we make a similar mistake over and over on Sunday mornings if our sermons put more confidence in trendy techniques than the Word of God?[3]

Are we prepared to stand before God for the words we speak, the messages we give, the books we write, and the songs we sing?

---

[2]James 3:1.

[3]The key is where we put the *most* confidence. Of course, we should seek to communicate in a way that audiences can best understand the Word of God. And the gospel should be contextualized and reflect a people's culture as much as is appropriate.

The angels long to look into the mystery of the gospel,[4] but have we considered what they hear every Sunday morning? Do they hear the mystery of God, His salvation, and His beauty? Or are they genuinely confused that a people called by God's name often seem to have little interest in His Person and His Word?

Absolute Fidelity to the Word of God

Many people eagerly speak the part of the Word they agree with but continue to cling to disagreements with other aspects of the Word. This filtering is an expression of our pride, and it must be broken. (God is very patient with us, but He must break this expression of our pride.) Furthermore, there are degrees of power God will not give as long as we are still filtering His Word through our own opinions.

Are you willing to put more trust in what the Word says than what you perceive with your own eyes? And are you willing to put more trust in what God has said than what you think?[5]

The fall in the Garden of Eden came about because Adam and Eve trusted their own perception more than what God had said. They saw that the fruit on the tree looked good, but God said it was not. In the end, they trusted what they perceived over what God had said.[6] Choosing our evaluation over what God has said is the fundamental human sin. Every sin flows from this.

God must break our fallen tendency to evaluate Him and trust our own wisdom over what He has said. Until He has broken this, the sin of Eden continues to live in our hearts.

Many people think they agree with God because they agree with many things they find in Scripture. For example, they may agree with what the Bible says about immortality because they have seen the negative consequences of sin. They are committed to the Word of God as long as it is reasonable to them, and they ignore, redefine, or

---

[4]1 Peter 1:12.

[5]For more on this, see *Have You Been Blinded? Facing Your Assumptions About God's Leadership.*

[6]Genesis 3:1–6.

actively resist aspects of the Word that seem unreasonable to them never realizing this is an expression of original sin.

You cannot operate in the full power of the Word as long as you filter it through your own wisdom.

Even Jesus passed through this test. In the Garden of Gethsemane, He offered up "loud cries" to God and asked the Father if the "cup" in front of Him could pass, but He put more confidence in the Father's wisdom than His own. When Jesus trusted the Father's evaluation of His suffering more than His own perception of what was coming, He demonstrated complete victory over the fundamental human sin:

> *"Father, if you are willing, remove this cup from me. Nevertheless, not my will, but yours, be done." (Luke 22:42)*

If you want to be fully useful to God, you must allow Him to break your confidence in your own perception of Him, His ways, and His Word. Because He loves you, God will take you to your own breaking point—the place where you have to choose whether to trust your own reason, understanding, logic, emotions, and perception or what He has said.

When God breaks a person, He will use something in their life to force a deep, internal conflict. That conflict will force a choice: *Are you willing to deny your own thinking and your own perception to believe what God has said, or will you deny God and instead put confidence in what you see, think, and feel?* He will press you to deny what you see and feel in your own wisdom and trust what He has said. This is the core of what it means to "deny yourself" and follow Jesus.[7]

When this conflict comes, you will feel you are on the edge of insanity, because no human wants to submit to a wisdom they do not fully agree with.

But the breaking must come, and when it does, you must stand on the edge of sanity if necessary, *deny* yourself, and choose His words over your wisdom, *especially* when His words do not make sense to you. If you do not pass through this process, the power on your words will be limited because you will continue to filter His words through your own wisdom and understanding.

---

[7]Matthew 10:17–22; 38–39; 16:24; 23:34; 24:9; Mark 13:9–13; Luke 21:12, 16–17; John 15:19–20; 16:2.

The Word of God must shatter your human paradigms and perspectives. If it doesn't extend beyond your human, mental capacity, then it is not the Word of God. Until we acknowledge our limited capacity as a creature and our inability to fully grasp His ways, the rebellion has not fully ended in our hearts. The judgments of God typically expose this issue more than any other thing because the judgments of God are *unreasonable* to many believers. However, God is very bold about His judgments. He is not ashamed of them and openly declares they are an expression of His glory.

Even the biblical prophets were challenged by God's wisdom. When they encountered the majesty of God, it instantly exposed the smallness and foolishness of human opinions. Some, like Habakkuk, argued with God's leadership of history. The prophets did not always understand what God said, and God did not always give them explanations, but they ultimately put their confidence in who God was when they could not fully grasp what He said.

Your ability to evaluate God's wisdom will never produce true confidence. Confidence in God comes from who He is, not in our ability to understand His ways. You can have absolute confidence in God because of the cross. Any God who is willing to become a man and suffer tremendously to give mercy to His enemies can be trusted in all His ways.

Today millions of Christians continue to interpret God's Word through the lens of their own wisdom. But it is not going to end this way.

Messengers like John speak with unusual authority because they have more confidence in the Word of God than their own perception. They do not view the world through their own wisdom; they view the world through the lens of what God has said. *What is your lens?*

Recovering the Prophetic

John was the first New Testament prophet, which means his life and ministry are the first expression of New Testament prophetic ministry. If you want to understand prophecy, and prophecy in the New Testament, you need to carefully examine John's ministry.

Jesus said no other biblical prophet had exceeded John, but John did not do many of the things we typically associate with a prophet. He did not make any new predictions, describe any mystical experiences, record unusual visions, or do any miracles.[1] In many ways, his life confronts stereotypes about prophetic ministry. John soaked himself in the Word of God and spoke the Word with insight and clarity, and Jesus said no prophet had exceeded him.

John allowed the Scripture to shape his life, and he proclaimed the Scripture with power. Jesus considered it the height of prophecy.

John's approach to the prophetic should not be surprising because he followed the ancient pattern of the biblical prophets. Many people think the prophets primarily predicted unknown events and new things, but this was not their main message. One Jewish scholar described the prophets' ministry this way:

> *Prophecy is not simply the application of timeless standards to particular human situations . . . but a divine understanding of a human situation. Prophecy, then, may be described as exegesis of existence from a divine perspective. Understanding prophecy is an understanding of an*

---

[1]John 10:41.

understanding rather than an understanding of knowledge; it is exegesis of exegesis. . . .[2]

According to this scholar, prophecy is a *divine understanding of a human situation* and fundamentally an *exegesis of existence from a divine perspective.*

The biblical prophets' prophetic perspective came in part from viewing the world through the lens of Scripture. Their messages were deeply rooted in Scripture because they were soaked in Scripture. Their main task was not to predict new things but to apply what God had already spoken (Scripture) in their generation. Men like Isaiah and Jeremiah are now part of our Scripture, but if you read their books carefully, you will notice their prophecies were based on the Scripture they already had.

Biblical prophecy begins with taking what God has already spoken and applying it correctly in a generation.

This is so fundamental to prophecy, Isaiah said prophets who do not speak according to the Word have no light in them:

> *To the law and to the testimony! If they do not speak according to this word, it is because there is no light in them. (Isaiah 8:20 NKJV)*

Notice Isaiah did not address prophetic statements; he addressed the prophets themselves. If prophetic messengers do not speak according to the Word, it is evidence *they* have no light—no true revelation—in their inner man. And if their inner man is not filled with revelation, then their words are not revelatory. They may genuinely love God, but they are not prophetic.

The Lord will allow prophetic words to test us[3] because our reaction to prophetic words exposes what is in our hearts. For example, if we are drawn to prophecies of personal success, blessing, and prosperity, it may indicate we crave these things more than we crave God. The prophets constantly had to deal with false prophets who

---

[2]Abraham Heschel, *The Prophets* (New York: Harper Perennial Modern Classics, 2001), xxvii.

[3]Psalm 105:19.

spoke according to what people wanted to hear, and we are no different.

We must recover the expression of prophecy John operated in because it is fundamental to prophecy.

God may give insight on future events, but the heart of prophecy is applying the Word of God in a generation with power to produce transformation in the hearer. Like the prophets of old, John repeated what God had already spoken with such power his audience cried out, *"What must we do?"* Believing Jews cried out. Corrupt tax collectors cried out. Pagan Roman soldiers cried out.[4]

In many parts of the church, there has been a renewed emphasis on the activity of the Holy Spirit and His gifts, including the gift of prophecy.[5] The emphasis is biblical because the New Testament expects prophetic ministry to continue. It gives us descriptions of prophets,[6] exhortations to value prophecy,[7] and instructions to carefully evaluate prophecy.[8] While the ability to reveal unknown information is intriguing, we must recover the *entire* gift of prophecy, which is much more than the ability to give a word of knowledge or predict an unknown event.

Many people seek to be "prophetic" in various ways, but biblical prophecy is not fortune-telling. Having a value for the "word of knowledge" or other prophetic insights is important, but these things are only part of the gift of prophecy.

The Essence of the Prophets

Many people have sought various things in their desire to be "prophetic." If you want to be biblically prophetic, your deepest need is not a hidden insight or someone else's anointing. The prophetic realm centers on the knowledge of God and our response to that

---

[4]Luke 3:10–14.

[5]Thankfully, there is a growing desire to avoid unbiblical approaches to the Spirit.

[6]Acts 11:27; 13:1; 15:32; 21:9–10.

[7]1 Corinthians 14:1–6, 39.

[8]1 Thessalonians 5:20–21.

knowledge, so if you want to be prophetic, you desperately need the knowledge of God. And that is a costly possession. No book can teach you that, and no one can lay hands on you and cause you to become a prophet in a moment.[9]

As we have seen, John's gift or prophecy matured through the three key elements of his lifestyle:

- The gift of the Spirit.
- The Word of God.
- An intentional way of life in a small place.

Biblical prophets do not merely carry messages. They are the message.

God does not want prophetic messengers who dispense unseen insights and information. He wants messengers who are the message. *Becoming prophetic will cost you your life.*

New information is not enough to make you "prophetic." God forms and instructs prophetic people through the way they live, and He wants to orchestrate your life so His words have power when you speak them. When you survey the biblical prophets, you find incredible variety. Daniel worked for a foreign king. Isaiah was a member of the royal family. Elijah seemed to be a rugged man from a small place. Amos was a shepherd. Moses was trained in a foreign empire. Samuel and Deborah governed a nation. Anna worked in the temple. Huldah was responsible for the priests' garments.

We imagine the prophets as near mythical individuals who are more like wizards in a *Lord of the Rings* novel than real people, so we have trouble seeing them as real people. However, what made the prophets unusual was not their appearance or their predictions but their deep zeal for God and their profound awareness of His majesty.

---

[9]There is, of course, great value in "laying on of hands" (Numbers 8:10; 27:18; Acts 6:6; 8:17; 13:3; 19:6; 1 Timothy 4:14; 5:22; 2 Timothy 1:6; Hebrews 6:1–2), and God does release things to us through impartation. However, impartation as an isolated or casual act is not a formula that can produce a "prophetic" messenger.

Biblical prophets are defined more by their vision of God[10] *than their ability to predict things.*

The prophets had a radically God-centered view of reality, and they viewed history through His perspective. Their view of reality was shaped by a high view of God that caused them to live differently and set the stage for messages.

The prophet views all reality through a God-saturated lens.

The prophet dares to take biblical verses literally and is deeply uncomfortable with any approach to God that is man-centered. A prophet is ultimately God's advocate, and he enters into God's raw and deep anguish over God's own people. Prophets are advocates for God's glory and God's honor above their own interests, and they are even willing to take God's side against their own people. They want everyone to see God the way they do, and when people do not, it perplexes them and causes deep pain in their hearts.

Prophets do not exist primarily as super-spiritual individuals but as ongoing gifts to the people of God. They exist to equip the church to have a prophetic perspective, not as demigods to be exalted because of the intriguing nature of their gift. We should not seek to make people "prophets" because they are chosen by God, not by man, and cannot be made by a predefined curriculum.

The New Testament assumes the existence of prophets in the church and affirms this gift as an ongoing grace from heaven.[11] For example, Paul is the best known missionary in the New Testament, and he was sent out from a group of "prophets and teachers"[12] in Antioch. The words and the lives of prophets must be evaluated according to

---

[10]When I say, "vision of God," I am referring to the way the prophet views God, not necessarily a mystical experience in which the prophet encounters God. These kinds of encounters profoundly affect prophets, but their vision of God is a bigger subject. John's high vision of God is obvious, and yet we have no mention of mystical encounters.

[11]Acts 2:17–18; 11:27; 13:1; 15:32; 19:6; 21:9–10; Romans 12:6; 1 Corinthians 11:4–5; 12:10; 12:28–29; 13:2, 9; 14:1, 3–6, 22, 24, 29, 31, 37, 39; Ephesians 2:20; 3:5; 4:11; 1 Timothy 1:18; 4:14.

[12]Acts 13:1.

Scripture, and we should only hold on to what is good.[13] We must not overemphasize ecstatic, mystical, or dramatic experiences.

God does not reveal information so prophets can build a following, nor does He give information. Nor will He give you information so you can use it to gain authority over others. That is witchcraft. Prophets only see in part.[14] They must be submitted to the body and share God's desire for His people. And they must also remember they exist to draw God's people to Him, not to themselves. The body is God's Bride, and in that sense, prophets are given power to influence another Man's wife to return to Him.

The Message Has Been Given

When God became man in Jesus, it was the most profound thing God had ever done. It was far greater than any event in the Old Testament, and John was given the unique task of preparing the way for it. It would be natural to expect the prophet with this assignment to have visions far beyond what Isaiah or Ezekiel saw. It would also be reasonable to anticipate this prophet would back up his message with powerful signs and wonders far beyond what prophets like Elijah did. All of this would be perfectly reasonable in light of God's history with Israel, and it makes John's ministry even more extraordinary.

It is almost unthinkable that God chose a man to prepare the way for His Son and did not give that man new visions to proclaim or miraculous signs to validate the message.[15] But God took a different approach with this unique prophet. The assignment was simple: Immerse yourself in My Word and proclaim it with power when I anoint you.

When God commissioned John, John had enough material in the Scripture to prepare the world for the arrival of God. He did not even need miracles.

There is no evidence John found the Scripture insufficient for his task, which provokes a question: *Do we share the same confidence in the Word John had?* If God used the Scripture already given to prepare the way

---

[13]1 Thessalonians 5:19–21.

[14]1 Corinthians 13:9.

[15]John 10:41.

for His Son's first coming, He will do the same for the second coming. In the days ahead, the church will rediscover the majesty of Jesus in the prophets' predictions and again proclaim the words of the prophets with power.

If John spoke the words of Scripture to prepare the way for Jesus, so should we.

The Message of Biblical Prophecy

Prophecy is not predominantly a collection of *predictions*. It is primarily a *witness* of Jesus. The predictions of the prophets exist to give us insight into Jesus—His kindness, His severity, His judgments, and His salvation:

The testimony of Jesus is the spirit of prophecy. (Revelation 19:10)

If you are more fascinated with future events than the Man those events revolve around, you are out of sync with God's agenda. And if your study of the prophets and the Word does not cause you to love and value Jesus more, you have missed the point because the heart of prophecy is the revelation of a Person not the prediction of events.

When you read the prophets' staggering words of judgment, you are reading descriptions of Jesus' unrelenting zeal for justice. When you read the prophets' majestic predictions of cosmic salvation, you are reading descriptions of Jesus' work of salvation. God is revealed by what He does, and the prophets have predicted what Jesus will do so we can discover who He is before He does all that He will do.

Many people are uncomfortable with the prophets. Their messages seem too extreme, too dramatic, too intense, and too emotional. These prophecies, however, were given to unveil Jesus. If you are uncomfortable with the messages of the Old Testament prophets, Jesus, not the prophets, is the source of your discomfort.

God's end-time agenda is very straightforward:

The revelation of Jesus Christ. . . . (Revelation 1:1)

In our generation, prophetic people sometimes bring attention to themselves through their unusual and spectacular revelations, but if a prophet's ministry brings more attention to them than it does to Jesus, something is deeply wrong. (And sometimes the problem is not the messenger, but the people who idolize the messenger.)

We tend to use the writings of the prophets to predict events, but John used them to proclaim Jesus and call people to repentance.

Predicting events alone is not the biblical prophetic. That is simply fortune-telling or divination. If predictions do not reveal something about God, they are not prophetic. Prophecy does not inform; it confronts. (This does not mean it is "prophetic" to be harsh or critical.) John's audience did not say, *"When will this happen?"* They said, *"What must we do?"*

If a prediction does not provoke a response toward Jesus, it is not biblical prophecy even if it correctly foretells an event. In fact, John's predictions did not happen the way he expected. He was confused by Jesus' ministry.[16] His predictions have yet to be fulfilled. The judgments he warned were imminent have still not come. God's timeline was different from John's, but John was listed in the top tier of all prophets, demonstrating prophecy is not an information game.

Biblical prophecy is not information about the future. It is a message about God and an invitation into the knowledge of God.

We have turned the prophetic ministry into people speaking about future events, but the prophetic ministry centers on speaking about God and, more specifically, God in the Person of Jesus. Prophets should be known by their insight into God, not their insight into world events. If your view of the prophetic becomes fixated on events, it will get off track.

Are you enamored with the future? Information? Spectacular events? Or God? Only one fascination is prophetic.[17]

---

[16]Matthew 11:2–3.

[17]Spiritual gifts like the word of knowledge (1 Corinthians 12:8) are powerful, and New Testament prophets did make predictions (Acts 11:28; 21:11). Insight into unknown information and future events is part of the prophetic, and we should value it in proper context. We should not dismiss these gifts because they are powerful when used correctly, but we must recover a biblical framework for the prophetic.

A Voice Crying in the Wilderness

Preachers often have a few messages that become their core messages throughout their lives, and they have unusual authority when they speak these messages. The message that defined John's ministry came from Isaiah 40:[1]

He said, "I am the voice of one crying out in the wilderness, 'Make straight the way of the Lord,' as the prophet Isaiah said." (John 1:23)

Isaiah 40 is a chapter about the second exodus and the return of the Bridegroom God, which explains why John chose this chapter. The chapter instructs a messenger to speak three themes:

- God's commitment to release salvation to Israel.
- The return of the God who came down on Sinai, the breathtaking nature of the second exodus, and the urgent need to prepare for it.
- The majesty of God and the foolishness of human pride.

The first few verses of the chapter introduce each of these themes and then command the messenger to proclaim them with increasing intensity.

First, it instructs a messenger to speak to Jerusalem and give comfort to Israel by predicting mercy will come to Israel after a final punishment for her sin:

Comfort, comfort my people, says your God. Speak tenderly to Jerusalem, and cry to her that her warfare is ended, that her iniquity is pardoned, that

---

[1]See also Matthew 3:3; Mark 1:3; Luke 3:4-6.

she has received from the LORD's hand double for all her sins. (Isaiah 40:1–2)

Second, it predicts a second exodus much greater in scope than the first exodus. The intensity increases with this second part of the message. This time a voice does not speak; it *cries* out:

A voice cries: "In the wilderness prepare the way of the LORD; make straight in the desert a highway for our God. Every valley shall be lifted up, and every mountain and hill be made low; the uneven ground shall become level, and the rough places a plain. And the glory of the LORD shall be revealed, and all flesh shall see it together, for the mouth of the LORD has spoken." (Isaiah 40:3–5)

Third, a command is given to declare the majesty of the Lord. The intensity increases again with a command to cry out:

A voice says, "Cry!" And I said, "What shall I cry?" All flesh is grass, and all its beauty is like the flower of the field. The grass withers, the flower fades when the breath of the LORD blows on it; surely the people are grass. The grass withers, the flower fades, but the word of our God will stand forever. (Isaiah 40:6–8)

The first eight verses of the chapter summarize the three main points of Isaiah 40, and the remaining verses expound on these points.

Isaiah describes two distinct aspects of God's commitment to Israel:

1. God is coming to Zion and Jerusalem to consummate the wedding He began with Israel on Mount Sinai.
2. God will save all Israel in a stunning way to dwell in her midst and make her His companion.[2]

He also described five different aspects of the second exodus:[3]

---

[2]Ezekiel 20:33; Hosea 2:14–20; Zechariah 14:9–11.

[3]Joel Richardson, *From Sinai to Zion* (Leawood: Winepress Media, 2020), 204.

1. The glory of the Lord will be revealed to the earth.[4]
2. The glory of the Lord will be visibly seen by all people.[5]
3. God will physically come just as the prophets have predicted.[6]
4. God will bring His rewards and His judgments.[7]
5. God's "arm" will rule, which is a reference to God's acts of power during the Exodus used to describe the acts of the future second exodus.[8]

Finally, he used analogies to confront the foolishness of human pride and the myth of human might:

1. The most powerful humans and human empires are little more than "grass" or "grasshoppers" in comparison to God.[9]
2. Humans are like "grass" when they face the consuming fire of God, a rebuke drawn from the imagery of God's appearance on Mount Sinai.[10]

Discovering John's Sermon Outline

The three themes in this chapter are all deeply connected by a single thread: the incomparable grandeur of God.

God's glory secures His promise to bring salvation. His glory will be demonstrated in the unprecedented drama of the second exodus.

---

[4]Matthew 16:27; 24:30; 25:31; Mark 13:26; Luke 21:27; 1 Corinthians 2:8; 2 Corinthians 4:4; Titus 2:13; Hebrews 1:3; Revelation 1:1.

[5]Isaiah 33:17; 35:2; 52:8, 10; 66:14, 18; Zechariah 12:10; Matthew 24:30; 26:64; Colossians 3:4; 1 Thessalonians 1:7–8; 2 Thessalonians 2:8; Revelation 1:7.

[6]Deuteronomy 33; Judges 5; cf. Daniel 7:13; Matthew 24:30; Mark 13:26; Luke 21:27; 2 Peter 3:4; Hebrews 10:37.

[7]Genesis 3:15; Numbers 24:17; Deuteronomy 32:35; 33:21; Judges 5:26–27; 1 Samuel 2:10; Psalm 58:10; 68:21; 110:5; Isaiah 63:3; Joel 3:13; Habakkuk 3:13; Matthew 25:23, 31–46; Jude 14; Revelation 14:20; 19:15.

[8]Exodus 3:19; 6:6; 13:3; 15:16; Deuteronomy 4:34; 5:15; 7:8, 19; 26:8; Isaiah 52:10; 53:1; Jeremiah 32:21; Ezekiel 20:33–34; Luke 1:51; John 12:38.

[9]Isaiah 40:22; Nahum 3:17.

[10]Exodus 19:18.

And His glory will be on full display when He brings Israel back to Himself and obtains her wholehearted love. Furthermore, His glory exposes the absurdity of human arrogance and idolatry.

John's tremendous view of God enabled him to proclaim Isaiah 40 with power.

John was a *God-centered* preacher, and his revelation of God's majesty provided the urgency for his call for repentance and his predictions of what was coming.

John's use of Isaiah 40 indicates his primary diet was the majesty of God.

A God-Centered Gospel

Isaiah 40 summarizes the end-time message of the church, and it revolves around the majesty of God. However, the glory of God is one of the most neglected subjects in the church. Tragically, the glory of God can even be viewed through a man-centered lens that emphasizes the ways in which God's glory benefits us.

John's message confronts the man-centered thinking that is pervasive in our time.

You must become a student of the majesty of God. Jesus considered John one of the greatest men ever born, but notice that Isaiah 40 simply referred to John as "a voice." The message is clear—the greatest human being is not even in the same category as the uncreated God. Compared to the majesty of God, the greatest human is nothing more than "a voice" and not worthy of a detailed description. When we glimpse the majesty of God, we lose sight of men and women—even great men and women.

Discovering and proclaiming[11] the beauty of God should be a central pursuit of our lives.

John's sermon fragments in the Gospels reveal that he studied and proclaimed the beauty of God from Scripture, but the tragic truth is many are more enamored with movies than the uncreated God. You must remember those who saw a glimpse of God's glory were nearly

---

[11]Proclaiming simply means sharing in whatever ways the Lord opens doors for you and gifts you. It can easily happen in conversations. Proclaiming is not only public preaching.

always either terrified or incapacitated. Consider Isaiah's encounter with Jesus' glory:[12]

In the year that King Uzziah died I saw the Lord sitting upon a throne, high and lifted up; and the train of his robe filled the temple. Above him stood the seraphim. Each had six wings: with two he covered his face, and with two he covered his feet, and with two he flew. And one called to another and said: "Holy, holy, holy is the LORD *of hosts; the whole earth is full of his glory!" And the foundations of the thresholds shook at the voice of him who called, and the house was filled with smoke. And I said: "Woe is me! For I am lost; for I am a man of unclean lips, and I dwell in the midst of a people of unclean lips; for my eyes have seen the King, the* LORD *of hosts!" (Isaiah 6:1–5)*

Try to imagine the scene. The temple is filled with smoke (incense) and incessant, thunderous shouts of "HOLY, HOLY, HOLY!" which literally means "completely and totally different, spectacular." The creatures are so overwhelmed, they instinctively cry out to each other in reaction to what they see. Their words demonstrate their minds are completely overwhelmed, and their voices must be deafening because their cries *shake* the foundation of this majestic temple.

Now imagine standing just outside this temple. If you could see the smoke, hear the creatures cry out, and feel the building shaking at their words, your mind would be completely overwhelmed with just one thought: *Who are they looking at? What is in there?*

Now compare this vision to our relative lack of fascination with the beauty of God.

The angels must be dumbfounded by our apathy. But the Holy Spirit is ready to give us revelation.

Uzziah was an impressive king, but when he died in humiliation and weakness, Isaiah had a vision of God that shattered his fascination with human achievement. With one glimpse of God, Isaiah immediately saw himself, his people, and even King Uzziah as little more than "people of unclean lips." When Isaiah saw divine glory, he cried out, "Woe is me!" which can also be translated "lost," "doomed," or "ruined."

---

[12]According to John 12:40–41, Isaiah saw Jesus.

When Isaiah suddenly saw he and the king he had been fascinated with were nothing more than "grass" that withers in comparison to the Lord of Hosts, he was so undone he pleaded to carry the message of God's grandeur to his people even though it would be a difficult assignment (and lead to his own execution):

And I heard the voice of the Lord saying, "Whom shall I send, and who will go for us?" Then I said, "Here I am! Send me." (Isaiah 6:8)

If you have revelation of God's majesty you will want to speak about it. What do you speak most about? God's majesty? Movies? Sports? Your ministry? The topic of your conversation reveals your heart's fascination.

Isaiah 40 is an exposition on the encounter of Isaiah 6, and it provokes a response like Isaiah's:

- If you have seen a glimpse of the beauty of Jesus, has your revelation of Him caused you to cry out, *"Woe is me?"* Until that cry emerges as a spontaneous reaction to the glory of God, you have not understood what Isaiah saw.
- Has your vision of Jesus caused you to petition heaven to carry the message of God's majesty to people who desperately need it? If we have the revelation Isaiah had, we will long to proclaim it so that men may be delivered from lesser things that hold their affections captive. If you are not burning to proclaim the majesty of God,[13] you have not understood what Isaiah saw.

You may not have the *encounter* Isaiah had, but you need the *revelation* Isaiah had. Isaiah 40 invites you to pursue that revelation and take up the message. Isaiah 40 is not directed to a single person like Isaiah 6; it instructs anyone who will hear to make a path for God and to speak His message. It is an invitation for us even if we do not share John's unique assignment.

It takes the revelation of God's majesty (Isaiah 6) to declare the Isaiah 40 message of the immensity of God and the fragility of man

---

[13]Proclaiming does not mean preaching. It means sharing the majesty of God according to your ability and opportunities.

with power. The vision of Isaiah 6 was a vision of Jesus,[14] which means the majesty of God proclaimed in Isaiah 40 is *Jesus'* majesty. Therefore, Isaiah 40 describes the unveiling of Jesus' majesty, which is the main theme of the end times and the spirit of all prophecy:[15]

> *The revelation of Jesus Christ, which God gave him to show to his servants the things that must soon take place. He made it known by sending his angel to his servant John. (Revelation 1:1)*
>
> *For the testimony of Jesus is the spirit of prophecy. (19:10)*

Messengers are not called to make much of themselves. When you stand before God, every illusion of your own glory will be shattered. No one will be captivated by your gifting in the presence of the uncreated God. You are called to make much of Jesus. John rejoiced when his glory faded because Jesus was revealed,[16] and Paul rejoiced when Jesus was proclaimed more widely as a result of his own imprisonment.[17]

Too many believers do not walk in the full strength of their calling because they are focused on *their calling*.

---

[14]John 12:41.

[15]Revelation 1:1.

[16]John 3:29–30.

[17]Philippians 1:12–18.

The Friend of the Bridegroom

John summarized his life, ministry, and ambition with one description. He was the *friend of the bridegroom*:[1]

> *The one who has the bride is the bridegroom. The friend of the bridegroom, who stands and hears him, rejoices greatly at the bridegroom's voice. Therefore this joy of mine is now complete. (John 3:29)*

John used this phrase to summarize who he was. It was more than a function—it was his identity. This title was very significant in light of Israel's unique history.

Throughout Israel's history, God had compared His relationship with Israel to the relationship between a bridegroom and a bride:[2]

> *For your Maker is your husband, the LORD of hosts is his name; and the Holy One of Israel is your Redeemer, the God of the whole earth he is called. (Isaiah 54:5)*

When John referred to Jesus as the Bridegroom, He identified Jesus as YHWH— the Bridegroom of Israel and the One who had made covenant with Israel on Sinai.

The Bridegroom God on the Mountain

When people recount the exodus story, they tend to spend the most time on Israel's deliverance from Egypt. That is not where the Bible puts the emphasis, though.

---

[1]This theme defined John's life and should define our lives as well. I dare say we have very little insight into God's identity as Bridegroom, and it limits our knowledge of God.

[2]Isaiah 54:4–6; Jeremiah 2:2; 3:1, 14; 31:32; Ezekiel 16:7–34; Hosea 2:19.

The crowning event of the exodus story is not the judgments on Egypt, it is Israel's unparalleled encounter with YHWH in the wilderness. The plagues released on Egypt were spectacular, but what followed was far more spectacular. God led Israel out of Egypt as a pillar of fire by night and a cloud by day, and when they camped around Sinai, God came down on the mountain *visibly*. He then spoke to a people *audibly* and entered into a covenant with humans that He compared to a marriage contract. No movie can adequately depict what happened there—the Israelites were terrified.

The fact God would *marry* Himself to humans is almost inconceivable, and Moses' description of the event is beyond spectacular:

> *On the morning of the third day there were thunders and lightnings and a thick cloud on the mountain and a very loud trumpet blast, so that all the people in the camp trembled. Then Moses brought the people out of the camp to meet God, and they took their stand at the foot of the mountain. Now Mount Sinai was wrapped in smoke because the LORD had descended on it in fire. The smoke of it went up like the smoke of a kiln, and the whole mountain trembled greatly. And as the sound of the trumpet grew louder and louder, Moses spoke, and God answered him in thunder. (Exodus 19:16–19)*

> *Now when all the people saw the thunder and the flashes of lightning and the sound of the trumpet and the mountain smoking, the people were afraid and trembled, and they stood far off and said to Moses, "You speak to us, and we will listen; but do not let God speak to us, lest we die." (20:18–19)*

When God came down on Mount Sinai in the sight of His people and spoke to them audibly, He came to them as a bridegroom.[3] God essentially came to a people and said, "I want to marry you, and I'm making a marriage covenant with you."

When YHWH led Israel into the wilderness to make covenant after the exodus, the event was compared to a betrothal which was the first step of a marriage:

---

[3]Jeremiah 2:2; Ezekiel 16:8.

"Go and proclaim in the hearing of Jerusalem, Thus says the LORD, *I remember the devotion of your youth, your love as a bride, how you followed me in the wilderness, in a land not sown." (Jeremiah 2:2)*

On the day when I took them by the hand to bring them out of the land of Egypt . . . I was their husband, declares the LORD. *(31:32)*

"When I passed by you again and saw you, behold, you were at the age for love, and I spread the corner of my garment over you and covered your nakedness; I made my vow to you and entered into a covenant with you, declares the Lord GOD, *and you became mine." (Ezekiel 16:8)*

Betrothal[4] was the first of two events necessary to complete an ancient Jewish wedding. Betrothal was different from the modern idea of being "engaged." After betrothal, the couple were legally married but lived apart. After a period of time, the couple would come together to complete their marriage in the second event which was the nuptials.[5] There would be a ceremony, a great celebration, and then the couple would consummate the marriage and begin living together. At this point, the marriage was fully established.

For example, Joseph and Mary were legally married (betrothed) when Mary became pregnant with Jesus, but they had not completed the second stage of marriage, so they still lived apart. Though they did not live together, if Joseph wanted to end his relationship with Mary, he had to divorce her because they had already passed through the first stage of marriage.

Mount Sinai was the first step of God's marriage to Israel. He gathered Israel under a massive cloud canopy, came down on Mount Sinai, and betrothed Himself to Israel as the divine Bridegroom. All of this meant He had to return to complete the wedding and dwell with His people. And when John began preaching, Israel had been waiting almost fifteen hundred years for YHWH to return to finish what He began at Sinai.

John's message focused on the return of the divine bridegroom to bring about a second exodus and finish His wedding.

---

[4]Also referred to as *kiddushin.*

[5]Typically referred to as *chuppah.*

The Second Exodus

The prophets had long predicted a second exodus so dramatic it would completely overshadow the first exodus.[6] They declared God was going to return to save His people, bring an end to all evil, and more importantly, finish His wedding:

> *Oh that you would rend the heavens and come down, that the mountains might quake at your presence . . . to make your name known to your adversaries, and that the nations might tremble at your presence! When you did awesome things that we did not look for, you came down, the mountains quaked at your presence. (Isaiah 64:1–3)*

> *"Therefore, behold, the days are coming, declares the LORD, when it shall no longer be said, 'As the LORD lives who brought up the people of Israel out of the land of Egypt.'" (Jeremiah 16:14)*

> *"Therefore, behold, the days are coming, declares the LORD, when they shall no longer say, 'As the LORD lives who brought up the people of Israel out of the land of Egypt.'" (23:7)*

When God initiated His marriage to His people, He came in a burning fire accompanied by earthquakes, thunder, and lightning.[7] His Bride (Israel) was terrified by His appearance, but this was only the first stage of marriage. It set up the next stage, which was consummation when the God of Sinai returned to dwell among His people. Accordingly, God's prediction of a "second exodus" overwhelmed the prophets, and they were unable to fully communicate the intensity of God's return using human language.

If God was this glorious (and terrifying) when He set His marriage into motion, what will He be like when He comes to consummate the marriage and dwell with His people?

When John proclaimed God was returning to baptize the earth in fire and the Holy Spirit, it evoked the memory of the exodus when

---

[6]Exodus 34:10; Deuteronomy 30:1–10; Isaiah 4:5; 11:11–16; 64:1–3; Jeremiah 3:16–17; 16:14–15; 23:7–8; 30:8–10; Joel 3; Habakkuk 3:3–15; Micah 7:15–17; Zechariah 10:8–9; 14.

[7]Exodus 19:16–19; 20:18.

God came in fire as Savior and Judge to deliver His people, destroy His enemies, and betroth Himself to Israel:

> *And in the morning watch the LORD in the pillar of fire and of cloud looked down on the Egyptian forces and threw the Egyptian forces into a panic. (Exodus 14:24)*
>
> *Now Mount Sinai was wrapped in smoke because the LORD had descended on it in fire. The smoke of it went up like the smoke of a kiln, and the whole mountain trembled greatly. (Exodus 19:18)*
>
> *"'Every valley shall be filled, and every mountain and hill shall be made low, and the crooked shall become straight, and the rough places shall become level ways, and all flesh shall see the salvation of God.'" . . . John answered them all, saying, "I baptize you with water, but he who is mightier than I is coming, the strap of whose sandals I am not worthy to untie. He will baptize you with the Holy Spirit and fire. His winnowing fork is in his hand, to clear his threshing floor and to gather the wheat into his barn, but the chaff he will burn with unquenchable fire." (Luke 3:5–6, 16–17)*

John's primary message was that Jesus would bring the second exodus that the prophets had promised. The baptism of the Holy Spirit was the promise of God's salvation,[8] and the baptism of fire was the promise of His judgments.[9]

When John spoke, his audience heard a staggering message: *YHWH who shattered Egypt, appeared in fire on Mount Sinai, and made covenant with Israel in the wilderness is coming to consummate His marriage to His people and dwell among them.*

This is one of the reasons John's audience cried out, *"What do we do?"* They knew the fierceness of His judgments on Egypt, and they were familiar with the terrifying descriptions of God when He appeared on Mount Sinai. They also knew many Israelites had resisted

---

[8]Isaiah 32:15; 44:3–4; 59:21; Ezekiel 36:27; 37:14; 39:29; Joel 2:28–29; Zechariah 12:10.

[9]Psalm 21:9; 97:1–5; Isaiah 4:4; 30:27, 33; 29:6; 34:9; 66:15–16; Jeremiah 15:14; Ezekiel 28:18; 30:8; 38:22; Daniel 7:9–10; Amos 1:4, 7, 10, 12, 14; 2:5; 7:4; Nahum 1:1–6; Zephaniah 1:18; Zechariah 13:9; Malachi 4:1; Matthew 25:41; 2 Thessalonians 1:6–9; Hebrews 10:27; 12:28–39; 2 Peter 3:7, 10–12.

God in the wilderness and ended up experiencing judgment instead of salvation. John's message that the God of Mount Sinai was returning was welcome news and terrifying.

It is especially remarkable the Roman soldiers cried out, *"What shall we do?"* when they heard John declare YHWH was coming. Israel was subservient to Rome at the time, so it was like Pharaoh's soldiers hearing Moses and asking him how to repent and become loyal to YHWH.

John's message was sobering: *The divine Bridegroom has waited long enough to consummate His wedding. He is coming again to bring about a second exodus and finish what He started. And this time, He's coming much closer than He did at Sinai.*

John's urgency and intensity did not come from his grasp of God's timeline. (In fact, John proclaimed events that still have not unfolded.) John felt the burning desire of God to return and finish His wedding, and that desire was the ultimate source of John's intensity.

We think of "urgency" primarily as a response to our interpretation of unfolding events. While you should know the times and seasons,[10] your urgency should flow from God's desire before it flows from your understanding of the prophetic timeline.

The *Shoshbin*

The "friend of the bridegroom" was a well-known role in an ancient Jewish wedding also known as the *shoshbin*. The shoshbin was similar to a best man, but he had additional responsibilities. For example, he would give gifts at the wedding and even help contribute to the cost of the celebration.

The shoshbin was the most trusted friend of the groom, and he would ensure the bride was taken care of and made it to the place where the wedding was to be consummated. The shoshbin might even stand guard for the couple to make sure no one disturbed them. The bridegroom would release a shout of joy when he took his bride and consummated the marriage. The shoshbin would stand by to hear this cry and rejoice that his friend now had his bride.

---

[10]Matthew 16:3; 24:32–33; Luke 21:31; 1 Thessalonians 5:1–6.

When John said he rejoiced at the bridegroom's voice, it was a reference to the shout of the bridegroom when he consummated his marriage:

> *The one who has the bride is the bridegroom. The friend of the bridegroom, who stands and hears him, rejoices greatly at the bridegroom's voice. Therefore this joy of mine is now complete. (John 3:29)*

John described himself as a shoshbin because his deepest joy flowed from giving his life to prepare a people for YHWH, so God could consummate His relationship with His people.

John's Message Was Not Fulfilled

John boldly proclaimed a second exodus and predicted God would come as a Bridegroom to deliver His people and judge His enemies by fire. The baptism of the Spirit John proclaimed included the salvation of all Israel because it referred to the day when the Spirit would be poured out on all Israel as the prophets had predicted.[11] While the Spirit was poured out on the day of Pentecost, it has not yet been poured out on *all Israel.*[12]

As long as Israel is not saved, John's prediction has not been fulfilled, and the apostles predicted this day of Israel's salvation would occur in the future when Jesus returned.[13] John's message of deliverance cannot be reduced to a spiritual or figurative deliverance. Spiritual deliverance is part of the message, but the baptism of fire includes judging the nations by fire and cleansing them from wickedness. These predictions were obviously not fulfilled in the first century.

God first revealed Himself as Bridegroom to Israel, and His identity as Bridegroom is so connected to Israel that gentile believers

---

[11]Deuteronomy 30:1–6; Isaiah 4:3–4; 45:17, 25; 54:13; 59:21; 60:4, 21; 61:8–9, 65:23; 66:22; Jeremiah 31:31–34; 32:40; Ezekiel 20:40; 36:10, 27–36; 37:25; 39:22, 28–29; Joel 2:26, 32; Zephaniah 3:9, 12; 12:13; Zechariah 12:10–13; Matthew 23:39; 24:30; Acts 1:6–7; 2:21; Romans 10:13; 11:26–27; Revelation 1:7.

[12]For more on this, see *It Must Be Finished.*

[13]Acts 3:19–21; Romans 11:12, 15, 26; Revelation 1:7.

are made part of Jesus' Bride by being brought *into* Israel.[14] Part of being a friend of the Bridegroom is sharing Jesus' pain over Israel's present condition and His longing to bring Israel back to Himself. God revealed Himself as Bridegroom to Israel first, and He wants those who have been grafted into Israel to become part of His pursuit of Israel.

If you look at the biblical context of John's message and what the apostles taught, it is plain Jesus' first coming set the stage for the second exodus but did not fulfill it.

There are three times in history when God:

- Comes down visibly.
- Speaks audibly to His people.
- Makes a covenant.
- Changes the way He relates to His people.

The three times are:

- The exodus
- The first coming of Jesus
- The second coming of Jesus

Every time, God comes as Bridegroom.

The gospel message is a declaration the Bridegroom wants to return to finish His wedding. He is the One who shook Sinai *and* the One who was fastened to a cross. And He will return as *both*. Our message remains the same as the prophets and John: He is coming. Prepare for Him.

Have you encountered the intensity of a divine Bridegroom who has waited 3,500 years to finish His wedding?

God's burning emotions led Him to the cross to do the unthinkable. Those same emotions will drive Him even further to return, reveal Himself again, judge evil, and transition the age. In fact, God summarized the unparalleled drama of the end of the age as the "unveiling of Jesus."[15]

---

[14]Ephesians 2:11–12; Romans 11:17.

[15]Revelation 1:1.

When He returns, the strength of His passion is going to shock us again. It will be a day unlike any other day.[16] *Mount Sinai and Mount Calvary both give us a glimpse of what what the Bridegroom will do to secure the object of His affection.*

A Bride Longing for the Bridegroom

The revelation of God as a Bridegroom reveals a lot about God, but it also reveals a lot about His people.

God designed marriage as an analogy for the mystery of Jesus and His church.[17] God is the Bridegroom, His people are the Bride, and He is returning for a wedding celebration:

> *"Let us rejoice and exult and give him the glory, for the marriage of the Lamb has come, and his Bride has made herself ready; it was granted her to clothe herself with fine linen, bright and pure"—for the fine linen is the righteous deeds of the saints. . . . Then I saw heaven opened, and behold, a white horse! The one sitting on it is called Faithful and True. (Revelation 19:7–8, 11)*

When you discover God's emotions as Bridegroom, it transforms the way you think about and relate to Him. God is not just a good Father; He is filled with passionate desire, compelled by His own longing for intimacy and communion. His desire is so strong He made covenant with His own blood so you will belong to Him forever.

If God relates to you as the Bridegroom, then you should relate to Him as the Bride.

A bride responds to the desire of the bridegroom. A bride is focused on the day she will be married to her bridegroom. She lives her life with great focus so she will be prepared for that day. She is completely loyal to her bridegroom, and she enjoys the fact that she belongs exclusively to him. Furthermore, she is filled with deep desire and affection for him. A bride does not fight for her own glory, but finds glory in joining herself to her bridegroom's assignment. His success is her success. She joyfully sacrifices for the sake of their union.

---

[16]Jeremiah 30:7; Daniel 12:1; Matthew 24:21; Revelation 16:18.

[17]Ephesians 5:31–32.

If you study God's affections as the Bridegroom but do not relate to Him as a wholehearted bride, you have an incomplete revelation of God as Bridegroom.

When a woman is separated from the man she loves, she longs for the day he will return. While they are separated, she does anything she can to communicate with him. She carefully reads every letter, email, or message he sends. She stays up at night to schedule a call and speak to him. The pain of absence provokes her to find every possible way to connect with him, and she longs for the day of his return. She makes every possible preparation for the day.

When the church does not long for the Bridegroom's voice, she is like a bride uninterested in her wedding day—it's abnormal.

Ministering to the Bride

The church belongs to Jesus, and you must always remember that every member of the body, regardless of their maturity, is part of Jesus' Bride. Therefore, when you engage with another believer, you are serving another Man's wife. If you are in a leadership role or unusually gifted, you have to be especially vigilant. *You must not compete for the affections of the Bride.* Your job is simply to direct her to Jesus.

Many draw the Bride to themselves by fascinating her with their spiritual gifts, and others are unnecessarily harsh with the Bride when a correction needs to be given. We must avoid both errors. When you deal with the church, even a compromised part of the body, you are handling Jesus' inheritance, His most precious possession. And you do not want stir His jealousy. As a friend of the Bridegroom, you must fight for the calling of the Bride.

- Do you address Jesus' Bride with the same tenderness and affection He does?
- Do you abuse the Bride and point out her deficiencies? Or do you speak with tenderness, aware of your own deficiencies and the Lord's kindness with you?
- Can you honestly say your words and your ministry are motivated by a desire to move the Bride closer to Jesus?
- Do you contend for the future of the Bride or only point out her failure?

- When you address failures, do you do it in a way that draws the Bride back to the Lord and leads her to growth and restoration? Or do you show how spiritual you are by exposing how weak and sinful others are?
- Do you speak flattering words that cause the Bride to be drawn to you? Do you use your spiritual gifts to do the same?
- Do you use your strength with restraint? The spirit of the prophet is subject to the prophet. When God gives you a burden, it should be communicated in a way that contends for the Bride and her future.
- Do you take joy in Jesus enjoying His Bride even if it does not bring any benefit to you?

Is Jesus's pursuit of His inheritance in competition with your own ministry ambitions?

How do you *feel* when:

- Jesus uses another person or another organization in a dramatic way?
- Another person's ministry or influence overshadows your own?
- God answers your prayer for revival by moving through someone else?

Do you deeply rejoice when Jesus receives His inheritance even if your sphere of influence declines? Do you treat the people of God the way you would another man's wife? Do you jealously direct the affections, loyalty, and devotion of God's people toward Him and Him alone? Do you have godly fear that keeps you from using people for your own benefit? Or do you struggle when Jesus' fame is not connected to your own?

Is Jesus' voice your deepest delight? If so, you will treasure the Word of God and spend time with it asking the Holy Spirit to speak to you through it. It will be more precious to you than food, will begin to fill your conversations, and will even become your entertainment. Many people are eager to speak on behalf of God, but longing for *His* voice makes you eager to *hear* what He wants to say through whomever it comes. When you love His Word, there is just as much delight in silence as speaking. There is a longing not to speak but to hear what God is saying even if it comes through someone else.

All of these struggles are normal, but we must admit them and face them together. We must let God expose us, transform us, and bring us to maturity if we want to become friends of the Bridegroom.

John's Grand Finale

John's life of extravagant devotion prepared him for his grande finale, and the end of his ministry demonstrated his greatness perhaps more than any other aspect of his life. In fact, Jesus' evaluation of John can only be fully understood in light of John's death. His death was so significant it is the only major story in the Gospel of Mark not about Jesus.[1]

John was a "burning and shining light"[2] who lived with fierce devotion and proclaimed the coming of Jesus in incredible power. And he had exceptional power resting on him when he proclaimed the Word of God. All of this makes the end of John's life the most perplexing part of John's life: *John lived an intentional life to proclaim the coming of the Bridegroom but did not play any role in the Bridegroom's ministry.*

John was one of the few men on the earth with prophetic insight into who Jesus truly was. John gave his entire life to prepare the way for Jesus, but John probably only met Jesus once briefly as an adult.[3] John was not self-seeking and was jealous for Jesus' glory over his own. He lived an intentional life in a small place rather than seeking influence and impact in Jerusalem. He was the obvious choice to be part of Jesus' inner circle, but when the time came, Jesus bypassed John and instead chose twelve disciples who did not fully know who Jesus was.

John's miraculous birth and thirty years of intentional living came to a climax in one moment. Jesus came to meet John, John baptized Him, and then Jesus walked away. And in that moment, John's ministry

---

[1] Mark 6:17–29.

[2] John 5:35.

[3] John 1:31–33.

was over. John prepared the way for Jesus, but he was not invited to join Jesus' disciples and never got to see Jesus' ministry. Instead of choosing the most powerful man in the nation, Jesus built His church on men who had not lived like John. This exclusion of John was a shocking decision.

Many people expect to share the stage with Jesus, but the beginning of Jesus' ministry meant the end of John's. John was in jail longer than he preached publicly.

After he baptized Jesus, John was quickly eclipsed by Jesus and became little more than a memory to most people while he was still alive. While Jesus drew large crowds, John sat in a dirty, filthy cell probably alone with little more than his own thoughts. The man who had lived a life in the wilderness finished his life in the loneliness of a prison cell. (Ironically, he was held at a prison in the wilderness.[4]) John did not end his life in a blaze of glory giving one final sermon in power. He was executed on the whim of a wicked family when a drunken king fueled by lust made a rash decision and a party went wrong.

This astonishing end to John's life contains the key to understanding who John really was.

Walking Out of the Spotlight

John's light burned extremely brightly, but it burned for a very short period of time. After six to eighteen months in the public ministry, John willingly let his ministry and influence fade when he was around thirty years of age and while he was at the height of his influence in the full strength of his anointing.

John not only surrendered his ministry, he took great delight in Jesus' success at his own expense. As Jesus began to eclipse him, John even encouraged his disciples to follow Jesus:

And they came to John and said to him, "Rabbi, he who was with you across the Jordan, to whom you bore witness—look, he is baptizing, and all are going to him." John answered, "A person cannot receive even one

---

[4]According to Josephus, John the Baptist was imprisoned in in the Machaerus fortress just east of the Dead Sea in the wilderness. F. F. Bruce, "Machaerus," ed. D. R. W. Wood et al., *New Bible Dictionary* (Leicester, England; Downers Grove, IL: InterVarsity Press, 1996), 712..

thing unless it is given him from heaven. You yourselves bear me witness, that I said, 'I am not the Christ, but I have been sent before him.' The one who has the bride is the bridegroom. The friend of the bridegroom, who stands and hears him, rejoices greatly at the bridegroom's voice. Therefore this joy of mine is now complete. He must increase, but I must decrease. . . ." The Father loves the Son and has given all things into his hand. (John 3:26–30, 35)

John's disciples were concerned with Jesus' prominence. They saw Jesus as a threat to John's ministry, but their concern went beyond John's future. They were accustomed to their own prominence as John's disciples, and they enjoyed the attention that came from their association with the wilderness prophet. His loss would become their loss, and they did not want to lose the notoriety they had enjoyed with John.

John's disciples confront *our* longing for prominence, even if it comes by association. Who are you trying to get close to? Who's spotlight are you hoping to share? What relationships do you have, or seek, that are based on enjoying benefits or a sense of importance from another person's prominence? Are you willing to do *your* assignment? Or do you want a share in someone else's assignment that seems more impressive?

We tend to love the stage. We love being important, known, and celebrated. We think our desire for the influence is primarily about spreading Jesus' fame, but we also expect to be onstage with Jesus, even if it's at the back of the stage. *What if walking off the stage will magnify Jesus more than staying in the spotlight?* Most people hope for the day they get to take centerstage, but there are times to walk offstage—even if it is a stage the Lord initially set. Some are willing to walk off the stage when they are tired and their strength is fading, but John was willing to be forgotten at the height of his strength at just thirty years old.

When Jesus came on the scene, John did not shine brightly as a part of Jesus' inner circle; John faded. We love to embrace the increase, but John eagerly embraced the decrease.

The way God bypassed John reveals just how much power was resting on John.[5] Before Jesus emerged, John was a brilliant light. Once Jesus emerged, John was a distraction. John's spotlight had to move to Jesus while John was in the prime of his life and at the height of his ministry. The staggering thing is that John was okay with this.

John was willing to walk off his public stage so that Jesus would not have any competition. How many are willing to embrace hiddenness when their own prominence threatens the Father's desire to glorify His Son?

There are few who can endure being set aside by the Lord while they are still in the prime of their life, but when the time came for John's ministry to end, John not only cooperated with God, he enjoyed Jesus' fame at his own expense. John's greatness was displayed by his burning zeal to see the Bridegroom take His Bride even if it meant John's demise.

Rare is the man who will extinguish his own public flame so that God alone can capture the affections of His people.

Paving the Way for Others

John labored a lifetime for things he never saw. As Jesus' fame grew, John sat in prison for approximately two years. However, John invested in at least two disciples who left him and went to follow Jesus.[6] In a shocking turn of events, John's spiritual sons would see what John had longed for and lived for. Sometimes, we walk out the vision the Lord puts in our hearts. Other times, we spend our lives to prepare others to walk out the vision the Lord has given us.

One of John's great achievements was preparing Andrew and another to go into the next season with Jesus. Are you willing to invest your entire life in others who get to fully experience something that may not be given to you?

Are you willing to give yourself for something you will not enjoy simply because God delights in it? Furthermore, would that be a *sacrifice* or a *joy* to you? If you follow John's path, you can become a person who loves Jesus so deeply His joy becomes your joy and what other men call a sacrifice fills you with deep delight. More specifically, God is

---

[5]At one point, Herod thought Jesus might be John risen from the dead, emphasizing the power that rested on John (see Matthew 14:1–2).

[6]John 1:37.

looking for a people who, like John, will give their lives for Israel's salvation, knowing they are deeply loved, but there is a unique salvation these sons of Abraham must come into. This is the central call to missions—lay down your life so God can enjoy something with other people.

Blessed Is He Who Is Not Offended

John's influence was so great that, when he criticized Herod's inappropriate relationship with his brother's wife, it was considered a political threat[7] and led to his imprisonment. John was imprisoned just as everything he had lived for, prayed for, hoped for, and predicted began to unfold. As he sat isolated in prison, John sent his disciples to Jesus with a critical question:

> *Now when John heard in prison about the deeds of the Christ, he sent word by his disciples and said to him, "Are you the one who is to come, or shall we look for another?" (Matthew 11:2–3)*

John likely had several reasons for sending his disciples to Jesus,[8] but these words were a profound expression of John's humanity. Elijah faced discouragement after battling the priests of Baal, and perhaps John faced a similar test after successfully fulfilling his ministry. As John sat in prison alone day after day, no doubt questions filled John's mind. Perhaps he questioned whether he should have publicly rebuked Herod for his marriage and wondered if he had cut his own life short.[9]

We can be reasonably sure that John was somewhat perplexed by Jesus' ministry. John predicted God would return in a dramatic way that far exceeded the exodus to pour out the Spirit and fire. John had the incredible revelation that Jesus was the "Lamb of God" (literally God's passover Lamb), but he combined the first and second coming in his

---

[7]Moisés Silva and Merrill Chapin Tenney, *The Zondervan Encyclopedia of the Bible,* H-L (Grand Rapids, MI: The Zondervan Corporation, 2009), 764.

[8]For example, by this time John had been in prison over a year, and some speculate John's question was a subtle attempt to encourage his disciples to move on now that Jesus had emerged.

[9]Gene Edwards classic book, *The Prisoner in the Third Cell,* is a fictional but provocative description of John's last days.

sermons, so there is no evidence John expected the first coming to unfold the way it did. John was likely confused by Jesus' ministry and seeking confirmation that the messianic ministry he gave his life to announce was in fact unfolding.

As a young boy, John probably did not expect he would announce the coming Messiah only to be moved out of the way when the Messiah appeared. In John's question, you can hear many questions: "Tell me that You really are doing all the things I predicted. Tell me what I predicted is coming to pass. Tell me what I proclaimed was right. Tell me I fulfilled my life's assignment. Tell me I did not make a massive mistake when I critiqued Herod's marriage." John was still a young man, but his life was over, and he knew it. As he sat in a cell day by day awaiting what he knew was coming, he had plenty of time to contemplate and examine his life. He needed Jesus' evaluation of his life.

John's final, critical question was essentially, "Please tell me I did my assignment and finished well."

Jesus knew what John was asking, so He sent a message to John through John's disciples:

> *Go and tell John what you hear and see: the blind receive their sight and the lame walk, lepers are cleansed and the deaf hear, and the dead are raised up, and the poor have good news preached to them. (Matthew 11:4–5)*

Jesus knew John would take great delight in His success, so Jesus told John's disciples to tell John what was happening. Jesus knew John's life had been defined by Scripture, so He chose to speak to John in John's own language. It is easy to sense the deep affection in Jesus' words as Jesus used the words of Isaiah to assure John he had successfully prepared the way for Jesus to take the stage.

The message Jesus sent John combined Isaiah 35:5 and Isaiah 61:1. If you consider the larger context, the message becomes clearer:

> *Say to those who have an anxious heart, "Be strong; fear not! Behold, your God will come with vengeance, with the recompense of God. He will come and save you." Then the eyes of the blind shall be opened, and the ears of the deaf unstopped; then shall the lame man leap like a deer, and the*

tongue of the mute sing for joy. . . . And the ransomed of the LORD *shall return and come to Zion with singing; everlasting joy shall be upon their heads; they shall obtain gladness and joy, and sorrow and sighing shall flee away. (Isaiah 35:4–6, 10)*

The Spirit of the Lord GOD *is upon me . . . to proclaim liberty to the captives, and the opening of the prison to those who are bound; to proclaim the year of the* LORD*'s favor, and the day of vengeance of our God; to comfort all who mourn. . . . (Isaiah 61:1–2)*

Both passages describe the results of the second exodus, so Jesus used them to tell John the second exodus was beginning even though it was unfolding in an unexpected way with extravagant mercy accompanied by acts of healing, deliverance, and salvation. John knew these passages well, and he understood the message.

However, Jesus did not quote all of Isaiah 61:1:

The Spirit of the Lord GOD *is upon me, because the* LORD *has anointed me to bring good news to the poor; he has sent me to bind up the brokenhearted, to proclaim liberty to the captives, and the opening of the prison to those who are bound.*

Jesus specifically excluded Isaiah's prediction of liberty for captives and release from prison to communicate a sober message. Jesus was healing the oppressed and proclaiming good news to the poor, but He was not going to open the doors to John's prison. John would die a captive. Instead of finishing Isaiah 61:1, Jesus sent John one final message:

And blessed is the one who is not offended by me. (Matthew 11:6)

This one statement must have cut John right to the heart. It reveals the real issue John was struggling with: John's story was not going to end the way he had thought it would. John had paid a great price to prepare the way for Jesus, but he would not see the Son of Man's success. Jesus did not even come to the prison to deliver the message personally. John heard Jesus' words secondhand in a prison cell.

Jesus' statement was both confrontational and liberating. John had to refuse bitterness and offense that his role was finished. By warning John not to be "offended by" Jesus, Jesus addressed John's challenge head on: Even the man Jesus called one of the greatest could be offended by Jesus' leadership of his life.

Instead of the opening John's prison, Jesus warned him against offense.

Jesus' words communicated a somber message: "John, I know this is not what you expected, but prepare for the end." Jesus' words were difficult to accept, and there was a possibility for deep pain. John had lived a consecrated life, but he would not see what he longed to see, nor be rewarded with proximity to the Bridegroom in this age. Instead, he was destined for a premature death. John's life had begun with great fanfare, but it would end suddenly on the whim of a lustful king.[10] It is hardly the end we would expect of a man whose birth was predicted by Gabriel.

Jesus could have delivered John, but He did not, and there are times God decides to direct our paths in a way that do not make sense to us.

Jesus' leadership does not make sense to us because we think in terms of success and productivity in this age, but God thinks very differently. He told King Hezekiah to get his affairs in order and prepare to die, but Hezekiah pled for a longer life. God gave it to him, and Hezekiah raised a son named Manasseh who became Judah's most wicked king. Manasseh's rule demonstrated God's wisdom in taking Hezekiah's life at an early age.

When Ananias and Sapphira lied about a donation to impress the church, they were struck dead. The sentence seems harsh, but what if God took their lives suddenly so their sin would not progress? Could it be that Ananias and Sapphira's deaths were a mercy to them to cut their lives short before darkness took deeper roots in their hearts? Our fixation on success in this age can keep us from grasping God's eternal purposes for His people.

Jesus' leadership over John's life can appear offensive, but Jesus deeply loved John. When Jesus heard John had died, Jesus was so emotional He went alone into the wilderness to mourn:

---

[10]Vanetha Rendal Risner, "Do You Wish You Had Accomplished More?" *desiringGod.org*, May 31, 2018, https://www.desiringgod.org/articles/do-you-wish-you-had-accomplished-more/.

He sent and had John beheaded in the prison. . . . Now when Jesus heard this, he withdrew from there in a boat to a desolate place by himself. (Matthew 14:10, 13)

Many of God's best friends have been rejected, abandoned, forgotten, and imprisoned. We simply do not have the capacity to evaluate our lives correctly at every moment. God's deep affection for you does not always correlate to whether or not you feel successful.

God's leadership of your life may, at times, feel deeply offensive, but that does not mean He does not deeply love you, nor does it mean you failed in your assignment.

When John heard Jesus' words, John knew he had fulfilled his assignment. As John thought about Jesus' ministry, John's joy in Jesus' success gave him the strength to avoid offense as he endured his thoughts and emotions in his final days. John had used his brief moment on the stage of history well, and now the Bridegroom of Israel had taken the stage.

John learned the message we must all learn: There's only one Man God is going to glorify when He comes in power.

God is looking for a people who delight when He exalts His Son, not a people hoping to share in His Son's exaltation. If you try to share His stage, the Father will resist you. Do you realize, when you pursue your own prominence, you risk provoking the jealousy of God over His Son?

The Danger of Offense

God has designed this age to reveal His Son and produce a people like Him,[11] but many continue to hope this age will be a stage for their own success. This discrepancy creates a massive occasion for offense. When God led Israel to the wilderness instead of the Promised Land, it caused so much offense that Israel engaged in pagan worship while God's presence was visibly in their midst. When Jesus came, He caused incredible offense. The idea that YHWH would be exalted through suffering was impossible to comprehend. As a result, Jesus was rejected by many in Israel. They simply could not fathom the idea that this Man was YHWH.

---

[11]Romans 8:29; Colossians 3:4; 1 Corinthians 15:49.

The Bridegroom is coming again, and we have been commissioned to prepare a people for Him. Have you settled the fact that God's leadership of your life may offend you? Are you preparing others to face their offense with God and His ways? If you have not resolved your own offense with God, you will not be able to prepare others.

Many were offended when God sent His Son to the cross. Will the church be offended when God allows His people to go to the cross during the time we typically call the "great tribulation"?[12] The man God chose to prepare the way for His Son only ministered publicly for a few months, and that man was not invited to even sit at Jesus' feet. From a purely human point of view, God's treatment of John is incredibly offensive, yet Jesus said no one had exceeded John. John's life shows the path to true greatness. Will you pursue that path?

Jesus warned that the "love of many would grow cold"[13] before He returned. There are a number of reasons love will grow cold, but offense is one of the most overlooked reasons. We often forget we serve the same God who sent His Son to the cross. Are we preparing ourselves and others not to be offended when we suffer by God's design?[14] Or are we trying to convince ourselves we will not suffer?

We tend to speak arrogantly about the stubbornness of the Israelites and the blindness of the Pharisees while assuming we will not be offended when the Bridegroom comes again. This is an extreme presumption. We easily agree with God's activity in the Bible because it did not happen to us. We would feel very differently if we had to live through similar trials. The days ahead of us will go far beyond any other time in human history,[15] and so will the opportunity for offense.

Many of us assume we will not be offended by God if we live through the most difficult crisis in history, but our offense at far smaller things indicates otherwise.

---

[12]Jeremiah 30:7; Daniel 12:1; Joel 2:2; Matthew 24:21.

[13]Matthew 24:12.

[14]Job 42:11; Daniel 7:25; Habakkuk 1:5–7; Philippians 1:29.

[15]Matthew 24:21–22.

Wrestling with Offense

Lasting offense exposes hidden things. When unmet expectations cause deep and lasting offense with God, it reveals you were not fully after God—you were after God *plus* something else. This exposure is God's gift to you. When these offenses come, you can turn to the Lord and allow Him to heal you, or you can nurture the offense and turn your expectations into culturally acceptable idols.

Are your dreams "sanctified" versions of the world's dreams? For example, do you dream of doing business for the kingdom and assume that will lead to success and affluence? Or are you a worship leader whose vision of success looks more like a rock star who sings moral lyrics? We easily forget that Jesus never promised success and notoriety in this age, but He did predict prison, persecution, and suffering:

Then they will deliver you up to tribulation and put you to death, and you will be hated by all nations for my name's sake. (Matthew 24:9)

Remember the word that I said to you: "A servant is not greater than his master." If they persecuted me, they will also persecute you. If they kept my word, they will also keep yours. (John 15:20)

For I will show him how much he must suffer for the sake of my name." (Acts 9:16)

It is hard to build a successful ministry when you are in prison, but this is where God has led a number of His friends.

We do not know all the reasons Judas ultimately betrayed Jesus, but it seems Judas allowed offense to grow in his heart when Jesus' ministry did not turn out the way he expected it. Do you realize that nurturing offense can lead us to betrayal?

John's Final Breath

Some people have a romantic view of martyrdom, but martyrdom is typically the last step of a life lived in consistent faithfulness over time. A life of daily devotion and simple obedience is far more important than pursuing a single moment of martyrdom.

John did not die in a "blaze of glory" in front of a grand audience. His prominence had faded years before. Like most martyrs, his death was not exciting or public. John was likely asleep in a dirty, dark cell. A drunken, aroused king made a rash promise, and his wife decided she wanted to silence John, so she asked for his head. In the middle of the night, soldiers suddenly woke John. There were no final words and no witnesses other than the soldiers. He did not get to preach one more time. He did not even see King Herod or Herod's wife. It probably happened so quickly John did not even fully grasp the situation before his life was over.

After languishing in prison for around two years, the man Jesus esteemed so highly was gone in a moment because a party went wrong.

John's Greatest Achievement

John's entire ministry existed for one moment that encapsulated his assignment. When Jesus approached John, John was so overwhelmed he did not want to baptize Jesus, but Jesus insisted. Jesus—as God—*submitted* to John's ministry,[1] a radical endorsement of John and his message.[2]

Jesus could not initially trust the disciples to accurately communicate who He was,[3] yet this man who had never met Jesus as an adult was given the privilege of publicly introducing Jesus. Like Simeon and Anna decades before,[4] John knew Jesus by the Spirit:

> *"I myself did not know him, but for this purpose I came baptizing with water, that he might be revealed to Israel." And John bore witness: "I saw the Spirit descend from heaven like a dove, and it remained on him. I myself did not know him, but he who sent me to baptize with water said to me, 'He on whom you see the Spirit descend and remain, this is he who baptizes with the Holy Spirit.' And I have seen and have borne witness that this is the Son of God." (John 1:31–34)*

John's intentional lifestyle enabled him to see what others could not see. And like John, you can know Jesus by the Spirit and the Word even if you have not seen Him.

---

[1]Matthew 3:13–15.

[2]Jesus inherited a stigma from John's ministry. His endorsement of John put Him in conflict with the religious leaders who had rejected John.

[3]Matthew 16:20; Mark 8:29–30.

[4]Luke 2:25–38.

When John baptized Jesus, the Father spoke audibly over His Son for the first time, and the Holy Spirit descended on Jesus.[5] It was an incredible validation of John's ministry by the Father, Son, and the Spirit:[6]

> *Then Jesus came from Galilee to the Jordan to John, to be baptized by him. John would have prevented him, saying, "I need to be baptized by you, and do you come to me?" But Jesus answered him, "Let it be so now, for thus it is fitting for us to fulfill all righteousness." Then he consented. And when Jesus was baptized, immediately he went up from the water, and behold, the heavens were opened to him, and he saw the Spirit of God descending like a dove and coming to rest on him; and behold, a voice from heaven said, "This is my beloved Son, with whom I am well pleased." (Matthew 3:13–17)*

This was the moment John had given his life for because he knew his assignment was to build a stage for the Father to magnify His Son:

> *"For this purpose I came baptizing with water, that he might be revealed to Israel." (John 1:31)*

John's greatest achievement was not his preaching. It was setting a stage for the Father to speak about His Son.

John had given his life for this moment, but God was silent about John's life in that moment. God only glorified His Son, and John was captured by *joy* as the Father spoke about His Son. John was not offended the Father did not acknowledge his sacrifice.

Are we living our lives to set a stage for the Father to speak over the Son? Is this our primary ministry objective? Are we willing like John to decrease when the Father speaks? Or do we seek to share His Son's stage?

Are you okay if God uses your entire life to publicly glorify His Son and does not publicly acknowledge you? The Lord will reward His people, and He loves us immensely, but what if God writes the story of your life and only puts Jesus' name on the cover of the book? Are you *satisfied* with that? Does that fill your heart with joy, or do you need

---

[5]Matthew 3:16–17; Mark 1:10–11; Luke 3:21–22; John 1:32.

[6]See also Mark 1:10–11; Luke 3:21–22.

your name on the cover as well? Is Jesus' fame your reward if you are not associated with that fame?

Jesus' baptism was not only the climax of John's ministry, it was also the beginning of the end. Once John baptized Jesus, his influence and ministry began to quickly fade. But John embraced his decrease with joy because Jesus had taken the stage and John knew his assignment was complete.

Our Incredible Privilege

Have you considered the immense privilege we have of preparing the earth for Jesus?

We are so self-absorbed it is easy for us to overlook the profound privilege we have been given. God could present His Son to the world any way He wants to, and yet He has chosen us to set the stage for His Son's glory. John grasped the weight of this assignment, and when Jesus came to him for baptism, John initially refused Jesus' request because John knew he did not deserve that kind of honor. Do you understand we also do not deserve the dignity of our assignment?

We are not worthy of the profound honor of presenting the divine Son to the world, and yet the Father has commissioned us to take up this task.

Humans have always sought fame, and our expectations are greater than any other time in history. Many expect fame and notoriety that would have been unthinkable just a few decades ago. The vast majority of humanity could never have dreamed of the fame we now consider normal. Two hundred years ago, a pastor would be thrilled to lead a church of a hundred people and even work another job to do it. In our time, many think leading a church of that size is "unsuccessful."

By modern definitions of "success" and "impact," nearly every believer in history has been a failure—including most of the most prominent figures in the Bible. Furthermore, our constant pursuit of internet and social media fame can hinder our ability to serve the Lord in places where Christian fame may hinder our ability to do the task God has given us.

John's labor did not secure a place for him on Jesus' team. Instead, Jesus chose the disciples as His leaders for the next several decades. Many pursue a life of devotion like John's, hoping they will be rewarded with anointing, influence, and prominence in a move of God. Yet the man Jesus esteemed as one of the greatest fulfilled his ministry by setting a stage for Jesus that resulted in his own demise. And that man took great pleasure in it.

Surrender Your Calling

John's public ministry was designed to set a stage for the Father to speak about His Son. Ministries are formed for a number of purposes, but how many are intentionally designed with this as the driving focus? We need to carefully and thoughtfully consider our ministry objectives and shift them until they align with this purpose. If we are not driven to create a context for the Father to demonstrate the worth of His Son, we need to reconsider the purpose and value of our ministries.

John surrendered his "calling" for Jesus' calling. John lived his life to see Jesus' calling emerge in strength. Once that happened, John was willing for his extremely brief ministry to fade because John's success was found in Jesus' success.

John is often called the "forerunner" of Jesus, and we have the same task of preparing the nations to love and welcome Jesus. This "forerunner" calling can be reduced to one ultimate question: ***Will you surrender your calling for Jesus' calling?***

So many of us are driven by our own callings, but it is time to shatter the illusions of our own grandeur and callings and live with all our strength for Jesus to receive His reward. Until He gets His reward, we are called to the wilderness because we cannot seek our inheritance when He does not have His. And I guarantee, if you give your life for His calling, you will not lose anything. The Father will make sure you receive everything He wants you to have.

Ultimately, the invitation to choose the wilderness is not about *where* you live, but *how* you live. At the center of the invitation is a probing question: Will you seek your own satisfaction in this age or lay aside the pursuit of your own satisfaction so that Jesus may receive His reward and be satisfied?

Jesus has been waiting for thousands of years to receive His inheritance, and it is time to challenge an entire generation to surrender their callings for Jesus' calling.

The Path into the Wilderness

A People Who Choose the Wilderness

As we have seen, John the Baptist was a foreshadowing of the church's task to prepare the way of the Lord. The early church understood they were a community continuing the task John had been given, so they referred to the church as "The Way," which was a reference to Isaiah 40:

> *A voice cries: "In the wilderness prepare the way of the LORD; make straight in the desert a highway for our God." (Isaiah 40:3)*

Like John, we should live peculiar lives in this age to "prepare the way" for the Lord. Like John, we are called to choose the wilderness. The wilderness we must choose is a way of life, not a geographic location.

The way of the wilderness is a reorientation of our spiritual walk according to Scripture. And John the Baptist is an example of the path we must choose.

In a generation that was filled with political complexity, religious zeal, sensuality, and raw ambition, John was captured by a different dream. He set his mind, his affections, and his joy on the return of God. God became John's dream over decades in the wilderness. For a few months, a nation was stunned when God revealed the inner intensity of a man who had lived an intentional life.

John was given the Spirit to allow him to burn, but we have access to more.[1] We live *after* the outpouring of the Spirit. We have *more* access to the Scripture. We simply need John's intentionality. We should not seek his assignment because God sovereignly chooses messengers for tasks like that. But we must be provoked by John's intentionality. The world is waiting for a people who will make the same kind of intentional decisions in their mundane, daily living.

---

[1] Matthew 11:11.

If John could burn brightly in the wilderness[2] before the cross and the outpouring of the Spirit, how much more can you burn?

God is not looking for elite Christians, but He is looking for those who will turn aside like John and allow the consuming flame of God to consume them through the same means John lived by. God is looking for those who are:

- Filled with the Spirit.
- Feeding on the Word of God.
- Living intentionally in small places.

When we draw close to God, we begin to feel what He feels. Feeling what God feels is not an emotional experience the way we typically encounter emotions. It is a settled sense of reality that comes as our spirits become aligned with God. When you get close to God, you will begin to feel His burning desire to finish His wedding, dwell among His people, and bring an end to the evil of this age.

You are called to be swept up into the strength of divine desire.

God's desire is an expression of His urgency, and you can encounter His urgency whether or not He returns in your lifetime. Jesus has "delayed" His great day to offer mercy to as many as possible,[3] but this delay has not diminished His desire. If you become consumed by God's desire, you can proclaim Jesus' return with incredible power. The church began as "The Way," and this age will end with a church that becomes "The Way" again.

Will you choose the wilderness?

We have seen the path to the wilderness, and now we need to dig a little deeper into John's life in the wilderness. His life leads us to confront issues we must deal with if we want to choose the wilderness.

---

[2] John 5:35.

[3] 2 Peter 3:9.

Weakness Is a Canvas for God's Glory

You were not made to demonstrate the glory of humanity. You were made to demonstrate the glory of God.

When you see a beautiful piece of artwork you are not enamored with the paint and the canvas. You appreciate the glory of the artist. Mankind is the work of a divine artist, and God designed humanity as *His image* meaning we reflect Him. We draw attention to Him. We allow His power to flow through us.

This age is enamored with the glory of man. We take deep delight in physical strength, mental strength, and physical beauty. However, this is not God's design for humanity. He wants humans to demonstrate something *higher* than human strength: the glory of God. Until you enter into the experience of your own weakness, you will not have a right view of yourself or God. In fact, our inability to accept our own weakness and dependence is one of the biggest obstacles to operating in the power of God in an unusual way.

Moses was called to liberate Israel, but we easily forget it took Moses eighty years to become weak enough to be useful to God.

When Moses was forty years old, he was so gripped by his destiny that he killed a man and then fled into the wilderness in disgrace. Moses was strong, gifted, and called by God, but he was not yet barren. Moses' failure at age forty required another forty years to prepare him for his assignment. He was prepared to liberate Israel by living among Gentiles, marrying a Gentile, and herding sheep for his gentile father-in-law. Moses' life in obscurity prepared him to fulfill one of the most unique assignments in history.

Moses was raised as royalty and had a profound sense of destiny, but he had to be emptied out by failure and live in a small place, herding sheep.

By age eighty, Moses had been completely emptied of ambition and became the "meekest man on earth."[1] When God came to Moses in the wilderness, He said, "I am going to give you unprecedented power to deliver Israel and confront the most powerful nation in your region." Moses' response was, "No, thank You. Get someone else." (God became angry with Moses because Moses refused to take on the assignment until God appointed Aaron as the mouthpiece.[2])

After eight decades, Moses had faced his own weakness and was aware of his own barrenness. He no longer carried the confidence of royalty, nor was he driven by the ambition to be a great liberator. Moses was dangerous at forty but useful at eighty because he was no longer driven by his own assignment and prominence. Believers who find their identity in their assignment can be dangerous. The bigger the assignment, the greater the danger.

Moses was ready to fulfill his assignment when he was no longer motivated by his assignment. Like Moses, messengers are often ready when they no longer want to speak.

Daniel was given some of the most unusual prophecies in the Bible, and his book was referenced by Jesus more than any book of the Bible.[3] However, his revelation was preceded by a painful process. He was carried away from his nation and his family as a slave. He was made a eunuch and forced to become physically "barren." He lived his life as a captive in a foreign land, separated from his people and serving the king who destroyed his nation. He was "greatly beloved" by God[4] and was given unique insight into God's plan. Daniel became one of the greatest messengers in the Bible, but his message came out of his barrenness.

The apostle Paul's achievements are remarkable, but he worked in a relatively small region. He wrote letters to encourage struggling

---

[1] Numbers 12:3.

[2] Exodus 3–4. Interestingly, this is the first time in the Bible God is described as angry.

[3] For more on this, see the book *Son of Man: The Gospel of Daniel 7*.

[4] Daniel 9:23; 10:10, 19.

congregations and probably never expected his letters to have far more impact after his death than during his ministry. In fact, many Christian leaders today are much better known than Paul was in his lifetime.

A. W. Pink is a recent example. After his death in 1952, Arthur Walkington Pink became "one of the most influential evangelical authors in the second half of the twentieth century,"[5] but he was virtually unknown in his lifetime. Like many of the prophets, he lived a life before the Lord that bore the greatest fruit after he died.

Would you be willing to live a life before God in order to write books that would be most useful after you are dead?

The biblical prophets were not popular conference speakers. Many were put into jail and rejected while they were alive. Isaiah was not celebrated in his generation—he was executed.[6] Daniel was not given a public platform during his life. Many of the most impactful men in biblical history had their greatest impact *after* their deaths. They did not live their lives according to our paradigms of success and impact. The wisdom of a life lived before God is often not evident for decades. In fact, the wisdom of Noah, Abraham, and Moses has not yet been fully vindicated.[7] A day is coming, however, when the wisdom of those who lived out of sync with this age will be demonstrated and rewarded.

A man with a settled identity is willing to take on the assignment the Lord gives him even if it means he does not live long enough to see his greatest contribution.

Embracing Weakness

We live in a generation that has unusual confidence in human strength, achievement, and intellect. We see every part of our universe as something to be conquered and every challenge something to be overcome through human ingenuity. Even when we disagree on the solution, we maintain incredible confidence in our ability to find the

---

[5]Ian Murray, *Life of Arthur W. Pink*, Banner of Truth; 2nd edition (November 1, 2004), xiii.

[6]Isaiah's death is not described in the Bible, but according to tradition, he was martyred.

[7]Hebrews 11:39–40.

solution. The rise of modern technology has given us even more ways to seek out power and a sense of control.

Men will continue to seek unprecedented power, but God is going to produce a people who embrace *weakness*. God will resist the strong,[8] and His power will instead rest on those who embrace weakness. Consequently, when Paul listed his apostolic credentials, he *boasted* in weakness:

> But he said to me, *"My grace is sufficient for you, for my power is made perfect in weakness." Therefore I will boast all the more gladly of my weaknesses, so that the power of Christ may rest upon me. For the sake of Christ, then, I am content with weaknesses, insults, hardships, persecutions, and calamities. For when I am weak, then I am strong. (2 Corinthians 12:9–10)*

Paul embraced weakness, but we continue to be seduced by human strength. Embracing weakness does not mean embracing half-heartedness, compromise, or passivity. It means abandoning human strength. One of the reasons we see so little miraculous power is that we are still too strong. There is an embrace of weakness that must come before God will release a greater measure of His power. If you want to operate in the power of God, you have to let go of the power of men. God does not want to anoint your strength.

We desperately need a church that has faced her own barrenness and, as a result, becomes a conduit for something greater than herself.

Coming to terms with weakness does not mean embracing moral compromise or indulging in sinful lifestyles with little concern about God's holiness. Weakness is recognizing the complete inability of our strength to produce what God has called us to produce. Ironically, the path to maximum fruitfulness is to be *reduced* first. God must break our confidence in our thinking, our strength, and our efforts before He can give us unusual power.

Do not be surprised by your own weakness. Your assignment will not be accomplished in your strength. The bigger your assignment, the more critical weakness becomes. Do not be surprised that the great

---

[8]Isaiah 2:11–12, 17; 57:15; Proverbs 3:34; Matthew 23:12; Luke 14:11; 1 Peter 5:5–6; James 4:6.

saints of the faith still carry human weakness. Moses was so weak when God offered him unprecedented power that he initially rejected the offer. Elijah was a man like us.[9] John was also a man like us. Do not try to find a way to be "strong" because human strength holds back God's purposes.

John's life began with a profound demonstration of human weakness, and this weakness was a defining aspect of John's life.

Zechariah and Elizabeth lived a life of weakness. They were unable to do a basic, human thing: have a child. However, their weakness ultimately became a conduit for God's glory. Their barrenness gave them a glory few parents have known.

John's impact did not come from his strength, wisdom, and natural ability. He did not speak publicly until the Word of the Lord came to him,[10] and when the Lord did come to him, John did not seek a place of influence or power. He remained in the wilderness content with whatever God chose to do through him. John affected a nation but lived in a small place with a handful of disciples and was not able to do miracles.[11] He was a vivid display of divine power through human weakness.

How much of your weekly activity and your church's weekly activity can be accomplished without the power of God? How much of our "prophetic" is merely a dramatic expression of human insights and desires? If the Holy Spirit was absent, could your services, programs, and ministries continue? I fear we have learned how to keep the show going in our own strength far more than we are willing to acknowledge. The Lord wants much more for us, so He is going to bring us face to face with our barrenness.

This age will not end with an unusually "strong" church. It will end with a church who, like John, is fully aware of her weakness and becomes a channel for divine power.

---

[9]James 5:17.

[10]Luke 3:1–3.

[11]John 10:41.

Waiting—A Public Display of Weakness

Very few things demonstrate weakness the way waiting does, so God often requires seasons of waiting to manifest your weakness. Waiting can be humiliating because it demonstrates you are unable to fulfill the assignment God has given you on your own initiative.

Waiting can produce something deep if we embrace it, so God almost always requires waiting when there is a significant assignment.

Joseph spent more than ten years in slavery unable to fulfill the assignment God gave him. Moses had to have his strength stripped from him over forty years *after* he had failed at forty years old. David waited over a decade to become king. Paul was called as an apostle but was not sent by the Spirit for fifteen years.

God always gives a sense of an assignment before the time of waiting because, without a sense of assignment, you are not waiting on God; you are simply passing time. When there is a deep sense of an assignment that we are unable to fulfill, waiting is agonizing, and it becomes the Lord's crucible. In that crucible, the Lord forces you to acknowledge your utter inability to do the thing He has asked you to do. In the process, you become truly dependent on His power and His timing.

If you resist this crucible, you will either forfeit your assignment or seek to fulfill it in your own strength. If you are especially gifted, you can produce something that may seem impressive to some, but anything born of human strength cannot hold the glory of God. Furthermore, anything born of human strength must be maintained in human strength.

Because the stakes are so high in waiting, God will often put you in situations that force you to wait if there is a significant assignment. Sometimes He will cut off every other option. Other times things that seemed right and good will fail. You will be left unable to fulfill the dream in your heart. *All of this is God's mercy.* He is saving you from yourself and from "successes" that produce confidence in human strength.

The Breaking Point

God will sometimes push you to the absolute breaking point to produce weakness. When He does, there is much more at stake than you realize. When He does this, you must obey the voice of God over your own wisdom or fears. You must choose His wisdom over your own. When you are in God's crucible, you cannot make decisions on the basis of logic. Decisions must be based on what God has said.

God especially pushes messengers to the breaking point because a messenger must have more confidence in God's voice than his own wisdom.

As we saw in a previous chapter, many people agree with Christianity and its morals because it seems reasonable to them. But you must go beyond this. You must have an intense loyalty to God that chooses to stand with His Word over and above your own reason. You must be loyal to God *especially* when it does not make sense. The central human sin—the sin of Adam and Even—was to choose their wisdom over God's Word. That sin must be rooted out of us if we want to carry God's glory in a profound way.

Perhaps you are prepared to stand with the Word of God when you are criticized by others. But are you prepared to stand with the Word of God when your own wisdom and your own thinking contradict it?

The events that will precede the return of Jesus are going to be far beyond what anyone can imagine.[12] The only people who can prepare others for these kind of events are the ones who have already faced this crisis in their own lives. They have already fought on the ultimate battlefield. They have already been forced to deny their own thinking, their own wisdom, and their own logic and choose the Word of God over everything their senses tell them.

Consider King Saul and King David. King Saul was put in a difficult spot because he needed Samuel to offer a sacrifice before he went out to war. However, Samuel was late, the enemy army was approaching, and time was running out. Saul could not bear the tension of waiting, so he decided to offer the sacrifice himself. Because he could not bear the tension of waiting, God brought an end to his kingly line.[13]

---

[12]Matthew 21:21.

[13]1 Samuel 13:8–14.

David, in contrast, refused to take the throne prematurely, even when it was put within his reach.[14] David chose to bear the agony of waiting rather than obtain God's promise by his own wisdom and strength. David was eventually given an eternal promise—one of his descendants would rule forever.[15]

When God pushes you to the breaking point, the stakes are far higher than they may seem in the moment. In that moment, we can forfeit our assignment or grow in God in a profound way.

God Will Force the Issue of Weakness

There are a number of reasons God forces the issues of weakness.

God does it to establish identity. You cling to your own strength when your identity is rooted in yourself and not in God. The greatest prophets in the Bible expressed deep pain at their profound weakness when they encountered the glory of God.[16] When you finally face your weakness, it produces a pain too deep for words. It cuts to the heart because it exposes the truth of who you really are.

When God uses weakness to break your pride, it opens up the wound of insecurity, and you feel the same shame and nakedness Adam and Eve felt. Most people rush to some sort of "covering" so they do not have to see who they truly are, but if you will face your true condition, God will reshape your identity in Him. Until you find your identity in God, you cannot fulfill your assignment because you will be constantly subject to the fear of man and human opinions.

The messenger is the message. Western culture tends to prize information, but God values *expression* over *information*. Who you are is ultimately demonstrated by what you are, not what you know. You must become an embodiment of the message you carry. Any messenger who communicates or demonstrates human strength communicates falsehoods about the gospel. Paul *chose* weakness for the sake of the

---

[14]1 Samuel 24; 2 Samuel 2:1–4.

[15]2 Samuel 7.

[16]Exodus 3:11; Isaiah 6:5; Jeremiah 1; Ezekiel 1:28.

gospel because he understood human strength obscures the glory of God.[17]

God is at war with man's pride, and His Word is designed to shatter your pride. We are called to declare the glory of God and the weakness of human pride, but if you have not had your own pride shattered, you cannot be a demonstration of the message you speak, and your words will lack a dimension of power. Weakness forces you to become a demonstration of the words you speak. When this happens, you can create a confrontation without speaking a word because you are a message.

A "strong" messenger is dangerous. If you do not have a profound sense of weakness, you will be dangerous to yourself and others. You are dangerous to yourself because you are easily deluded into thinking you are something you are not. You will have a difficult time separating yourself from the anointing which creates a context for incredible pride. You will tend to use power for your own purposes and enjoy the praise of man.

If you are "strong," you are also an incredible danger to others because your infatuation with yourself will cause you to use the power flowing through you for your own benefit. Instead of serving people and pointing them to God, you will tend to attract people to yourself and use people for your own purposes.

Our Humanism Is Still Too Strong

The issue of weakness is more profound than we know. People imagine there is some kind of "superior human" that God is looking for to accomplish His work and that God's work is held back by the kinds of humans He works with.

This thinking reveals our humanism is still too strong.

We do everything we can to avoid any indication of weakness:

- We become obsessed with comparison and disqualify ourselves in our own minds from our assignments. We draw back from God until a time when we feel more confident in our own

---

[17]1 Corinthians 2:1–5.

condition, which is ironically the opposite of the gospel. God does not respect human strength or achievement.[18]

- We do everything we can to present ourselves to God and others as strong. We are obsessed with our image and what people think of us. In the process, we become susceptible to self-righteousness.
- We evaluate others according to our perception of their strength and gifting.
- We become angry and impatient with those who fail or come up short.
- We are disillusioned when leaders demonstrate weakness because we assumed they were "superior" and their God-given gifts were rewards rather than sovereignly chosen gifts.
- We strive with everything we can to accomplish the work of God in our own strength.
- We are unable to bear periods of waiting.

We expect the messengers that God uses to be some sort of exalted people—people who have achieved some sort of perfection. As a result, we turn gifted leaders into idols and are disillusioned when we discover their own weaknesses, shortcomings, and failures. We also disqualify others and are unable to see the grace of God in others because we assume God is looking for a "better" kind of human.

The truth is we are uncomfortable with weakness in others because we are uncomfortable with the weakness in our own souls.

God wants to remove this deeply rooted pride. Some are proud because they are confident in their own strength and ability. Others are trapped in pride because their obsession with their own weaknesses drive them to become stronger, more gifted, and more capable so God will "use" them. This despair over the way God has made a person is also an expression of pride. It's a desire to be something stronger. More capable. More impressive. More independent.

You will not able to walk in everything God has for you until you fully come to terms with your weakness.

---

[18]Job 34:19; Matthew 22:16; Luke 20:21; Acts 10:34; Romans 2:11; Galatians 2:2–6; Ephesians 6:9.

More Than a Prophet

When Jesus spoke about John, He asked the audience three times who John was, indicating the people had not understood who John truly was:

> *As they went away, Jesus began to speak to the crowds concerning John: "What did you go out into the wilderness to see? A reed shaken by the wind? What then did you go out to see? A man dressed in soft clothing? Behold, those who wear soft clothing are in kings' houses. What then did you go out to see? A prophet? Yes, I tell you, and more than a prophet. (Matthew 11:7–9)*

Notice Jesus did not ask what they went out to *hear*. He asked what did they go out to *see* because John was the message. When Jesus asked the question a third time, He repeated the crowd's answer to His questions: John was a prophet. And then Jesus added another phrase: "and more than a prophet."

The crowds defined John as a prophet, but the word *prophet* did not define John's core identity. There was something else, something that had been overlooked by the crowds.

If you see John primarily as a prophet, you will miss something significant. Furthermore, "more than a prophet" does not merely mean "a special prophet." Jesus did not say John was an "honored prophet" —though that of course was true. He said John was *more* than a prophet. He was not simply an oracle. Something else defined John.

If the term *prophet* was not adequate to explain who John was, then who or what was he?

Jesus explained why John was "more than a prophet" by quoting Malachi 3:1:

This is he of whom it is written, "Behold, I send my messenger before your face, who will prepare your way before you." (Matthew 11:10)

"Behold, I send my messenger, and he will prepare the way before me. And the Lord whom you seek will suddenly come to his temple; and the messenger of the covenant in whom you delight, behold, he is coming, says the LORD of hosts." (Malachi 3:1)

This quotation was especially significant because it is the only Old Testament quotation Jesus directly applied to John.[1] Isaiah 40 is typically associated with John because the Gospels apply it to him and it was his main message, but Jesus never applied Isaiah 40 to John in the Gospels. The reason is simple: Isaiah 40 summarized John's public *ministry*, but Jesus used Malachi to summarize John's *identity*.

Jesus did not quote Malachi to state the obvious—John was a messenger (prophet). He quoted Malachi to reveal why John was *more* than a prophet. To understand Jesus' saying about John, we need to know what the book of Malachi says about this "messenger."

My Messenger

When a Jewish teacher in the first-century referenced part of a biblical passage, he expected you to know the context of the reference and use the entire passage to understand his message. Consequently, we have to know the book of Malachi to grasp why Jesus used Malachi to describe John as more than a prophet. The book of Malachi contains the last prophetic message Israel was given before John was born. For several centuries, Israel had waited for the one Malachi called "my messenger" to emerge. If John was this messenger, it meant Malachi's prophecy was unfolding in front of everyone's eyes.

The phrase *my messenger* is very significant because the word translated *my messenger* in Malachi 3:1 is the same word typically translated *Malachi* in Malachi 1:1:

The oracle of the word of the LORD to Israel by Malachi ("my messenger"). (Malachi 1:1)

---

[1] Jesus also alluded to Malachi 4:5 in His description of John in Matthew 11:14, making Malachi the only book Jesus applied to John.

The word *Malachi* (מַלְאָכִי, *mal'ākî*) is a not a proper name; it is a word that simply means "my messenger." As a result, commentators debate whether the "Malachi" in Malachi 1:1 was an actual person's name or a title. Whether Malachi was a person's name or a title, whoever wrote the book made a direct and intentional connection between 1:1 and 3:1 by using the same word in both places to describe a messenger.

The author described the message of the book as the message delivered to "my messenger" (Malachi 1:1) and then predicted that a person also known as "my messenger" (Malachi 3:1) was coming. This connection indicates the message given in the book (Malachi 1:1–4:6) is the message that the messenger of Malachi 3:1 will carry. Therefore, when Jesus applied Malachi 3:1 to John, He applied the entire book to John.

If John was the messenger of Malachi 3:1, the book of Malachi was his message. As a result, you have to understand Malachi's message to understand John.

This word *Malachi* (my messenger) is used a few times in the book to emphasize the main theme of the book, but this connection is easily missed when the word is not translated consistently. However, if you trace the use of the word in the book, you can discover who John really was.

The Failure of the Priesthood

The message in Malachi begins with a declaration of the Lord's constant, covenantal love for Israel and a rebuke to the Israelites who questioned God's love because of what they had experienced. God contrasted His covenantal love for Israel with His hatred toward Esau.[2] Esau was a reference to the nation of Edom, and when John prophesied, Israel was being ruled by King Herod who was an Edomite. This formed a backdrop for John's message—God's covenant love for Israel continued even though her people were being ruled by an Edomite.[3]

---

[2]The book of Obadiah explains why God hated Esau (Edom). In short, the Edomites tried to take advantage of Judah's trouble and take Israel's inheritance for themselves.

[3]Ironically, it was the failure of Israel's Hasmonean kingdom that led to Herod becoming king.

God directed His primary rebuke at a priesthood that was going through the motions of priestly service and did not have any genuine desire or affection for the Lord. They were doing the bare minimum necessary to secure God's favor by offering what God called "polluted" sacrifices.[4] As a result, God accused the priests of "despising" Him and His sanctuary.[5]

The state of the priesthood was so offensive to God that He wanted them to shut down the worship sanctuary rather than continue in a half-hearted condition:

> *Oh that there were one among you who would shut the doors, that you might not kindle fire on my altar in vain! I have no pleasure in you, says the LORD of hosts, and I will not accept an offering from your hand. (Malachi 1:10)*

This statement was incredibly shocking because God established the priesthood and temple worship during the exodus when He had appeared in fire on Mount Sinai and spoken audibly to Israel.[6] God had set this ministry in place so Israel could host His presence, but He wanted Israel to disobey His commands rather than maintain a sanctuary out of a sense of obligation.

While the rebuke may seem harsh, it was a statement of the Lord's desire for real relationship. Ancient priests in the surrounding nations had a transactional relationship with their gods. They performed sacrifices and other rituals to secure favor and blessing from their gods. Whenever a relationship is transactional, either party offers the bare minimum to secure the desired result, and the priests of Israel had begun relating to YHWH this way.

The priests were offering sacrifices to secure YHWH's favor, but YHWH did not want a transactional relationship with His people.

---

[4]Malachi 1:7.

[5]Malachi 1:6–7.

[6]Exodus 19:7–9, 16–18; 20:19; Deuteronomy 4:9-13, 32–36, 5:1–4, 20–23.

God had made covenant with Israel as a Bridegroom,[7] and He wanted the passionate, covenantal love of a wife, not transactional services that resembled prostitution. Because the priests were functioning like the pagan priests—like a prostitute rather than a wife —YHWH wanted someone to be bold enough to shut the system down. This crisis is repeated when people seek blessing and an eternity in heaven in return for attending church services, donating some money, avoiding bad habits, and doing a few other religious acts, but have no real interest in the person of God.

YHWH is a bridegroom with deep desire for His people, and He expects us to relate to Him as a bride filled with deep emotion and desire for Him. He wants a people who enjoy Him.

We typically evaluate ourselves and others on the basis of outward behavior, but God cares little for outward acts of devotion if the heart is not interested in a fiery relationship of love. As we have seen, John referred to Jesus as the Bridegroom. That phrase communicated a lot, and Malachi 1 provided part of the basis for John's preaching. John called Israel to repent because she was not relating to God as a bridegroom.

God reminded Israel she had been given a privileged place as the first priests of a coming global priesthood,[8] and He tried to provoke her to return to the heart of the priesthood by predicting the priesthood would expand into the nations:

> *For from the rising of the sun to its setting my name will be great among the nations, and in every place incense will be offered to my name, and a pure offering. For my name will be great among the nations, says the* LORD *of hosts. (Malachi 1:11)*

In Malachi 1, we discover the message is primarily about the failure of the priesthood and God's plan to purify and restore it.

---

[7]Isaiah 54:4–12; 62:2–5; Jer. 2:2; 3:14; 31:32; Ezekiel 16:13–15, 32; 23:1–45; Hosea 1:2; 2:7, 14–23; 3:1–5.

[8]Mysteriously, this expansion of the priesthood will ultimately play a part in God's plan to restore Israel's priestly call.

Priestly Messengers

God's rebuke to the priesthood continued in Malachi 2, and He used the word *Malachi* again to describe the role of the priests:

> *For the lips of a priest should guard knowledge, and people should seek instruction from his mouth, for he is the messenger [Malachi] of the LORD of hosts. (Malachi 2:7)*

Because the priests had access to God's presence and His Word, their words were to "guard knowledge" so people could "find instruction" in their teaching. They were to be God's spokesmen, instructing the people to preserve a true knowledge of who God was.

Because the priests stood before the Lord and taught the nation, they were called to be *messengers* of the Lord. But the priesthood had become corrupt, and the priests were not functioning as His messengers, and the people were not being instructed in the knowledge of God:

> *"And now, O priests, this command is for you. . . . you have turned aside from the way. You have caused many to stumble by your instruction. You have corrupted the covenant of Levi, says the LORD of hosts." (Malachi 2:1, 8)*

Malachi 2 ended with God's response to priests who did not take their assignment seriously and delight in the knowledge of God:

> *You have wearied the LORD with your words. . . . (Malachi 2:17)*

There is a divine poetry between Malachi 1 and Malachi 2. In Malachi 1, the priests considered their service to the Lord a burden. In Malachi 2, the Lord considered the priests a burden.

The message of Malachi 2 is straightforward: A messenger must be a priest because the central message is the knowledge of God.

The knowledge of God is not optional. Without it, you are not useful to God, and you cannot become His messenger. The knowledge of God is the primary arena for spiritual warfare in your life:

> *For the weapons of our warfare are not of the flesh but have divine power to destroy strongholds. We destroy arguments and every lofty opinion raised against the knowledge of God. (2 Corinthians 10:4–5)*

If you do not wage war in this area, you have abandoned the heart of the battle. God gave Israel the Levites as teachers, and He has given the church ministry gifts so we will come into the knowledge of God:

> *And he gave the apostles, the prophets, the evangelists, the shepherds and teachers, to equip the saints . . . until we all attain to the unity of the faith and of the knowledge of the Son of God. (Ephesians 4:11–13)*

The knowledge of God is so serious John referred to priests without the knowledge of God as a "brood of vipers."[9] *Do we consider the knowledge of God this serious?* Do you believe you are a "dangerous snake" if you try to lead people without the knowledge of God?

If you do not carry the knowledge of God, your ministry is irrelevant and can become harmful.

Are you willing to adjust your life—radically if necessary—to obtain the knowledge of God? Or do other pursuits still captivate you more? What is your fascination? What do you treasure in your heart? What do you meditate and daydream about? These are the things you will communicate to others. As Jesus said, *"Out of the abundance of the heart the mouth speaks."*[10]

What flows out of the abundance of your heart?

I Will Send My Messenger

The failure of the priesthood to delight in God and become His messengers sets the context for Malachi 3:1 and explains Jesus' summary of John's life.

Because the priests were burdened by their ministry and did not have the knowledge of God, they could not prepare the way for Him to come. Therefore, God predicted He would raise up a person He called "my messenger:"

---

[9]Matthew 3:7; Luke 3:7.

[10]Matthew 12:34.

Behold, I send my messenger, and he will prepare the way before me. And the Lord whom you seek will suddenly come to his temple; and the messenger of the covenant in whom you delight, behold, he is coming, says the LORD of hosts. (Malachi 3:1)

Because God wanted the priests to be His messengers,[11] it indicates the messenger of Malachi 3 would be a priest. This messenger would emerge in a generation where the priesthood had failed, and he would be a priest who would not despise his task but instead fear God and stand in awe of God's name.[12] This messenger would be a sharp contrast to the corrupt priests who despised their ministry:

You have said, "It is vain to serve God. What is the profit of our keeping his charge or of walking as in mourning before the LORD of hosts?" (Malachi 3:14)

The corrupt priesthood had no delight in keeping the temple and ministering to God, neither did they see any benefit in mourning over the condition of the nation. As a result, God referred to them as "arrogant" and "against Him." They were "strong" and "hard" in their resistance of Him.[13]

However, Malachi predicted a messenger would be accompanied by a people who feared the Lord:

Then those who feared the LORD spoke with one another. The LORD paid attention and heard them, and a book of remembrance was written before him of those who feared the LORD and esteemed his name. "They shall be mine, says the LORD of hosts, in the day when I make up my treasured possession, and I will spare them as a man spares his son who serves him." (Malachi 3:16–17)

This people would take Malachi's message seriously and speak to each other in response to the message because they feared the Lord and

---

[11]Malachi 2:7

[12]Malachi 2:5.

[13]See Malachi 3:13, quotations combine the ESV and NASB.

treasured His words. God will record the devotion of this people, spare them when He comes in judgment, and take them as His "treasured possession."[14] God referred to Israel as His treasured possession and a priestly people,[15] so this is an indicator these people will be part of the true remnant of Israel—the true priesthood. And the first chapter of Malachi hints these priests will emerge in the nations as well as Israel:

> *For from the rising of the sun to its setting my name will be great among the nations, and in every place incense will be offered to my name. . . . For my name will be great among the nations. . . . For I am a great King, says the* LORD *of hosts, and my name will be feared among the nations. (vv. 11, 14)*

God's longing for a people who are His "treasured possession" forces you to ask a serious question: Are you in sync with His desire?

The application is obvious. We still need priestly messengers to call us back to our priestly occupation. Whenever we despise our priestly assignment, the church languishes, and God's word to us is, "Do you have courage to shut it down? Or will you continue devoid of a true priesthood and satisfied with an imitation of what I want?"

If you are comfortable with a Christianity that is not priestly, it is evidence you do not grasp what God wants. If we do not train our people to minister to God *before* they minister to people, we do not understand the ministry. Tragically, in many places we have "priests" who despise or neglect the essence of their calling.

God's answer two thousand years ago is His answer today: *Behold I will raise up my messengers—people who are true priests and can feed people with the Word of God.* Some will be in vocational ministry, but most will be

---

[14]God has designed this age to produce a people who will become His treasured possession. God expresses His commitment and desire throughout Scripture by reminding His people, "I will be your God, and you will be My people." This phrase encapsulates one of God's deepest desires, and as a result, it is found in various forms in the Bible at least 35 times (Genesis 17:8; Exodus 6:7; 19:5; 29:45; Leviticus 11:44–45; 26:11–12; Numbers 8:14–17; Deuteronomy 29:13; Ruth 1:16; Song of Songs 2:16; 6:3; Isaiah 51:15–16; Jeremiah 7:23; 11:4; 24:7; 30:22; 30:24–31:1, 33; 32:38; Ezekiel 11:20; 14:11; 36:28; 37:26–28; Hosea 1:9; 2:23; Zechariah 2:10–12; 8:8; 13:9; Malachi 3:17; John 14:17, 20, 23; 2 Corinthians 6:16; Romans 9:25; Hebrews 8:10; 11:16; Revelation 21:3, 7).

[15]Exodus 19:5–6; Deuteronomy 7:6; 14:2; 26:19; 28:9.

not be. As in John's day, Israel's priesthood has failed. But God is going to answer the crisis with a people who, like John, are priests throughout the wilderness of the nations in a time when the priesthood in Jerusalem has failed.

The priesthood is our permanent calling, yet we spend far more time on our temporary assignments than our eternal calling. This must change.

The Priest Who Became a Messenger

The message of Malachi summarized John's life and message:

- The priesthood had become compromised and politicized.
- Priests were to be God's messengers, but the priesthood had failed and did not instruct the people in the knowledge of God.
- YHWH was going to send a priest who would be His messenger to prepare the way for the Lord to come to His temple and purify the priesthood.
- There would be a company who treasured the Lord, feared His name, and became His treasured possession.
- God was going to expand the priesthood beyond the city of Jerusalem out into the nations.

John was the messenger of Malachi 3:1 and a prototype of a priestly people who would fear the Lord, serve as His messengers, and become His treasured possession.
John's preaching carried allusions to Malachi 3 and Malachi 4:1, indicating John knew who he was.[1] When the crowds heard John, they assumed he was a prophet, but in reality, he was a lifelong priest who became the Lord's public messenger for a few months. His assignment as a messenger was significant, but it was not his core identity. John was more than a preacher and more than a prophet. In the wilderness, John lived as a priest and had become the Lord's "treasured possession."[2]
John's lifelong assignment was to live as a priest before the Lord in a small place in a generation where the priesthood in Jerusalem had failed.

---

[1]Matthew 3:10–12; Luke 3:16–17.

[2]Malachi 3:17.

John's life was defined by the priesthood. He was the child of a priest. His miraculous birth was predicted in a priestly context. He lived His entire life as a priest, but a priest of a different kind. And he was given the Holy Spirit in his mother's womb as a prototype of a new people who would be priests by virtue of the gift of the Spirit.

John was a preview of the priesthood Malachi predicted would emerge in the nations because he ministered on the far side of the Jordan.[3] Israel officially entered the land by crossing the Jordan as a people,[4] so John was ministering outside the land.

Symbolically, people had to go "outside the land" into the wilderness to hear John, and after repenting and being baptized, they then "returned" to the land. In this way, John's ministry pointed toward priests who would live before the Lord outside the land of Israel and prepare the way for the Bridegroom of Israel to come.

John was a prototype of a new priesthood ministering to God in the wilderness of the nations outside the land and preparing the way for Him to come while Jerusalem was not yet saved and her priesthood not yet purified.

John was a picture of a priestly people who will love the Word of God, dwell in the nations, and become messengers of the God of Israel. Like John, this priestly people from all nations are called to speak Isaiah 40 to Israel and provoke her to return to her priestly calling:

> *Go on up to a high mountain, O Zion, herald of good news; lift up your voice with strength, O Jerusalem, herald of good news; lift it up, fear not; say to the cities of Judah, "Behold your God!" Behold, the Lord GOD comes with might, and his arm rules for him; behold, his reward is with him, and his recompense before him. (vv. 9–10)*

In John, the Lord had a priest in the wilderness—outside the land—who was more priestly than the priests in Jerusalem. John was like the sons of Zadok who were faithful to the Lord even when the people had gone astray:

---

[3]John 1:28; 10:40.

[4]Joshua 3–4.

"But the Levitical priests, the sons of Zadok, who kept the charge of my sanctuary when the people of Israel went astray from me, shall come near to me to minister to me." (Ezekiel 44:15)

All of this was behind Jesus' probing question: *"What did you go out to see?"* If John had simply been a prophet, Jesus would have asked, "What did you go out to *hear?"* Instead, Jesus asked, "What did you go out to *see?"* because John did not just speak a message to Israel; he *was* a message to Israel. People thought they were looking at a prophet, but they were looking at a priest. John was an embodiment of the message of Malachi calling the people to be a priestly people, and he was a demonstration of what God wanted from His people. He was also a prediction of where the priesthood was going.

If the crowds did not see John as a priest, they had missed the message. And if you see John only as a prophet, you will miss the message as well.

No Man Greater

John was obviously an anointed preacher and one of the greatest messengers in biblical history, but Jesus' evaluation of John as one of the greatest was not based on John's preaching gift. It was connected to Malachi's prophecy:

This is he of whom it is written, "Behold, I send my messenger before your face, who will prepare your way before you." Truly, I say to you, among those born of women there has arisen no one greater than John the Baptist." (Matthew 11:10–11)

John was not great simply because his public ministry was powerful. There are other examples of powerful ministry in the Bible. Nor did his greatness flow exclusively from the assignment he was given to prepare the way for Jesus.

John was great because he stood before the Lord in a small place, treasured the Lord's words, and ministered to the Lord in a generation where Jerusalem's priesthood had failed.[5] As we have seen, John's life gives us insight into what Jesus considers great.

---

[5]This is not to suggest all the priests were corrupt, but the conflict between Jesus and some of the religious leaders indicates the leadership of the priesthood was not functioning the way it was designed to.

Does your life align with this definition of greatness?

John and Elijah

Jesus also used Malachi to compare John to Elijah:

> *"Behold, I will send you Elijah the prophet before the great and awesome day of the LORD comes." (Malachi 4:5)*
>
> *And if you are willing to accept it, he is Elijah who is to come. (Matthew 11:14)*

This connection further enforced John's priestly identity, because Elijah also lived in a time when Israel's priesthood had failed by abandoning the God of Israel for the worship of idols. The most famous story about Elijah is his contest with the prophets of Baal on Mount Carmel, and that conflict was a battle of the priests. The false priests offered their sacrifices, and God's priest offered his.

Like John, Elijah suddenly appeared to Israel and had one qualification: *Elijah stood before the Lord:*

> *Now Elijah the Tishbite, of Tishbe in Gilead, said to Ahab, "As the LORD, the God of Israel, lives, before whom I stand. . . ." (1 Kings 17:1)*

Neither John nor Elijah were in Jerusalem or part of the temple ministry, but both had the same qualification: *They stood before the Lord in a small place in a generation when Israel's priesthood had failed.* Both lived out Malachi 2:7. Elijah was a wilderness priest raised up to confront a compromised priesthood so Israel would return to her proper priestly identity, and John's life followed the same pattern.

John and Elijah were deeply connected in many ways,[6] but most of all they both were priestly men who ministered to the Lord in the wilderness (nations) and confronted false priesthoods. As a result, fire fell when Elijah prayed, and the Spirit fell on Jesus when John baptized Him.

---

[6]John and Elijah were both connected to the Jordan River. They both wore similar clothing, preached a message of repentance, and were persecuted by a wicked king.

There is one way John and Elijah were very different: Elijah was primarily known as a man of power, signs, and wonders. He prophesied shifts in weather and called down fire from heaven, but John did not do any miraculous signs.[7] Instead, John was known for powerfully proclaiming the prophets' messages. John the Baptist was a man in the *spirit* of Elijah who lacked one of the principal characteristics of Elijah's ministry.

The fact John was in the spirit of Elijah but lacking what Elijah is primarily known for indicates he was not the full and final fulfillment of the spirit of Elijah.

When we consider what Jesus said about John and Elijah,[8] it leads us to a sobering conclusion: *John is a prototype of an end-time ministry of preparation that will combine powerful proclamation of the Scripture with the kind of power Elijah demonstrated.* These two will come together again to release a witness of Jesus and prepare the way again.[9]

Standing in the Lord's Council

John and Elijah both provoke a question: *Do you stand before the Lord?* Obviously, not everyone will be a prophet, but we all have the invitation and the access to stand before the Lord because of the blood of Jesus.[10]

Many people want to be the Lord's messenger, but how many will stand in His council? Jeremiah rebuked false prophets in Jerusalem because they spoke *without standing in His council:*

> *Thus says the LORD of hosts: "Do not listen to the words of the prophets who prophesy to you, filling you with vain hopes. They speak visions of their own minds, not from the mouth of the LORD. . . . For who among them has stood in the council of the LORD to see and to hear his word, or who has paid attention to his word and listened?" (Jeremiah 23:16, 18)*

Are you trying to to speak for the Lord without standing in His council?

---

[7]John 10:41.

[8]Matthew 17:10–13.

[9]We see a picture of this in Revelation 11.

[10]Hebrews 4:16; 10:19–23.

Elijah did unusual signs and wonders, but he described himself as one who stood before the Lord. Do you pursue a lifestyle of standing before the Lord with the same tenacity you pursue signs, wonders, and other things? This is not a small issue. Do you realize some people will operate in power and then hear Jesus say, "I never knew you":

> *"On that day many will say to me, 'Lord, Lord, did we not prophesy in your name, and cast out demons in your name, and do many mighty works in your name?' And then will I declare to them, 'I never knew you; depart from me, you workers of lawlessness.'" (Matthew 7:22–23)*

The blood of Jesus was not simply shed so you could escape hell. It was shed so you can approach God. Do you seek a life before God? Or are you more enamored with the opportunity to stand before men?

The biblical prophets stood before God, and you must follow their example. Jesus shed His own blood so you could have the awesome privilege of standing before the Lord, and if you do not, it demonstrates a lack of appreciation for His blood.

God is not casual and flippant. He loves to speak to His people,[11] but He will not speak to you so you can expand your influence, promote your "prophetic" gifting, or find your identity in ministry. Many people long to hear God's voice so they can go speak and become a celebrated "messenger," but God is not your agent. He will not give you a weighty word so you can expand your influence.

Standing in God's council also means not speaking for Him when He is not speaking.

Many are quick to give their opinion in the Lord's name, assuming He agrees with their opinions, but this is a serious error.[12] Part of standing before the Lord is waiting when He is silent, but many cannot bear the tension of silence, so they come up with something they think sounds prophetic or just abandon the process of standing before Him when He has not spoken.

---

[11]Genesis 18:17; Amos 3:7.

[12]For more on this, see *Have You Been Blinded? Facing Your Assumptions with God's Leadership.*

The deepest friendships are those who can stand together in silence, but tragically, the Lord has few friends who can endure His silence.

We are so quick to speak in our generation that we often cannot clearly discern what the Lord is saying. Many times, God simply wants us to hold our tongues and be silent before Him until He chooses to speak. Sometimes He speaks for the purpose of intercession or communion. He may want you to share in His pain. Every word God speaks is not a ministry opportunity. God is looking for *communion*, but too many are seeking Him for ministry. What does God feel when we take words that were meant for communion and rush to microphones hoping to be honored and celebrated for our insight?

If we want to stand in His council, we must give ourselves to the words God has already spoken. God's words are timeless and eternal, and our obsession with the "new" and "novel" can lead us to look endlessly for something "fresh" when God wants us to meditate on what He has already said. God is not obligated to speak to you again if you do not treasure what He has already said.

The Call to a Priestly Life

Malachi was the only book Jesus used to describe John because it perfectly defined John's life.

Like the book of Malachi, John directly confronted the priesthood:

> *But when he saw many of the Pharisees and Sadducees coming to his baptism, he said to them, "You brood of vipers! Who warned you to flee from the wrath to come? Bear fruit in keeping with repentance. And do not presume to say to yourselves, 'We have Abraham as our father,' for I tell you, God is able from these stones to raise up children for Abraham."* (Matthew 3:7–9)

You can hear the words of Malachi in John's rebuke:

> *And if I am a master, where is my fear? says the LORD of hosts to you, O priests, who despise my name. . . . Oh that there were one among you who would shut the doors, that you might not kindle fire on my altar in vain! I have no pleasure in you, says the LORD of hosts, and I will not accept an offering from your hand.* (Malachi 1:6, 10)

John was not arrogant. He confronted these leaders because they had no desire to consider his message. They were threatened by John's influence and saw him as a political threat.

John used the analogy, "brood of vipers," for a very specific reason. Vipers are unusual among snakes because they do not lay eggs. Instead, baby snakes hatch inside the mother and emerge from the mother as small snakes. This unusual process caused people in the ancient world to conclude these baby snakes ate their way out of their mother. John's analogy was a shocking accusation: "You are like a bunch of baby snakes eating their way through the mother—destroying the very thing that gives you life."

John accused the corrupt priesthood of destroying Israel—the very entity that created the context for the priestly ministry. The same thing happens any time anyone uses the church for their own benefit. The church is not an organization to be leveraged for influence, success, or wealth. Anyone who does is like a baby snake destroying the thing that was designed by God to be a context for His people to live together as priests.

John's life as a priest, his call for repentance, and his baptisms put him in direct conflict with the priests who governed the temple:[1]

John's family was priestly, and his activity of offering a baptism for forgiveness out in the desert presented a clear alternative to the temple.[2]

Like Malachi, John warned God was coming in judgment:

But who can endure the day of his coming, and who can stand when he appears? For he is like a refiner's fire and like fullers' soap. (Malachi 3:2)

"I baptize you with water for repentance, but he who is coming after me is mightier than I, whose sandals I am not worthy to carry. He will baptize you with the Holy Spirit and fire. His winnowing fork is in his hand, and he will clear his threshing floor and gather his wheat into the barn, but the chaff he will burn with unquenchable fire." (Matthew 3:11–12)

The Lord's prediction had come to pass: A priest who treasured His Word had become His messenger. The God of the temple was coming, but He would not appear first at the temple. He would be publicly introduced by the priest in the wilderness. God chose a priest in the wilderness to prepare Israel for Jesus' first coming, and He is looking for a priestly people to prepare the nations for Jesus' second coming.

---

[1]Webb, in his book on John the Baptist, also writes: "John's baptism, functioning to mediate forgiveness, offered an alternative to a primary function of the temple, and so was a threat to the temple establishment. As John grew in popularity, he would probably have been perceived as a real threat to those whose authority was grounded in the temple." Robert L. Webb, *John the Baptizer and Prophet: A Socio-Historical Study* (Sheffield: Sheffield Academic Press), 204.

[2]N. T. Wright, *Jesus and the Victory of God*, Christian Origins and the Question of God (London: Society for Promoting Christian Knowledge, 1996), 161.

God is not waiting for you to become a messenger; He wants you to become one of His priests. God will raise up His messengers from His priests.

As a priest in the wilderness, John was a prophetic picture of God's plan to radically enlarge the priesthood and form a company of priests in the nations. The "priesthood of all believers"[3] is now a familiar phrase, so it is easy to overlook how radical John's life was.

If we read Malachi as little more than a rebuke of an ancient priesthood that had become corrupt, we miss a significant part of the message. Malachi's book forces us to confront some uncomfortable questions: *Are we truly living as priests and functioning as a priesthood? Is it even in our thinking to live a priestly life? Do we prioritize it?*

Obviously, we are not called to maintain the same kind of sanctuary ancient Israel had, but we are meant to be priestly as John was. The priestly calling is our only permanent assignment, but far too many of us are trying to become messengers when we need to become priests. John was only a messenger for six to eighteen months of his life, but he lived as a priest all his days.

It would have been a tragic waste of a life if John had lived thirty years hoping for a few moments of notoriety, but the greater tragedy is that countless Christians live this way every day.

Day in and day out, people live their lives hoping for some future day when they achieve their dream of fame or success. When the desired success does not come, they retreat into halfhearted lives marked by disappointment and unmet expectations. Some leave the faith entirely. Because there is no vision for a priestly life, years are wasted as people seek the illusion of ministry, success, comfort, and popularity. It's a colossal waste of human life more tragic than we can comprehend.

Calling and Assignment

People often confuse their *calling* with their *assignments*. The word *calling* is frequently used to refer to a person's vocation, but this is better referred to as an assignment. God cares about our assignments, but they are not our primary calling. Furthermore, the Lord can bring you into your calling as you engage in different vocations or assignments.

---

[3] 1 Peter 2:9; Revelation 1:6; 5:9.

Your assignment is not your inheritance, nor is it your reward. It is simply a way you express your love for God and partner with Him.

Your calling is to become like Jesus and embrace your priestly identity.[4] Your vocation and assignments may change throughout your life, but your calling does not. This confusion can cause those in occupational ministry to find identity and purpose in what they do instead of who they are. It has also led many not in occupational ministry to feel their lives are not as spiritual as a full-time minister's even though most prominent biblical figures were not in occupational ministry.

Unlike John, we tend to be more obsessed with our temporary assignments than we are our priestly calling.

When God appointed the priests, He did not give them an inheritance or reward in the land. Even their priestly ministry was limited to twenty-five years of service in the tabernacle.[5] Most of their lives were not spent in the spotlight of ministry.

The priests had one reward: *God Himself.*

And the LORD said to Aaron, "You shall have no inheritance in their land, neither shall you have any portion among them. I am your portion and your inheritance among the people of Israel." (Numbers 18:20)

The priests were a reminder that God did not liberate Israel from Egypt primarily so Israel could escape oppression. He liberated Israel so she would become His treasured possession:[6]

Now therefore, if you will indeed obey my voice and keep my covenant, you shall be my treasured possession among all peoples, for all the earth is mine. (Exodus 19:5)

"But the LORD has taken you and brought you out of the iron furnace, out of Egypt, to be a people of his own inheritance, as you are this day." (Deuteronomy 4:20)

---

[4] 1 Peter 2:9; Revelation 1:6; 5:10; 20:6.

[5] Numbers 8:24–26.

[6] Deuteronomy 4:20; 14:2, 21; 26:18; 32:8–9; 1 Kings 8:53; Psalm 135:4; Isaiah 41:8; 43:1; Jeremiah 10:16; Malachi 3:17.

"For you are a people holy to the LORD *your God. The* LORD *your God has chosen you to be a people for his treasured possession, out of all the peoples who are on the face of the earth." (7:6)*

Israel's priests were a witness to the entire nation that they were called to be a priestly people with an inheritance in God Himself.[7] Like these ancient priests, you are called to be a priest, and your reward is not found in your assignments or possessions in this age.[8] We are part of a "kingdom of priests,"[9] which means God is our inheritance and we have no other inheritance in this age.

When you make assignments and success your destiny, you become susceptible to idolatry and often use other people and opportunities to obtain the success you want.

Is God Enough?

John's life forces you to ask a question: Do you truly value God as your reward, or are you constantly searching for and enamored with lesser rewards? Is God enough for you?

Moses left the comfort of the palace in Egypt because he preferred the reward of knowing Jesus more than the pleasures of Egypt:

By faith Moses, when he was grown up, refused to be called the son of Pharaoh's daughter, choosing rather to be mistreated with the people of God than to enjoy the fleeting pleasures of sin. He considered the reproach of Christ greater wealth than the treasures of Egypt, for he was looking to the reward. (Hebrews 11:24–26)

Moses not only rejected the pleasures of Egypt, Moses also considered the riches of Jesus a greater treasure than his God-ordained inheritance in the Promised Land. When Israel rebelled, God came to Moses and told him He would still give Israel the Promised Land, but His presence would not go with Moses and the people.[10] Moses was offered the

---

[7]Exodus 19:6.

[8]Romans 8:15–17, 23. 1 Corinthians 7:31; 2 Corinthians 1:22; Ephesians 1:14; 1 John 2:17.

[9]1 Peter 2:9; Revelation 1:6; 5:10; 20:6.

[10]Exodus 33:3.

fulfillment of God's promise without the presence of God, and Moses said *"No!"* Moses preferred living in the wilderness without his promise to receiving the inheritance but losing the presence of the Lord.

If God offered you an inheritance and the fulfillment of His promises to you at the cost of relationship, would you take it or refuse it for the sake of knowing Him?

God wants to fill the earth with a message: *I am enough. I am a greater treasure than all other treasures.* To carry that message with authority, it must be formed in the way we live. Moses was tested on this issue. John was tested on this issue. God is going to produce a mature church that also passes this test.

Do you pursue a priestly life with zeal, or do you find your public assignments more exciting than a hidden life of ministry to God?

John was the most powerful preacher in his generation, one of the most powerful messengers in history, and he lived his life in a small place. If you wanted to hear John, you had to go out to the wilderness to see him. John made it difficult for people to get to him because he had a priestly life in the wilderness that he did not want to surrender.

What is more beautiful to you—your assignment or God Himself?

If God offered you an increase in access to His beauty through hiddenness or a public stage, which would you take?[11] Many people will likely immediately say "intimacy," but actions often indicate otherwise, so you need to soberly ponder this question. Are you more captivated by opportunities to become students of the beauty of God or by opportunities for notoriety and the possibility of "success"?

Paul was a brilliant man. His intellect was towering, and he could have used it in any way he wanted. He could have left behind profound books of theology and philosophy instead of a few small letters. He could have become one of the leading thinkers of his day. Instead, he took the full force of his intellect and limited it to one captivating subject:

For I decided to know nothing among you except Jesus Christ and him crucified. (1 Corinthians 2:2)

---

[11]This, of course, does not mean public ministry is always at odds with intimacy.

Paul did not focus the strength of his intellect on ambition, strategic thinking, or ministry objectives. Paul did all those things, but he focused on just one thing: *Jesus and Him crucified.* Paul made a commitment to *limit* himself to the knowledge of God. (It must be said that the pursuit of the knowledge of Jesus includes more than study and meditation—it includes engaging in the biblical life of the church where we discover aspects of Jesus' beauty among His people. Nor does this require a vocation in "ministry."[12])

Have you consciously decided to focus your strength, meditation, thinking, and pursuits on Jesus and His beauty?

Messengers who are fixated on their assignments limit their usefulness to God, but those who set their minds and imaginations on the pursuit of the beauty of God will be incredibly useful to God, whether they are publicly known in this age or not.

Do you treasure and enjoy the priestly life, or are you more like the priests in Malachi's book? Do you seek communion and deep relationship with YHWH through His Spirit, or do you do what is necessary to obtain some blessing and benefits and escape the judgment of hell? Do you long for God, or are you content with a little "anointing"?

Are you transactional with God like the priests? If God challenged the priests to stop their ministry, would God challenge us to shut down our church meetings?

If God gave a warning to the priesthood formed by the Mosaic covenant, what would He say to the priesthood formed by the gift of His own Spirit? Are we priests like John? Or are we more like the priests Malachi rebuked?

John's entire life made a statement. John was a priest who could not enjoy his "inheritance" in the temple. Instead, he lived a limited lifestyle in a small place gripped by anticipation for God to come to His people. All of John's hope was connected to the return of the Bridegroom who had appeared on Mount Sinai. John had no other inheritance, no other reward, and no other joy. John's life was a statement to the nation —a prophetic call to live by the same values.

John's life was unusual, but his life was similar to all those listed in Hebrews 11. The life of faith is uncomfortable and unsettled because it

---

[12]For more on this see, *Discipleship Begins with Beholding.*

demonstrates we have set all our hope on a divine Person who is not presently here but is coming. The great saints of Hebrews 11 had very different lives, but this is the one common theme that marked all their lives.

If you want to follow the ancient path of faith, your life will be defined by a permanent ache, a dissatisfaction cured only by the return of the Bridegroom.

What If God Reduces You?

If you choose the wilderness, it will slowly close in on you and lead you to make a conscious choice to pursue communion with God first, reject self-promotion, and delight in the exaltation of Jesus.

You will know the wilderness has done its work in your heart when you do not want to leave.

Embracing the wilderness does not mean pursuing isolation. It means you confront your pursuit of a public profile and the hunger for attention and notoriety. It is not a decision to ignore people; it is a decision to embrace things that seem "small," like discipling a few people in front of you. In the process, you discover a path to life and experience a life that is not possible as long as you are living for crowds and influence.

If you have an assignment for public ministry, you *especially* need to embrace the wilderness and find your identity in standing before the Lord. You must minister to God first and become content with whatever public ministry He causes to flow out of that. Those who avoid the wilderness and find their identity in their assignment become a danger to themselves and God's people because they crave crowds and attention. And that appetite is destructive. God may or may not hide you to fulfill your assignment. That is His prerogative. However, if you are unwilling to embrace His hiddenness, it is a major warning sign that your identity is not yet settled in God.

What if God uses you in intercession to bring revival, but He uses someone else as the visible messenger? Is that okay with you? Or do you need the attention that comes with being the public messenger? Can you rejoice if Jesus' fame increases and it does not bring any secondary benefit for your profile? Jesus never invited John to join His team. What if Jesus does not share His stage with you? *Is that okay with you?* Or are you living for Jesus' fame *and* your own?

John had a national assignment, but he had to be cut off from the crowds to settle the issues in his own soul. Too many people pursue crowds to fill a void that is still lacking in their own soul. And many find significance in notoriety, so they define impact by human attention rather than the eye of God.

Perhaps God will use you in a public way. If so, you better embrace the wilderness now, or you can become destructive to yourself and others when accolades come. Perhaps He will keep you hidden. If so, you need to realize your public profile is not a statement of His affection for you or your impact.

God often keeps some of His favorite messengers primarily for Himself.

What if God appoints another messenger to the public stage because He values communion with you more than public ministry? Would that be okay with you? *There are times God will not appoint you to a public ministry simply because He is jealous for you.*

Daniel was given some of the most profound prophecies in the New Testament, wrote the book referenced by Jesus more than any other book,[13] and became a biblical prototype of the end-time church. However, he was never a public messenger, and his prominence seems to have faded as he grew older. *Perhaps God loved Daniel so much He kept more and more of Daniel for Himself.* Far too many people constantly chase an illusion of success, thinking the more prominent they are, the more successful they will be. God may frustrate their attempts to "succeed" because He wants more of them for Himself.

What if God wants to pull you aside for Himself? What if God wants to *reduce* you? What if God wants you to see *His* vision and forget your own? Typically, the prophets in the Bible were not leaders with great responsibility. Sometimes God does not give people aspects of leadership because He wants more of them for Himself.[14]

I know a man who can only speak an hour or two a day because of a vocal injury. Many people see that injury as a tragedy, but the inability to engage in human conversation has forced him to seek internal

---

[13]See *Son of Man: The Gospel of Daniel 7.*

[14]This, of course, does not mean God is less interested in people with demanding assignments. God deeply loved Moses and David, and both had demanding assignments.

communion. What if God took his voice to limit his human conversations because God was jealous for his attention? Ironically, this man has become a global speaker who is sought out across the world, even though he can barely speak for an hour or two a day. His inability to spend hours speaking with humans has produced a life of fellowship with God which has given the few words that he can speak profound weight. Do we know this kind of God? Do we grasp the depth of God's desire for communion?

When you choose the wilderness, God may lead you to a place of weakness. Many people resist this because they love strength, but strength is not the way of the cross. Do you want power, strength, and grandeur? Or are you willing to embrace weakness? If you have strength, you may get human accolades. If you embrace weakness, you may be embarrassed at times, but you will experience the power and life of God.

Perhaps you have not been able to understand what God is doing in your life because you are seeking public impact, but He is inviting you to embrace the wilderness and allow Him to fulfill your assignment His way.

The Lord may fulfill your assignment by reducing you.

God Knows Your Address

It can be easy to embrace an assignment from the Lord while difficult to surrender to His leadership over that assignment. Anything you make happen in your own strength, you will have to maintain in your own strength.

God knows your address. If God has spoken something, He can bring it to pass.

Moses was in the wilderness as a failure moments before God sent him back to Egypt. Elijah suddenly appeared when he was needed. David was destined to be king but herded sheep as a young man. John the Baptist was hidden away in the wilderness for decades. Paul was in a small prayer meeting in Antioch when the Holy Spirit spoke and set him and Barnabas on a course that changed world history.

You must submit to God's sovereignty over your assignment.

Time after time, the Bible demonstrates, if God needs a person, He knows where to find them and how to raise them up. If He wants you to be a public voice to a people, He knows how and when to put you in front of those people. When you have a promise from God, you do not need to try to get His attention or impress Him. Your part is faithfulness, especially in the small and the mundane. Joseph was destined to rule Egypt but was forgotten in a prison due to an unjust accusation. However, in a single day, God moved Joseph from the prison to Pharaoh's palace. Not everyone has that kind of assignment, but if you have a promise from God, you do not need to make it happen.

Breaking Free of Fear

Many people who truly want to serve God live in fear of missing their assignment. They are concerned their own weakness or one wrong decision will keep them from fulfilling what God has for them. Fear of missing an assignment is typically connected to three main issues:

- *Lack of confidence in God's sovereignty*—We often have more confidence in our weakness and our ability to hinder the purposes of God than we do in God's ability to bring to pass what He has spoken. We overlook the fact that God demonstrates His glory in using the unqualified—and we are *all* unqualified.
- *Finding fulfillment in our assignment*—Sometimes we fear missing an assignment because our sense of identity and fulfillment is more tied to the assignment than it is to God. Our fear of missing our assignment is really the fear of living an unfulfilled life.
- *An incorrect definition of success*—Many people are burdened with unbiblical definitions of success, which cause them to misinterpret their assignment. This comes from evaluating our situation based on human wisdom rather than God's perspective. It is possible to be successful in your assignment but unable to see it because you consider your assignment too small or too ordinary.

John's entire life was small. Most of Paul's ministry was in small contexts. We assume small things have no impact, so we have little vision for them. However, most of Jesus' life was "small." Our God loves the small, and the visible scope of your assignment might be smaller than you imagine it to be. If God has given you a larger assignment, you still need a vision to embrace the small because God prepares people for larger more public assignments through faithfulness in small, hidden things. If you skip this step, it will cause significant issues when you are given more to steward.

God may lead you on a path that does not seem to make sense, and if you are not confident in His leadership, you will avoid things you think are too small for you or things you think do not advance your assignment. Anyone who despises the small has an overinflated view of their own importance and holds back the fullness of their assignment by avoiding the process God has prescribed.

Many people neglect the small things because they have unbiblical definitions of impact. Because we are too easily impressed with human definitions of success, we forget Jesus warned much of what we consider great is not truly great and much of what we overlook is actually great.[1] Our definitions of greatness are so distorted many would not consider Paul a success if he had lived in our generation.

This is particularly a problem in this generation. Because of the rise of mass media, megacities, and megachurches, a pastor can now feel like a failure pastoring a few hundred people even though his congregation is larger than the vast majority of churches in human history. Virtually every Christian in history is unsuccessful when evaluated according to modern definitions of success that dominate Instagram.

Virtually everything in the this age is small in light of what is coming in the age to come.[2] You must abandon the idea that you only do the small things so you can graduate to the bigger things. While there can certainly be a progression in an assignment and in the grace of God on a person, you do not necessarily do small things so you can move on to bigger things. God delights in what humans see as small, and wrong views of success cause you to devalue what God values.

Submitting to God's Leadership

You must submit to God's leadership of your life in every area—even in your mistakes. You must have more confidence in His sovereignty than your failures because God often uses failure as part of the process of preparation. Failure leads you to know your own weakness and encounter the strength and mercy of God. Without failure, you have too much confidence in our own strength and ability.[3]

God will use success, failure, excitement, and disappointment to make you like Himself if you will cooperate with Him. Your weakness does not automatically disqualify you because God did not choose you on the basis of your strength. Peter was a bold, brash leader until he

[1] 1 Samuel 16:7; Matthew 8:11–12; 20:16; 19:30; Mark 10:31; Luke 13:28–30.

[2] 1 Corinthians 2:9

[3] Obviously, we should not pursue failures.

failed by publicly denying Jesus three times.[4] Peter's failure prepared him to serve the people because it broke his pride. If Jesus matured Peter through failure, He can do the same for you. God will use the crucible of failure to expose issues and to prepare you for an assignment.

Sometimes God will advance your assignment. Sometimes He will bring it to an end. Sometimes He will promote you. Sometimes He will reduce you. If you belong to Him, He gets to do what He wants with you. You have been bought with a price.[5] Your life, message, ministry, business, body, past, present, and future do not belong to you. God gets to do whatever He wants with you. Your assignment is important to Him, but it is not the basis of your relationship with Him. God frequently delays an assignment for His purposes, and these delays are excruciating if your identity is wrapped up in your assignment. *God will use your fixation on your assignment, and your frustration over it, to purge and mature you.*

The Illusion of Human Potential

One of the great deceptions in this generation is the illusion that anyone can be anything they want. While we should advocate for equal opportunity, the reality is humans are not equal in any way when it comes to gifts and abilities. God simply does not give each person the same gifts, abilities, or assignments.

The illusion that anyone can be anything fuels a subtle lie that our destinies are in our hands. This lie is endlessly propagated by stories of men and women who seem to be self-made and fulfill their dreams through their own endurance and fortitude. When people believe this lie, they waste years trying to become "successful." Many imagine an endless ocean of possibilities, and this is often paralyzing. Human envy causes us to compete with others. Sometimes we despise their gifts, and other times we desire their gifts.

You cannot be anything you want to be, and when your identity is settled, you will begin to enjoy who you are.

---

[4]Matthew 26:69–75; Mark 14:66–72; Luke 22:54–62; John 18:15–18, 25–27.

[5]Acts 20:28; 1 Corinthians 6:19–20.

If you want to completely fulfill your assignment, you must allow God to reduce you to the gifts He has given you. You have to have courage to break the fantasy of human potential and operate in the gifts He has given you. You cannot do everything in life, but you can do well what you have been given.

God's gifts and His rewards are two very different things. The gifts God gives are not a statement of His affection. They are not given for our sake; they are for the sake of the body.[6] We often try to use our gifts for the sake of our own success, but this is not a biblical way of thinking. Our gifts were not given to us for our success; they were given for the benefit of the body. The body needs us, and we need the body,[7] so if we neglect our gift, the body suffers. The health of the body is at stake in whether we will choose to fully steward the gifts we have been given instead of longing for the gifts given to others.

You have to break free of envy, realizing that the gifts we have been given are given *by God*.[8] The vast majority of what you can do and the potential you have were determined by your birth and by the gifts God has given you. What God has given you comes with limitations and opportunities. You must submit to the limitations and embrace the opportunities.

Embrace the Small

Many people will embrace a process if it secures a desired outcome, but God asks you to submit to His process for the sake of transformation and let Him determine the outcome of your life.

God is incredibly patient and willing to endure delays, failures, and shortcomings to produce His nature in a person. God typically matures people through a mix of heightened spiritual activity and longer periods of growth and development. God will often speak clearly accompanied by an unusual experience of His power to produce a sudden shift in your life.

---

[6] 1 Corinthians 12:7; Ephesians 4:7–12; 1 Peter 4:10–11.

[7] Romans 12:4–5; 1 Corinthians 12:12–26.

[8] Romans 12:6; 1 Corinthians 7:7; 12:7, 11; Ephesians 4:7.

After speaking dramatically, God will lead you through a period of growth and development where life seems more normal and mundane. For example, John's and Jesus' births were both miraculous and highly unusual. But then each of them had to grow in wisdom and stature[9] for three decades before the next season of unusual power.

You have to learn to value the moment when God releases His power on you and the long period of growth and development. People tend to value one or the other, but both are a critical part of formation. You must receive something that only comes from heaven, but you also have to cooperate with His process of maturity.

Faithfulness in the ordinary and mundane over time is what positions you for what God has for you. *"He who is faithful in little will be given much."*[10] A series of small obediences in the same direction is what prepares you to fulfill your assignment. Sometimes big decisions are required, but the small, consistent decisions move you in the direction God wants you to go.

Your spirit grows stronger the way the body does. Small, consistent actions over time produce profound physical strength, and the same is true for the spirit. Many people have a body in poor shape because they do not want to embrace routine daily exercise, and the same is true for the spirit. Many people expect to be great if they live through something dramatic like the end of the age, but they are not living carefully and faithfully now. This is like a teenager who expects to play in the World Cup but has never played sports.

Far more is at stake in your seemingly small daily decisions than you think.

You can become so driven by your sense of an assignment that you will be tempted to "fulfill" that ministry at all costs. When this happens, you begin to view people, resources, and relationships as assets for your own "calling." This produces a tremendous amount of networking, and relationships become very utilitarian. It's a subtle deception that feels godly because it often includes tremendous time and sacrifice for the sake of the "mission."

---

[9]Luke 1:80; 2:40

[10]Matthew 25:21; Luke 16:10–12; 19:17.

When people become an end to your means, even a "ministry" end, you have lost the way of the cross. The reality is that serving people is inefficient. It involves joy, patience, pain, and discouragement, and it takes tremendous time. We do not always see an immediate benefit from our investment in others. Many times the people God puts in your life will not help you advance your assignment.

Enjoying God's Leadership of Your Assignment

When you let the Lord control the scope of your assignment, it liberates you:

- It liberates you to joyfully engage in things that seem small.
- It liberates you to embrace the people in front of you even if they do not seem "useful" to your assignment.
- It liberates you from using human strategies to accomplish something.

This is why you must embrace weakness. It takes profound weakness to acknowledge you cannot fulfill your assignment and have to depend on God to do what only He can do.

There are the two paths to burnout for Christian workers:

- If you use human wisdom, strategies, and networking to "fulfill" your assignment, you will have to continue your assignment in your own strength, and it will exhaust you.
- If you step into your assignment through God's leadership yet neglect the place of ongoing communion, you will also become exhausted.

When God gives someone an assignment, God frequently gives a person a summary of their assignment before they are ready to fulfill that assignment. For example, Joseph had dreams about his future, and Paul was told he would be an apostle to the Gentiles fifteen years before he was sent.

While this seems confusing, God does this for a number of reasons:

- An assignment is usually accompanied by tests and trials, and the assignment is one form of motivation to continue through difficult seasons of preparation.
- God will use your desire to fulfill an assignment to motivate you to pursue Him. In the process, He will transform you so that you love Him more than an assignment.
- Knowing an assignment can help you make decisions that shape your direction in life.
- The process of fulfilling your assignment tests you and exposes the key issues in your life that need to be addressed.

God frequently initiates opposition to test and train us. Joseph was sold into slavery, put into prison, and forgotten, but he recognized it all as the design of God.[11] David was put under the leadership of an envious king who pursued him to take his life. However, the test David faced with Saul prepared David to be king. Daniel was carried away as a slave as a young man, but his life in Babylon produced the book of Daniel.

Sometimes the thing you think is the primary hindrance to your assignment is God's tool to prepare you for your assignment.

If you do not understand God's ways, you can resist His wisdom. The key to being successful is *perseverance*. God does not evaluate us the way we evaluate ourselves. The great heroes of the faith fulfilled their assignment through perseverance, not through perfection. It is easy for the Lord to fulfill an assignment, and much more difficult to shape a person to be in agreement with Him, fully submitted to Him, and more interested in His glory than their own. John fulfilled his assignment in a few months, but God shaped John over a lifetime.

A mature vessel:

- Actively pursues obedience but is internally at rest about their assignment because they realize their assignment is for God's glory and not their own.
- Is content with God's sovereign leadership over their assignment. They are willing for the assignment to be bigger or smaller than they imagined.

---

[11]Genesis 45:5–8.

- Finds their satisfaction in their obedience and not in their prominence. They are settled in God's sovereignty over their life, but not passive.

The Deadly Enemy of Comparison

If you do not define impact correctly, over time you will succumb to the deadly enemy of comparison. When you come under the influence of comparison, you begin chasing other people's assignments. When someone else prospers in their assignment, you will either burn with jealousy or desperately seek to imitate their assignment to obtain the same "success" and accolades they receive.

Never take on someone else's assignment for the sake of impact.

Comparison is the fastest way out of your assignment. It drives you to pursue what is popular in the moment, and you cannot steward your assignment if you are chasing everyone else's. If John had compared his circle of influence in the wilderness to the priests in Jerusalem, he would have abandoned his assignment.

Everyone likes to think they are "cutting edge," but the reality is the vast majority of people want to be part of what is popular and accepted. It is a very, very small number of people who are willing to truly step outside what is accepted and celebrated. Being different has little value in and of itself, but John lived differently because he saw something coming that others did not see. He lived in light of what he saw, and that made him seem strange to most people.[12]

You cannot gain clarity from the Scripture, live in light of Jesus' return, speak with weight, or be prophetic if you are chasing the trends of the moment with everyone else.

Identity and Comparison

God may delay your assignment until the issue of identity has been settled because He wants you to labor with Him as a son or a daughter, not as a hired servant.

When God delays your assignment, it is a profound act of kindness that demonstrates He is more concerned with who you become than what you can produce.

If you allow God to settle your identity, you will find:

---

[12]Matthew 11:18.

- *Freedom to be yourself and operate in the way God has gifted you*—Far too many people try to emulate the gifting God has given other people because they are not yet comfortable in the way God has made them.

- *Freedom to receive from and enjoy the gifts God has put in others*—When you are insecure, it hinders your ability to receive from others because you evaluate their gifts with envious eyes.

- *Freedom to celebrate the success of others and work for their success*—Insecurity causes us to see others as competition and seek to protect ourselves from any loss from another's success instead of liberating people to enter their calling.

- *Freedom to take on whatever assignment the Lord gives*—Many people avoid assignments the Lord gives because they seem too small or too insignificant.

- *Freedom to succeed or fail*—The fear of failure can be paralyzing when the issue of identity is not settled, but the truth is God enjoys us in success and failure. In fact, God may enjoy our willingness to risk even when it results in failure more than the safety of a comfortable success.

Your identity must be in the fact God loves you and values you.

When your identity is settled, you will find the courage to choose the wilderness and walk the ancient paths that many avoid. If your identity is not settled, you will constantly be chasing wrong definitions of success and seeking affirmation.

The Path to John's Joy

John understood who he was. He was not the Bridegroom. He was the *friend* of the Bridegroom—the shoshbin. The shoshbin's primary joy was in someone else's inheritance, not his own. John was able to enter into God's joy because he knew who he was, he knew who Jesus was, and he took delight in Jesus receiving what belonged to Him alone.

John found his primary joy in God's joy.

Only deep, authentic love can take more pleasure in someone else's success than our own. Only deep love can take genuine joy in someone else receiving a reward that does not benefit us. John had cultivated this kind of love for YHWH during his years in the wilderness.

John loved Jesus so deeply he was delighted by Jesus' success and his loss. Do we love Jesus the same way? We have the testimony of Jesus' suffering for our sake that John did not have. We have received eternal life, the indwelling Spirit, and fellowship with God. How much *more* should we delight in Jesus' receiving His inheritance?

He Must Increase

John took great delight in Jesus' success, but as we saw, his disciples were deeply bothered by it. They did not fully perceive the value of who Jesus was, so they preferred their influence as part of John's ministry to pursuing Jesus. Their pain over their loss of influence kept them from enjoying Jesus' ministry.

If the loss of influence or perceived impact is more important to you than the invitation for greater intimacy with God, your life is out of alignment.

John knew that a man can only receive true spiritual authority if it is given from heaven, so he was content with what heaven had given him, and he could freely celebrate what had been given to Jesus. John's disciples could not yet celebrate Jesus' success because they feared it would come at their own expense.

Far too many are trying to protect their influence and their gift. As a result, they do not fully support and celebrate others. Envy poisons the way we relate to each other, and it is a significant hindrance in the kingdom. Imagine how quickly the church could advance if we all truly enjoyed seeing everyone operate in their maximum capacity and gave our lives to see *others* maximize their own gifting in God?

The church is not a zero-sum game. We do not need others to "lose" so we can "win."

Can you imagine a school teacher who wanted to withhold certain subjects from students in order to maintain an advantage over them? This would be ludicrous, and yet it happens in the church any time a person wants to gather people to their gifting. It is not biblical to try to gather people to yourself on the basis of your gifting and make them dependent on your ministry. The biblical model is to invest your gifting in others with the hope that they will receive everything they can and, if possible, exceed you. As we have seen, this is exactly what John did. He poured his life into his disciples, and two of them went on and became a part of Jesus' team—a privilege denied to John.

Government in the church should be on the basis of the witness of the Spirit, not gifting. Of course, some gifting must be present for a person to lead, but a leader may or may not be the most gifted person. A leader exists to empower others to mature in their gifts. A pastor needs to be able to teach but may or may not be the best Bible teacher in the congregation. Leaders must be secure enough to allow the gifts of the body to flow (with proper order, of course.)[1] Likewise, people must honor and submit to those the Lord has set in place[2] and not use their gifts to supplant or undermine leaders.

Finding True Joy

We need more examples of men and women driven—compelled—by Jesus' worth and not their own success.

---

[1] 1 Corinthians 14:26–40.

[2] 1 Thessalonians 5:12–13; 1 Timothy 5:17–20; Hebrews 13:7, 17.

If you relentlessly pursue joy in yourself, it will remain elusive because you were not created to be self-centered, but when you find your joy in Him, you access an ocean of infinite joy—joy unspeakable and full of glory.[3]

The seraphim around the throne are captured by the beauty of the One on the throne. He fascinates them endlessly, and they find great delight in Him. They are so overcome by His majesty that they do not find delight in themselves, nor do they seek to because they are focused on a superior pleasure. If this is true of the seraphim who look at God, how much more should it be true of humans who have the living God dwelling inside them and were created to reflect His image?

The seraphim cry out, "Holy, holy, holy," *endlessly*[4] in response to His beauty. Their cry is a witness to us that any human who embarks on an unbridled pursuit of joy in God will discover a realm of beauty, pleasure, and joy most humans cannot fathom.

The Tyranny of Your Own Assignment

If you want to live New Testament Christianity, you must think like Jesus:

> *Have this mind among yourselves, which is yours in Christ Jesus, who, though he was in the form of God, did not count equality with God a thing to be grasped, but emptied himself, by taking the form of a servant, being born in the likeness of men. And being found in human form, he humbled himself by becoming obedient to the point of death, even death on a cross. Therefore God has highly exalted him and bestowed on him the name that is above every name. (Philippians 2:5–9)*

Jesus was exalted because He willingly used His power and privilege for the sake of others. This is what the Father is looking for in His people. Those who think like this will be exalted with Jesus to rule in the kingdom. You are called to lay down your life for the body. You should take great delight in surrendering your own honor and success for the

---

[3] 1 Peter 1:8.

[4] Revelation 4:8.

sake of another who may surpass you. There should be no competition or envy among us.[5]

If your own destiny dominates your thinking, you will make decisions that preserve your life, business, ministries, and future. This is not the way of the cross, nor the path to life.

Self-preservation hinders the work of God. It was true for Jesus, and it is true for us. The way to find freedom from self-preservation is to find a higher love and a higher joy than what you have found in yourself. Jesus did not preserve His life. He laid it down to secure His joy.[6] Should your path be any different?

There are three main ways your obsession with your own life hinders God's work through you:

1. *You will hold on to things God would have you lay down.* This includes good things, successful things, and even ministry assignments. It can include a personal dream that may not be God's dream for you. There are times He asks you to lay something down. There are times things need to die. There are times influence needs to fade and something "big" needs to be traded for something "small." There may be times He will ask you to start over.

2. *You will tend to avoid things God asks you to do.* This may be a specific assignment or simply instructions you find in the Scripture. You may avoid a task you need to take on because it seems difficult and may involve suffering or sacrifice with no visible reward in this age. Or you may avoid an assignment simply because it seems small. This is especially a problem in our generation because of the seducing possibilities of popularity.

3. *You live by your own expectations.* People tend to form expectations about how their assignment will come to pass, when the assignment will come to pass, and what the assignment will look like when it is fulfilled. These assumptions about the

---

[5] 1 Corinthians 3:1–4; 11:18; 2 Corinthians 12:20; Galatians 5:15, 19–21; James 3:16; 4:1–2.

[6] Hebrews 12:2.

future can keep you from wholeheartedly embracing your present assignment. The Bible repeatedly demonstrates God's promises are often fulfilled in ways we would never expect. In reality, your assignment will be more difficult than you imagined, take longer than you anticipated, and feel smaller than you imagined. It is likely your assignment will not match your expectations.

John's entire life was small. He lived in a small community, discipled a small group of young men, and never left the wilderness. Furthermore, his assignment did not bring any great reward or personal benefits. It led him to prison and an early death. His prophecies were not fulfilled in his lifetime, and the nation did not ultimately repent. He lived his entire life to prepare the way for Jesus, but he apparently only met Jesus one time,[7] and Jesus did not invite John to become a disciple. When John's assignment was finished, he ended up in jail and was then executed when Herod made a rash promise at a drunken party. We do not know what the Lord revealed to John, but it is likely John's assignment did not end the way he expected.

John embraced a way of life we normally avoid, and his life was not successful by our standards. However, as John's success began to fade, he spoke about Jesus and said, *"I am filled with joy at His success."*[8] Could it be that we find it so difficult to find true joy because we are looking for that joy in *our* assignments rather than in *Jesus'* success? Overflowing, abundant joy is available to us if we live like John regardless of the way our lives unfold.

It's time to join the Father in His glorious plan to exalt His Son, and it's time to discover the joy and freedom of no longer living under the tyranny of your assignment.

---

[7]John's comment that He did not know Jesus until the Spirit rested on Him (John 1:33–34) indicates John did not know Jesus at least not as an adult.

[8]John 3:29 (NLT).

Living for His Reward

If Jesus' joy and His reward became your driving obsession what assignment would you eagerly embrace that up until now you have neglected, resisted, or not even considered? What would you let go of that you are still clinging to?

If you are a slave to your own assignment, you will likely refuse the difficult and small assignments which are the heart of the kingdom. Furthermore, you will not manage risk properly. Some avoid *necessary* risks because of the fear of loss while others embrace *unnecessary* risks hoping for attention and accolades. It is easy to pursue safety in a life that is too comfortable or to seek an "exciting" life to avoid boredom.

When you become a friend of the Bridegroom and delight in His voice, you begin to make very different decisions. You will become a joyful laborer in the Father's plan to exalt His Son, and your life will begin to break free of the self-centeredness that dominates this age. You will discover a new realm of freedom and joy when you are no longer slave to your own reputation and your own success. You will find small assignments are just as meaningful as large ones because they bring Jesus great delight. Your "profile" and "success" may go up or go down, but it will not disrupt your joy.

Many people rejoice more in their voice and their ministry than in Jesus' voice.

John found his ultimate satisfaction when YHWH received what He wanted from His people. We can hardly imagine what could be accomplished if an entire generation decided to seek our joy in Him. We would find it just as joyful to have a worldwide "impact" as to stay hidden if it advances Jesus' joy. We would not fear death or avoid difficulty. Poverty or riches would be the same to us if they advanced His kingdom. Fame or obscurity would not matter one bit. "Small" or "big" would not be a factor in our decision making. If He wanted to reduce our influence or comfort for the sake of His purposes, we would gladly comply and enjoy the increase in his fame.

In short, when Jesus' joy becomes our great ambition, the church will be an unstoppable force in the world.

It's time to stop looking for hidden wilderness seasons that prepare us for seasons of blessing. It's time for an entire generation to choose a life in the wilderness for the sake of Jesus' joy.

Seeking Our Reward When Jesus Does Not Have His

God has committed to partner with His people to exalt His Son, and we hinder the purposes of God when we find more joy in our success than in Jesus' reward.

It is especially tragic that we rarely recognize this error or seek to correct it. Instead, we continue to eagerly pursue it. Year after year, innumerable books are written, sermons preached, and conferences convened to help us find *our* destiny, *our* calling, and *our* inheritance. Based on the conferences and books which permeate the affluent Christian world, many of us are obsessed with finding fulfillment in this life. There seems to be an insatiable appetite for *our* destiny and *our* inheritance while we pursue *our* passions.

In light of all this, we need to ask a serious question: How can we possibly seek our own fulfillment and "destiny" when Jesus has not yet received His inheritance?

If Jesus is the uncreated God, if He literally gave His own life for our sake, and if He is the One we love more than any other, how can we possibly pursue our inheritance when He has not yet received His? What do the angels think when they see Jesus the crucified and exalted Man sitting at the right hand of the Father and *waiting* for His inheritance while the people He purchased with His own blood are consumed by the frenzied pursuit of their personal destiny?

Our lives demonstrate we lack revelation of who Jesus is, what He has done for us, and what He deserves. Jesus is the only Human who deserves His destiny, and He has not yet received it.

The fact that people tirelessly labor for their own reward and success while Jesus does not yet have His is sheer madness. It is a treadmill of frantic activity that is ultimately not going anywhere. Tragically, by the time most people grasp this, they are either offended by unmet expectations or so old most of the strength of their lives has already been expended.

I guarantee you, if you prioritize Jesus' inheritance, He will take care of yours.

We should be driven by one agenda in this age: for Jesus to receive the reward of His suffering. It does not make any sense to spend our lives pursuing *our* fulfillment and destiny when Jesus has not received His reward. We need to commit now to live "unfulfilled" lives of ache and longing until Jesus receives His inheritance. We are pilgrims and strangers without an inheritance in this age.[9] This must affect how we build ministries and how we think about our assignments.

It's time to disciple a generation to embrace a truly radical cause: *It's time to challenge an entire generation to make Jesus' inheritance its primary goal and to forget about its inheritance when Jesus does not have His.*

---

[9]Hebrews 11:9–10, 16, 24–26, 36–40.

Information without Demonstration Is Hypocrisy

You have far more affordable access to the Bible, resources about the Bible, and translations of the Bible than any other generation. Because of the digital revolution in the last decade, access to the Bible has now grown far beyond what anyone in history could have imagined. The world has never been this immersed in Scripture, and it is increasing rapidly.[1]

Most believers throughout history had limited access to the Bible. Often, there was only one complete copy in a local church or synagogue. In the last few centuries, some had access to one copy of the Bible in a home. The saints of the past would be shocked at the access we have to the Bible. It would stun them to know that we can read or listen to the Bible with very little effort at any time and in any place, and they would be equally astounded at the number of biblical resources we have access to.

You have nearly unlimited access to the Bible in a multitude of translations, along with innumerable resources. The prophets did not have what you have. The disciples did not have what you have. The reformers did not have what you have. Can you imagine how excited the apostle Paul would be if he had the tools you have?

Have you recognized the riches that have been freely handed to you? Right now God is flooding the earth with the Word of God, and it is totally unprecedented.

The challenge of our unequaled access to the Bible is that people tend not to value things that are free and easily available. To use an idiom, "Familiarity breeds contempt." For example, a couple who is

---

[1] Tools like the https://bibleproject.com/ could not be imagined just a few years ago, and yet now they are instantly and freely available worldwide.

dating deeply values every moment they can get together because time together is precious and limited. When they are married and have constant access to each other, though, they begin to devalue each other over time. Can you honestly say that you value the Bible on your smartphone as much as you would value the Word if there were only a single, shared copy in your entire church?

You have an unprecedented opportunity to deeply meditate on the Word of God, and you must seize the opportunity.

God leads history, and He is flooding the world with the Bible because He has a very specific purpose in mind. The Lord wants this generation to devour His Word in a way no previous generation has been able to. It is time to seize this extraordinary opportunity to devour the Word of God and immerse yourself in it. The Word needs to become like food to you, and you need to "eat the scroll" like the prophets of old.[2] Our computers, tablets, and smartphones must become modern scrolls as we take this unparalleled opportunity to meditate on the Word night and day.

God is handing us unprecedented access to the Word so an entire generation can devour the Word the way John did. But if you want to respond to the invitation you need to choose the wilderness.

You may hope the Holy Spirit will give you a new insight or revelation through some sort of astonishing encounter. But you cannot expect God to speak new things if you do not value what He has already spoken. While some may overlook the treasure we have been given, millions are going to recognize the riches we hold in our hands, and a people are going to emerge who are more soaked in Scripture than any generation in history. Think about that carefully: *God is about to produce the most Bible-soaked generation in all history.*

We should seek to make the Word of God, not just a matter of discipline, but a source of entertainment. We should read the Word, sing the Word, meditate on the Word, and speak it to each other. We should also take the Word and turn it into prayer because it has been given to us as conversation material. Loving the Word does not mean reading as quickly as possible; it means loving meditation on the Word and allowing that Word to affect our spirits and bring the

---

[2]Jeremiah 15:16; Ezekiel 3:1–3; Revelation 10:9–11.

transformation God wants. God wants a people to take the Word so seriously that they cooperate with the Holy Spirit and allow Him to produce something only He can produce—a life that is a living demonstration of the Word of God.

Biblical information is good, but information without a demonstration is hypocrisy.

It is obviously hypocritical when a minister speaks out against certain expressions of immorality but freely indulges in pornography or affairs. However, hypocrisy is not always this overt. It can be subtle. If you challenge the culture by what you say, but not by how you live, then you are in hypocrisy.

Hypocrisy exists whenever the way you live is out of sync with what you say you believe.

By this definition, we all have a degree of hypocrisy. However, do we recognize our hypocrisy, and are we allowing God to remove it? The vast majority of Christians *say* Jesus will return, judge this age, reward His people, and produce a new earth in which what is valued in this age will become worthless. However, these "beliefs" have almost no effect on their daily lifestyles. Churches continue to operate as though the present condition is permanent rather than an aberration—a strange moment in time during which Jesus is not on the planet.

Is this not hypocrisy?

The church is meant to be a living witness of the truth that provokes and confronts, but too often we have settled for trying to confront people with ideas. Until our ideas and beliefs radically shape who we are and we become a living, breathing demonstration of those ideas, we cannot challenge the darkness in this age. Sometimes the truth we speak is rejected as empty and hollow words because it has not transformed us and people easily see through this façade.

We may argue passionately for certain aspects of morality, but do we have the same zeal of words of Scripture that confront our own lifestyles? If we only submit to the elements of the Word which seem reasonable to us, why can others not do the same?

Could it be that our gospel preaching produces so little transformation because that word has not truly transformed us?

Do we connect people to beliefs and doctrines but not necessarily to a way of living that is a wholehearted expression of those beliefs?

The sad truth is that we often live nearly the same as the culture and society around us. You are not called to argue with others about what they believe; you are called to *demonstrate* the nature of God in the way you live.

As Leonard Ravenhill used to say:

The world does not need a new definition of Christianity, it needs a new demonstration of Christianity.[3]

The Biblical Witness of the Gospel

The Bible says the Word of God does not return void,[4] but when read in context, it means the promises of God are not empty—they will be fulfilled by God. In reality, information about God can be spoken with little effect when it is delivered by a messenger in whom that information has not produced any transformation.

The church is designed to be God's witness, a legal evidence of His Word in the courtroom of this age.[5] Are you living evidence of the validity of the Word of God? Do you confront the world with the way you live, or do you live a better (more moral) version of what the world aspires to? Have you exchanged morality for the true transformation of the Spirit?

The gospel is not validated or primarily communicated by the logic of the message. The gospel is designed to be communicated by people who have been so transformed by that gospel that they are the living embodiment of their message and obvious demonstration of its power. People are meant to *see* the gospel not simply *hear* it. We have written endless books trying to perfect what we *say*, but have we given the same tenacity to what people *see*?

A person can explain the effects of a jet engine with charts, graphs, diagrams, and numbers. That is nothing, though, compared to standing next to a runway when a jet races down the runway and the roar of the

---

[3]A phrase often repeated by Leonard Ravenhill.

[4]Isaiah 46:10; 55:11.

[5]For more on this, see *What Does God Want? Aligning Your Life with God's Desire.*

jet's engines shakes your entire being. The *experience* of a jet engine is completely different from the *explanation* of a jet engine.

The gospel was never meant to be a technical analysis of theological information that gives people a lot of explanations but no real experience of the thing being explained. God always intended the gospel to be communicated by people who have been transformed by the message and now live that message out.

How do you know when the Word becomes flesh? Heaven responds when you speak Bible verses.

Ministry to God

We are accustomed to forming *communicators*, but we need to learn how to form *priests*. John's priestly life set him apart in his generation and positioned him to fulfill his messenger assignment.

When the temple was destroyed and Israel was sent into exile, the synagogue was the structure utilized to maintain the teaching of the Word and Israel's national identity. The synagogue was not wrong, but it gained prominence because the temple had been lost. The synagogue was a place of teaching, prayer, and community. The temple included those elements, but it was not defined by them. It was defined by ongoing ministry around God's presence.

We have forgotten the church is not modeled after the synagogue, but after the temple.[6]

When the leaders were gathered at the church in Antioch, Luke said they were "ministering" to the Lord,[7] using a word that described the priestly ministry in Jerusalem. The point was clear—the church in Antioch was a temple, and its people were priests. The temple had gone viral into the nations, and Paul and Barnabas were sent out by the Spirit to reproduce what was happening in Antioch. All too often we have followed a "synagogue" model instead of a "temple" model.

Synagogues need leaders who can teach and administrate. Temples require priests who minister to God and then teach and lead. The difference is critical. We know how to train people to think and to teach, but do we know

---

[6]For more on this see *Discipleship Begins with Beholding.*

[7]Acts 13:2.

how to train priests to minister to God? The priesthood is our only eternal assignment and yet we given little focused attention to it.

You can teach people to craft messages, but you cannot make them messengers.

Ministry to God sets the context for properly handling the Word of God, because whatever we focus our primary attention on is what we will begin to imitate. If ministers do not prioritize ministry to God, their preaching begins to resemble popular motivational speakers.

John was clearly one of the most powerful messengers in biblical history. However, if we fixate on his powerful preaching, we miss who he was and how he spent his time. John was only a public preacher somewhere between 1.6 percent to 5 percent of his life. Biblical priests ministered to God and then served the people so the people could approach God. This was John's pattern. And it should be ours as well.

We have a lot of contexts to teach ministry to people—what context have we established to train our people in ministry to God? Do we even have a vision for it?

When people fix their gaze on God, they begin to resemble Him.[8] And then when they give themselves to His Word, the Holy Spirit begins to shape and mold them into a manifestation of that Word. And they begin to escape the grip of humanism. Until this transformation takes place, a messenger is limited. However, as this transformation takes place, their ministry begins to produce life because, when they speak, they communicate *God* instead of only information about Him.

The Word is more than lessons for instruction. It is first and foremost conversational material for communion with God. Many people study the Word of God to speak it to people, but first we must learn to speak that Word back to God. If you do that, the Holy Spirit will make the Word alive.

Formation or Information

Modern ministry tends to be more focused on the transfer and assimilation of information than the formation of a messenger.

Modern theological training is typically classroom and research based. We tend to prioritize information and knowledge transfer. Showing careful attention to the Word and instructing others in it are a

---

[8] 1 Corinthians 2:2.

central expression of loving God with our strength,[9] so rigorous study should not be despised or neglected but only be part of the process of growing in God. Biblical learning must happen in an immersive context where information learned from the Word also produces transformation.

We need to consider the way in which we are doing training and development.

We do not need to discard everything that presently exists. Our training institutions are filled with teachers who value deep spirituality and give their lives to see it imparted to their students. However, we need to ask honest questions about our programs and curriculum to rightly evaluate whether formation (the Word becoming flesh) has equal or greater focus than the assimilation of information about the Word.

The Pharisees in John's day knew the same Scriptures John did, but their lives demonstrated a radically different response to the same information.

We need to honestly ask if our programs and our communities primarily *form* or *inform* people. Both are required to produce the kind of church the Lord wants to prepare the way for His Son.

The biblical model requires the shaping of a person into a demonstration of the Word. God alone can ultimately shape and form His people, but our part is to create a context where that shaping can occur. That context is the church, and it is important we lay proper biblical foundations in the church.

When we emphasize information over formation, messengers like John the Baptist still seem odd. They become *enigmas* when in fact they should be an expected outcome of our training and discipling systems. Not everyone will be spiritually gifted the way John was, but the values he lived by should not be exceptional.

---

[9]Deuteronomy 6:5–9.

The Fasted Lifestyle

John's life was associated with fasting,[1] but he was not known for periodic fasts. He was known for a fasted *lifestyle*. John embraced a simple lifestyle and did not pursue typical delights for one simple reason: John could not fully enjoy life until Jesus received His inheritance.

Biblical fasting is not all about self-denial and asceticism. Fasting should not be used to prove something to God or convince Him to do something. The cross has fully secured God's favor for believers. We do not need to secure His favor by proving something through our ability to deny ourselves.

The fasted lifestyle can be compared to what happens to a young man when he is captured by the beauty of a young woman and begins to pursue her. A man in love will ultimately abstain from some previous pleasures and limit his experience of other pleasures to enlarge his capacity to pursue a superior pleasure. *This is the purpose of a fasted lifestyle.*

The fasted lifestyle is a consistent, regular, and ongoing approach to life that limits our experience of certain pleasures to create more space for the pleasures of God.

Food is a core part of fasting, but a fasted lifestyle extends beyond food. For example, what about fasting beauty? Job made a covenant with his eyes not to gaze at young women.[2] Job's covenant was part of his commitment to avoid immorality, but it was more than that. Job was putting limits on his search for beauty. He knew if he satisfied his

---

[1]Matthew 9:14; 11:18; Mark 2:18; Luke 5:33; 7:33.

[2]Job 31:1.

eyes with female beauty, it would blunt his desire for the beauty of God.

You were born with "greedy eyes." Your physical eyes, and the eyes of our heart, relentlessly search for beauty, and most people are constantly indulging their eyes and their imagination with every sort of visual delight they can find. As a result, their imaginations are saturated, and they have little capacity to search out the beauty of God. There is nothing wrong with the beauty that God has created in this age, but if we overindulge in the beauty of this age, we will not have capacity to gaze at the beauty of God.

You choose the wilderness to cut off distractions that attempt to satisfy your appetite for divine beauty.

You should carefully consider every area of life: time, entertainment, housing, money, purchases, consumption, possessions, work, etc. None of these areas are intrinsically bad, but you should intentionally moderate your lifestyle to create more capacity to pursue and receive from God. This is the fasted lifestyle.

The reality is that we are starving because we are overfed. We keep trying to pursue God *and* everything else, but it will not work. People who are full do not have an appetite even when they are offered something superior. Furthermore, God will not simply be one more amusement on your list of amusements. There are things He simply will not give you as long as He is just another one of your delights.

No spouse wants to be just one of many in whom their spouse finds deep delight. If this is true for human spouses, how much more is it true for the divine Husband?

Fasting and Mourning

Jesus predicted His people would fast and mourn out of pain over His absence:

> *Can the wedding guests mourn as long as the bridegroom is with them? The days will come when the bridegroom is taken away from them, and then they will fast. (Matthew 9:15)*

Fasting is not the avoidance of harmful things. That is basic self-discipline. Fasting is abstaining in some measure from good things, things God has given for our blessing and enjoyment, as a statement things are not normal. For example, when a crisis or tragedy occurs, people miss meals and skip entertainment. They "fast" out of mourning because things are not quite right.

We often act like Jesus' absence is normal, but it is not.

In a billion years, we will look back in wonder at just how abnormal this age was. We will say to each other, "Do you remember that very strange time when God was not on the earth?" However, right now there is little mourning over Jesus' absence and longing for His return. Astonishingly, many believers seem content if things continue as they are and Jesus does not return. The angels are shocked by our indifference. They cannot grasp why so many in the church seem content with Jesus' absence.

This will change. The Father is not going to send Jesus back to a church that does not miss Him. Before Jesus returns, the Father will stir the affections of the church until we begin to fast *and* mourn over His absence the way Jesus predicted we would.

As the church becomes more captured by the beauty of Jesus, she will begin to mourn. New Testament mourning is not simply sorrow. *It is pain over Jesus' absence that affects our lifestyles.* This kind of mourning is not a *sad* mourning but a *joy-filled* mourning because we know a day is coming when we will see the object of our affection.

This mourning produces a *fasted lifestyle*. A fasted lifestyle is a mindset of intentional restraint with regard to the pleasures in this age as a statement that even God-given pleasures cannot be fully enjoyed while Jesus remains absent. It may be expressed differently by different people, and it does not have to be something everyone notices. It is a simple alteration in our lifestyle fueled by mourning over Jesus' absence.

The tragic truth is that may Christians would never think about the return of Jesus if the economy was strong, their bodies were healthy, and their local church offered enough programs to fulfill their desire for activity and friendship. Millions of Christians think about the return of Jesus as a heavenly retirement plan. They agree with the doctrine of His return, but there is very little mourning.

If we are fully enjoying the pleasures of life and fully content in this age, how can we carry the message of the superior pleasure of

God, the glory that accompanies Jesus' return, and the hope of the age to come?

How can you provoke those around you to long for Jesus if you do not live with longing?

Most men are consumed by their impact and their inheritance in this age, but God is going to make a profound statement through His church before the end of the age. The Bible predicts there will be tremendous prosperity and peace just before Jesus returns.[3] In the middle of economic prosperity and great comfort, there will be a people who willingly embrace fasting. Most people fast during a crisis, but the end-time church will become a sign and a wonder fasting, fasting and mourning with longing, in the middle of unprecedented prosperity.

Does your life demonstrate to others that things are not okay in this age? Is it okay with you if Jesus never returns? Are you more burdened by your own impact or His absence?

We easily forget that Jesus has been fasting in some way for two thousand years. Jesus loves His people so much there are things He will not indulge in until He is with us again. If He has adopted a fasted lifestyle until the day of His wedding,[4] shouldn't we?

A Joyful Wilderness People

Instead of periodically breaking up our overcrowded lives with fasting, why not live a life of fasting—a life of simplicity and pleasure? Why not embrace the wilderness for the sake of joy?

Beloved, when you taste sweetness in a lifestyle of fasting, *you do not have to stop.* John ate, but his lifestyle included a lifelong restriction on his diet as an expression of fasting. His life is an invitation to consider abstaining from certain foods, not because they are wrong, but because Jesus is not here to enjoy them with us. For example, perhaps the Lord will give grace to a company of people to cut desserts out of their diet until Jesus returns. This will not make them more holy; it will simply be their expression of pain over His absence.

---

[3]Matthew 24:37–39; 1 Thessalonians 5:3.

[4]Matthew 26:29; Mark 14:25; Luke 22:16–18.

Longterm fasting is not a requirement and does not indicate spirituality. It is not a tool by which we evaluate each other. It is simply one of many ways to cultivate longing and express our affection for Jesus.

Of course, you must eat properly and not abuse your body, but much of what we think is normal is not required and would have been unthinkable a generation or two ago. You should not do something rash (such as avoiding all food for an unhealthy amount of time), but you can experience freedom and joy through a fasted lifestyle. The pull of the culture is strong, but it is not unbreakable. The demands of this age are simply the enemy's scarecrows—lifeless things trying to frighten us away from fields of delight.

If the Lord is stirring desire for fasting and simple living, do not hesitate— your joy is at stake.

Do not be bothered by failures in fasting, and do not be driven by comparison with others. Simply pursue the joy of the Bridegroom's voice and engage the process. God is not evaluating your performance. He is moved by your desire however imperfectly it is expressed.

Fasting will not make you feel strong, for it will produce real weakness. As we have seen, John was not marked by strength. His life's message, Isaiah 40, emphasizes human frailty. John's fasted lifestyle produced weakness, and in the midst of his weakness, he grew strong in spirit.[5]

John's lifestyle did not earn Him favor with God, but it created space in his soul, mind, and emotions and positioned him to hear God's voice. Embracing JOMO and a fasted life does not make you "elite." It simply removes clutter in your soul so you can experience more.

John and Moses lived fasted lives in the wilderness for the sake of pleasure. Both men lived without an inheritance in this age, but neither one lived a life of sacrifice. Their joy in the wilderness was superior to every other treasure. The call to the wilderness and a fasted life is not ultimately a call to sacrifice. It is not primarily a call to discipline, though intentionality is required. It is an invitation to joy.

How much is available to us in God but being forfeited because we are too afraid to cut other things off? We tend to think about the

---

[5]Luke 1:80.

wilderness as a discipline and a sacrifice. It may take some discipline to get to the wilderness and to stay there, but a life in the wilderness is not a life of sacrifice. It's a life of joy and pleasure.

What if you stand before the uncreated God and hear Him say, "I had so much for you, but you were overfed. There was no room to give you what I wanted to give you."

Will you choose intentional restraint as an expression of desire for an absent Bridegroom?

John's Life Must Inform the Church's Assignment

Jesus predicted the good news of the kingdom must be proclaimed throughout the whole world before His return.

And this gospel of the kingdom will be proclaimed throughout the whole world as a testimony to all nations, and then the end will come. (Matthew 24:14)

The word *proclaimed* (κηρύσσω, *kēryssō*) was a very specific word that referred to the task of an ancient herald. A herald was a person who received a message from the king and then spoke for the king. He was the king's public mouthpiece. When a king wanted to visit a city, he would give a herald a message for that city. The message would contain information about the king's visit and instructions on how to prepare for that visit. The herald would proclaim the message to the city so the people of the city could prepare for the arrival of the king. This task was very similar to modern diplomacy where diplomatic officials are sent ahead of a president or prime minister to prepare a host nation to properly receive a head of state.

With this in mind, we can reword Matthew 24:14 this way:

The good news of the kingdom and the coming King must be proclaimed to every people to instruct them to prepare for the arrival of the King.

Like John, we are heralds of the coming King, conveying the King's message so the nations will be prepared for His coming.

Many believe it is possible to fulfill Matthew 24:14 through mass evangelism, but we cannot fulfill Matthew 24:14 until we grasp the nature of the task given to us. Evangelism is just one part of the task.

The ultimate task of missions is to partner with the Father to prepare the nations for the return of Jesus.

John's individual assignment was unique, and we should not seek to replicate it, but his ministry gives us insight into what will be necessary to prepare the nations for the return of Jesus. Just as we can learn foundations for the church from studying the life of Paul without having Paul's assignment, we should study how John prepared Israel as we seek to partner with the Father to see the earth prepared for Jesus' return.

The life of John the Baptist must shape the way we understand the end of the missions movement.

We need a fresh revelation of John's burden for Israel because Israel must be prepared again for the return of her Bridegroom and her God. At the moment, there is an incredible amount of energy being expended to reach every people group. This is good and right, but not the end. Before the age is over, the global church will focus her strength on one specific people group: *Israel.* The global church will speak directly and passionately to Israel about her God from her Scriptures.

Until this witness is given, the task of the church in this age has not finished.

The task of missions will conclude with an unprecedented witness about the return of the Lord. This witness will be given to every people group but will conclude with an unprecedented witness to Israel. God is going to give the global church an unprecedented burden for the people He began His redemptive plan with. Very few have anticipated how serious God is about this witness, but He is leading history to produce it. He has not forgotten Israel thousands of years after He made covenant with her as the Bridegroom on the mountain.

An Unprecedented Moment Requires an Unprecedented Response

We live at an unprecedented moment in history. There are two key events unfolding that have never occurred before and are simultaneously occurring in our generation:

- *The gospel could reach every people within a generation*—There are still billions who need to hear the gospel, but for the first time in history, it is possible a witness could be given to every people group within a generation if the church prioritizes it. A few decades ago, we did not know where every people group was, and now they are within reach.

- *Israel exists as a sovereign state, and the city of Jerusalem has become a global controversy*—The prophets predicted Jerusalem would become an international controversy. For two thousand years, the idea of Israel re-emerging was inconceivable, but suddenly within a generation, Jerusalem has become a global issue for the first time in history.

It is easy to overlook the significance of the moment we are living in, but we live in an unprecedented moment predicted thousands of years ago. As a result, we no longer have the option of whether or not we consider how missions must end. We do not know when Jesus will return, nor should we seek to time it precisely. However, we are commanded to know the season we are living in,[1] and it is obvious we are in a unique season. As a result, we must begin to understand what Scripture says about missions and the preparation of the earth for the return of the Bridegroom. Because John is the prototype, that includes understanding the life, message, and ministry of John the Baptist.

There is a growing interest in studying the prophets and the return of Jesus in a responsible and biblical way. People sincerely want to avoid unbiblical emphases in the study of the end times, but more and more believers realize we have neglected a significant part of our faith. Hunger is stirring to grasp what the Bible says about the return of the Bridegroom. If we have eyes to see it, the Lord is beginning to shape and form a corporate John the Baptist. He wants to stir our emotions for the return of His Son, because He is going to produce a church that is no longer content with the absence of the Bridegroom.

There are three dramatic moments in this age when God reveals Himself in a new way and suddenly shifts the way He relates to His people: the exodus, the first coming of Jesus, and the second coming of Jesus. Two of these transitions are behind us, and one is in front of us. Of the three transitions, the second coming is by far the most

---

[1]Matthew 16:3; 24:32–33; Luke 21:31; 1 Thessalonians 5:1–6.

dramatic. Nothing in history past is comparable. It will be far more dramatic than the flood and the exodus.[2]

God takes centuries to prepare for a transition, but when the time for transition comes, it comes suddenly, and it is too late to prepare.[3] Centuries of slavery set the stage for the exodus from Egypt. Thousands of years set the stage for Jesus to shift history through a three-year ministry, and ultimately a three-day suffering. A small moment changed everything. The second coming is similar. Thousands of years have set the stage for an event that will come suddenly.[4]

When God was ready to bring the exodus, He put His hand on Moses. He took him into the wilderness for forty years and prepared Moses with a gentile priest. God then brought Moses out of the wilderness when God was ready to visit His people. When God was ready to bring His Son into the world, He again laid hold of a man. He hid John in the wilderness for thirty years and then used him like Moses to prepare the people for what was coming.

The pattern has been set.

Jesus predicted the nations will be prepared before the second coming. The second coming will be far more dramatic than anything in history, and the preparation for that event must also go far beyond anything in history. God will give messengers unusual anointing, but He is going to prepare the nations through a corporate witness—His church. The end-time church will function like John, but on a scale far beyond the limited scope of John's ministry.

The time is right for the church again to embrace the "wilderness" to finish the task Jesus has given us to prepare the nations for His return. The apostles understood this task two thousand years ago, but we have largely forgotten it. The Father is going to set the stage for the

---

[2]Exodus 34:10; Deuteronomy 30:1–10; Isaiah 4:5; 11:11–16; 64:1–3; Jeremiah 3:16–17; 16:14–15; 23:7–8; 30:8–10; Joel 3; Habakkuk 3:3–15; Micah 7:15–17; Zechariah 10:8–9; 14.

[3]Matthew 24:42–44; 25:1–13.

[4]Matthew 24:36–39; 1 Thessalonians 5:3.

revelation of His Son, and it is time for us to build that stage with Him.[5]

---

[5]Revelation 1:1.

The Forerunner Community

In the decades before John was born, communities began to form in the wilderness with a deep longing for the coming of Messiah and a radical commitment to live according to what they saw in the Word. We should not imitate all the practices of these communities, but we should imitate their devotion.

These communities carefully studied the prophets and had a deep desire for the Messiah to come. They saw the compromise in the temple priesthood and hoped their wholehearted devotion to the Word would prepare the way for the Messiah to come. Because John lived in the wilderness, it seems likely John spent at least part of his life in one of these communities.

> *And the child grew and became strong in spirit, and he was in the wilderness until the day of his public appearance to Israel. (Luke 1:80)*

John's early life only merited one statement in Luke's Gospel. The word *wilderness* can communicate the idea John was living alone as some sort of hermit, but this was not the case. It was a sparsely inhabited place, but there were small communities of people seeking to live very focused lives. John was given an incredibly unique assignment and a stunning evaluation by Jesus, but he was not formed in isolation. John was formed by the Lord in a community.

John is typically studied as an individual, but we must not overlook the community dimension of John's life which began with his parents.

God's choice of Zechariah and Elizabeth was not accidental:

> *In the days of Herod, king of Judea, there was a priest named Zechariah, of the division of Abijah. And he had a wife from the daughters of Aaron, and her name was Elizabeth. And they were both righteous before*

God, walking blamelessly in all the commandments and statutes of the Lord. (Luke 1:5–6)

John was a miraculous child chosen for a unique assignment, so God put John in a priestly family that would play a significant part in shaping John's life. Though John would not carry on his father's priestly assignment, Zechariah and Elizabeth created a context for John to grow in the knowledge of God.

John was forged first in his home. Do we establish homes as parents in such a way that one of our children could live before the Lord as John did?

John's parents probably died when he was relatively young, and after their deaths, John continued to live in a small community that had a deep value for the Word of God. While John's parents and his community did not share his unique assignment, they sustained a context where John grew in the knowledge of God. As we have seen, John also engaged in community by discipling and leading a small group of young men. John was not idle or isolated in the wilderness. Though he had a national calling and a miraculous birth, he lived in a small place and was faithful to invest in a small number of young men who were attracted to his life and his message.

Messengers Do Not Emerge in Isolation

We tend to forget messengers do not emerge in isolation. God disciples them in community.

Western romanticism has caused us to fixate on individual callings, but this is not a biblical view. God is so committed to the community that Hebrews tells us Abraham has not yet received his inheritance because his reward is connected to us.[1] Even Jesus' glory is connected to His people. God does give individual rewards, but aspects of our inheritance are connected to the community. Individuals are shaped in community, their gifts are for the sake of building up the community, and their rewards are connected to their community.

God is not looking for gifted individuals. He is looking for a corporate people who carry the glory of God.

---

[1] Hebrews 11:39–40.

The powers and principalities will be instructed by the church—the corporate expression of Jesus—not spectacular individuals.[2] Without a vision for the corporate family, we will not grasp the true purpose of our assignments and become very self-centered in the way we view our anointing. Even our individual gifts are given so others can come into their calling.[3] There may be moments it seems a prophetic person has to stand alone in their assignment, but prophets are meant to live in community and emerge out of community. The idea of prophets as isolated individuals is not biblical.

We tend to read many of the stories in the Bible as isolated stories of impressive individuals and forget that God shapes and forms His vessels as they live in a spiritual community. Who taught John the Word of God? Who trained Daniel to survive Nebuchadnezzar's arrogance? Often, God trains His messengers in small communities that serve as "greenhouses" where the Lord can grow men and women for His purposes. This begins in the family and extends to the broader church family.

We are quick to give accolades to a person God uses in a prominent way, but we quickly forget the parents, friends, pastors, teachers, and mentors who shaped and discipled that person. We are going to be shocked in the age to come when God displays His affection for every role in the body and He gives great dignity and great reward to those who were not prominent but served His purposes by parenting and discipling others who were more prominent.

Perhaps we lack prophetic messengers like John because we lack the communities necessary for their formation and sending.

Perhaps a burning desire the Lord has given you will be fulfilled through the ministry of someone else you disciple. Are you okay with that? Are you willing to invest your life into another for the sake of the glory of God? Sometimes God gives us a burning desire for something to be expressed through our own lives, but other times that burning desire is something we impart to others God has chosen. Either way, we fulfill our assignment, and God's reward will be the same.

---

[2] Ephesians 3:10.

[3] 1 Corinthians 12:7–13; Ephesians 4:11–14.

Perhaps Zechariah and Elizabeth were in deep pain over the priesthood, and their intercession produced John's life. Perhaps John's gift as a messenger was a gift Zechariah had longed for but was not given.

God is going to prepare a people to prepare the way for His Son's return. Churches will emerge with a deep devotion to the Word of God, people will alter their lifestyles out of desire to obey the Word wholeheartedly, and there will be a longing to prepare the nations for the return of Jesus. These communities (churches) will become places of formation where people are matured and formed for the days ahead. These churches are God's provision for the coming storm, *and* they are His great inheritance.[4]

Perhaps you long to be anointed like John when you speak the Word. That desire is good, but that longing should mature into the desire for a community in which everyone, according to their gifting, speaks the Word of God with power.

Events are coming that are far beyond what any of us can imagine. No other time in history is comparable to what will come before the Lord returns.[5] *Let that sink in.* Are you discipling people with this in mind? Are you engaging in your local church with this sobriety? Or is your church merely an extension of your social life and part of a lifestyle that is largely consumed with other things?

Messengers Formed in Community

God chooses and sends messengers with unusual anointing when a crisis is looming. Noah was sent before the flood. Moses was sent before the exodus. The biblical prophets were sent to Israel for decades before calamity came. If God raised up Isaiah, Ezekiel, and Jeremiah to prepare Israel for Babylon's invasion, will He not raise up messengers to prepare Israel and the nations before the most difficult crisis in history?

Incredible events like the flood, the exodus, and the Babylonian invasion were all foreshadowings of the end of the age. What they were in measure, the end of the age will be in fullness. When we consider the immensity of the end of the age, we should anticipate the

---

[4]Ephesians 1:18.

[5]Jeremiah 30:7; Daniel 12:1; Joel 2:2; Matthew 24:21.

Lord to release an unprecedented witness and warning before the final trouble. He will send messengers like the ancient prophets again before the age ends. And because the mystery has been revealed,[6] they will proclaim Jesus' beauty with an understanding the ancient prophets could not have known.

The coming moment in time that is far beyond every other period of history[7] will be preceded by a prophetic witness that goes far beyond every other witness in history.

These messengers will not predict new things or write new Scripture. They will follow the example of John and speak the things already in the Scripture with incredible weight and authority. Like John, they will use what is written in Scripture to prepare the nations for the return of Jesus. God released a measure of power in the book of Acts to establish the church, and He will release far more to mature the church and enable her to stand against the most wicked man in all of history. The spirit of Elijah will come to fullness in powerful proclamation *and* power.[8]

God alone will choose who will represent Him in this way. It is not something that can be earned because there are no "superior" humans. You cannot choose this assignment, nor can you make people into messengers or prophets. However, we all participate in this witness by establishing biblical communities where the Word of God is valued and people can be shaped and formed to fulfill their assignments.

With that in mind, we need to ask a question: *Are we building churches that can shape a Daniel, an Isaiah, a Jeremiah, a John the Baptist, or an apostle Paul?*

---

[6]Romans 16:25; 1 Corinthians 2:7; 4:1; Ephesians 1:9; 3:2–5, 9; 6:19; Colossians 1:26–27; 2:2; 4:3; 1 Peter 1:10–12, 20.

[7]Jeremiah 30:7; Daniel 12:1; Joel 2:2; Matthew 24:21.

[8]The two witnesses in Revelation 11 provide a glimpse of this witness.

God's Delight in Hiddenness

God fully enjoyed John for thirty years—not just for the few months John preached.

God did not invest thirty years in John to get a few months of preaching. God enjoyed communion with John for decades. God enjoyed the process as John was discipled and then discipled others. God also *enjoys* you, and He is forming you to be His eternal companion. God is relational, and He is more interested in who you become than how well-known you are.

Ambition and insecurity can easily cloak themselves in religious activity. The pursuit of productivity and ministry "success" can be a smokescreen that allows us to "work for God" instead of giving God full access to the parts of our inner man He wants to transform. Prioritizing relationship with God does not mean a life of devotional passivity. It will ultimately require more of you than religious activities because God will confront what you want to avoid so He can make you like Himself.

If you become like God, you will have far more impact than you can ever have by seeking more influence.

People often endure seasons of life hoping to get to the next "significant" season, but God intensively enjoys every stage of your life, and He is fully present in each season. God fully enjoys an immature believer progressing in discipleship in the same way good parents treasure each stage of their child's life, even if that child cannot make any substantial contributions to the household. God is not anxiously waiting for you to do something "bigger." If you are cooperating with Him, He fully enjoys your present season. Sadly, we tend to despise the stages of our growth hoping for the next big thing.

We need to become like children[1] who typically enjoy each stage of their growth.

Life in God is the "big" thing. Steward it. Enjoy it.

John shook the nation, but he never abandoned his life of communion. *He never left the wilderness.* As a result, his words had such power unreligious men cried out, *"What should we do?"*[2]

We have been taught to pursue prayer to come *out* of the wilderness with power. What would happen if a generation committed to pursue prayer to *stay* in the wilderness with power? The Lord may assign people different tasks and move them to different places, but what could the Lord do with a people committed to living wilderness lifestyles wherever the Lord sends them and in whatever dimension of power He releases?

What if God offered you a choice between a life defined by public prominence and a life defined by hidden communion? Which would you choose? If you were given an option between impact in heaven and influence before men, which would you choose? Would you choose the wilderness?

God chose a man who embraced the wilderness to prepare Israel for Jesus' first coming, and He will use a people who live the same way to prepare the way for Jesus' second coming.

The Far-Reaching Effects of the Wilderness

John never left the wilderness, but his life of communion reached far beyond the wilderness, and his message took root in other cities. One of the most powerful New Testament preachers was a man named Apollos who was from Alexandria. When he came to Ephesus, he came proclaiming the baptism of John the Baptist.[3] Paul also encountered a company of disciples in Ephesus who were following John's message.[4]

---

[1]Matthew 18:3; Mark 10:14–15; Luke 18:16–17.

[2]Luke 3:10–14.

[3]Acts 18:24–26.

[4]Acts 19:1–6.

Twenty years after John died, people were still following his message in regions he never traveled to.

Many people assume it takes publicity, networking, and travel to make an impact, but John made his maximum impact by staying in the wilderness and doing his primary assignment. The truth is impact is a difficult thing to measure properly.

If you do what God calls you to do where He places you, He will handle the impact.

When God reduces a person's sphere of influence and activity, many people do everything they can to expand their ministry and get things going again. However, if your ministry expression shrinks or even dies, inquire of the Lord to see if He has something to say. He could be reducing you for your benefit and for the sake of your longterm assignment. He could be giving you the invitation to hiddenness and life in the wilderness.

John was given the most significant assignment in his generation, but he did not live in the most influential city in his region. He was born to be a priest, but he did not have the privilege of being part of the vast temple operation in Jerusalem. Ironically, being cut off from Jerusalem made John the priest with the greatest impact in his generation.

Urgency Comes from Intimacy

You must know the difference between *urgency* and *immediacy*.[1] Urgency is biblical. Immediacy can be reckless. John lived with the tension of urgency for decades. John knew the Lord had given him an assignment to be a messenger, but because he knew how to steward urgency, he was able to live before the Lord and submit to God's processes rather than take his assignment into his own hands.

When we put more confidence in our ability than God's leadership, we become vulnerable to immediacy.

If John had been driven by immediacy, he would have networked, made plans, and done everything he could to initiate the public season of his life. While there is wisdom to stewarding an assignment, that wisdom is secondary to the sovereign activity of the Lord. When immediacy begins driving us, we short-circuit the process of God, and our impact is significantly reduced, even if we are pursuing an assignment God has for us.

Immediacy and passivity are both errors on the opposite ends of the spectrum. The solution is to steward urgency. Urgency propels us into God to hear His voice and cooperate with Him. It also propels us to engage early in a life of consistent faithfulness in things that others consider "small," doing so with confidence that God will bring about everything He has spoken.

We need to recover biblical urgency. Biblical urgency is informed by times and seasons, but it is not based on timelines. It is not a product of fear of what may come. We do not know the day of Jesus' return. He may come more quickly than we expect, and He may take longer

---

[1] The concept of "urgency" vs "immediacy" is drawn from a teaching by Stuart Greaves' on the subject.

than we anticipate. Biblical urgency is not dependent on our grasp of the biblical timeline; it is based on the burning emotions of God to exalt His Son and finish His wedding.

Biblical urgency is a response to divine desire. It is the natural product of intimacy.

The prophets were some of the most urgent humans who ever lived, and yet their greatest predictions have not be fulfilled thousands of years later. They did not live through the events associated with their urgency, but they encountered God's emotions through His Word, and it consumed them until they became overwhelmed by urgency and spoke for God. They lived with a shocking urgency for events that were a very long way away.

When you discover God's emotions, you will begin to feel incredible urgency.

Urgency is a frequent byproduct of revival. When God comes in revival, people typically speak urgently and passionately about the return of Jesus. For example, during the Azusa Street revival, people spoke as though the return of Jesus was imminent, nearly 120 years ago. Their urgency did not come from their insight into God's timeline. They felt urgency because God's manifest presence was near, and when you encounter Him, you feel His urgency which transcends time.

It's time to move on from predicting the return of Jesus or being fearful of the last days. We need an urgency that flows from God's burning desire to return.

An Urgent Response to Divine Desire

John was a messenger, but he was *more* than a messenger.[2] He had one of the shortest prophetic careers for any of the biblical prophets, and yet Jesus said no one had gone beyond him. John's words were powerful, but *he* was the message.

- John was a priest in the dessert. *But what made him a burning priest?*
- John devoured the Word. *But what made John devour the Word?*
- John lived an intentional life in a small place. *But what made him leave Jerusalem for the desert?*
- John was a prophet. *But what made him prophesy?*

---

[2]Matthew 11:9.

- John did not predict new things; he cried out. *But what made him cry out?*

We can examine the Scriptures to see what John *said,* but if John is a prototype of the mature end-time church, we must know who John *was.*

- John was not the only holy man in that generation. God always has a remnant.[3]
- He was not the only intercessor. There were others like Simeon and Anna.[4]
- He was not the only one looking for the Messiah to come. Many were expecting the Messiah to come at any moment.
- John did not have more information than other people. He had the same Bible everyone else read.
- John was not more disciplined than any other man. The desert where he lived was filled with small communities of people who devoured the Word and lived extremely austere lives to prepare a path for the Messiah.

John was transformed by his knowledge of God and his understanding of God's emotions, and God is giving this same invitation to this generation.

Will you choose, like John, to be consumed by the emotions of the divine Bridegroom?

This is an ultimate question that requires an ultimate response. If you say *yes,* you will be transformed. Like John, your life will become a message regardless of your notoriety. If you say *no,* God will still love you, but you will find yourself increasingly out of step with Him.

The end of the age is not defined by charts, timelines, and information. The end of the age is defined by a single question: **What will it take to satisfy God's emotions?**

---

[3]For example, the Lord rebuked Elijah when Elijah thought he was the only faithful man left (1 Kings 19:10–18).

[4]Luke 2:25–38.

This question is so significant you must not answer it quickly. You must search this question out, and if you do, the answer will consume your life.

God's emotions drive all His activity and His emotions led Him to the cross,[5] where He poured out His life to obtain the object of His desire. God does not act out of obligation; He acts out of desire. And His desire will be satisfied.

God declared His burning desire in Song of Solomon 8, and He is looking for a people, like John, who declare that same desire back to Him with their words and their lives:

> For love is strong as death, jealousy is fierce as the grave. Its flashes are flashes of fire, the very flame of the LORD. Many waters cannot quench love, neither can floods drown it. . . . (Song of Solomon 8:6–7)

The age will not end until this people emerge because Jesus will not return for a disinterested bride.

It's Time

It's time to preach John's message again. While we want to avoid unbiblical teaching about Jesus' return, the biggest event in human history is looming large in front of us, and it's time to proclaim it again. We must proclaim it in a biblical way to call men to repentance before that dreadful day.

It's time for us to embrace John's lifestyle again. John lived according to a set of values that shaped him into who he became. We will not all live the same kind of life John lived, but we are called to live according to His values.

It's time for John's approach to ministry. John described his approach to ministry as a "friend of the bridegroom." The apostle Paul adopted this same approach, and so should we. We easily forget the church is Jesus' wife. She is not to be treated harshly, and she is not to be used for our own agendas.

It's time to stop taking shortcuts. We have tried to advance the gospel, gain influence, and achieve objectives by every human scheme imaginable. In many cases, this was well meaning, but human strength

---

[5]John 3:16.

cannot meet the demands of what is coming. We still have too much confidence in our own ability despite the fact we lack John's authority and often experience very little in the way of results. It's time to embrace John's path again.

It's time to treat the Bible seriously. We usually hold to certain core doctrines in the Bible, but we tend not live as though the Bible is entirely and completely true. We tend to "innovate" and define success in ways that are not biblical. Many of the greatest men in the Bible would not be successful according to our ideas of success. We need to carefully consider messengers like John and determine we will live with the same confidence in the Word they had. We need fresh confidence in God and His leadership, not just confidence in doctrines.

People have embraced the wilderness as a season, but the Lord is looking for a people who embrace it as a lifestyle.

So that leaves us with one question: *Will you choose the wilderness?*

Made in the USA
Coppell, TX
09 October 2023

22599564R00154